Arabian Assignment

David Smiley
With
Peter Kemp

SAPERE
BOOKS

Arabian Assignment

Published by Sapere Books.

20 Windermere Drive, Leeds, England, LS17 7UZ,
United Kingdom

saperebooks.com

eBook ISBN: 978-1-80055-009-4.

To Moy

Table of Contents

Preface

It is almost impossible to translate Arabic words into English and, whenever I could, I have avoided using any, except in the names of people and places; throughout the book I have spelt the names phonetically.

The Arabic of Oman is quite different from the Arabic of Yemen; for example the word for 'thank you' in Oman is *assant* and in Yemen *shukran*. In the case of people's names, I have followed the custom of the country and used *bin* (the son of) in Omani names and *ibn* in Yemeni ones.

Many place names can have more than one spelling; for example Nizwa was more often used when I was in Oman, but Nazwa is now more common. Jizan could equally well be spelt Jizzan and Salala could be Salalah.

Part I: Muscat & Oman

Chapter I: A Harsh and Hostile Land

I was a latecomer to Arabia. It was not until 1958, when I was in my forties, that I arrived in Muscat and began an association with the peninsula which was to continue with little interruption for nearly ten years. I already knew something of the Middle East because, as a subaltern in the Blues, I had accompanied the 1st Household Cavalry Regiment to Palestine at the beginning of the Second World War, and for a large part of the ensuing five years that theatre of operations had been either my battleground or my base.

Although a Regular soldier — I was commissioned from Sandhurst in September, 1936 — I had spent the greater part of the war working with irregulars.[1] Recruited two years later into the Special Operations Executive, I had parachuted from North Africa into Greece in April, 1943, with an old friend, Billy McLean,[2] from the Royal Scots Greys, with whom I had served in Palestine. A good-looking, blond extrovert of 25, with all the panache attributed in romantic fiction to cavalry officers, McLean had already gained useful paramilitary experience under Wingate in the Ethiopian campaign of 1941. A keen and unconventional mind, unusual courage and great powers of mental and physical endurance had equipped him well for the role of a guerrilla leader, and his natural exuberance and charm made him an ideal companion in conditions of hardship and danger. He entered Parliament after

---

[1] In 1941 I had led a company in commando operations behind the Italian lines in Abyssinia.

[2] Lt.-Col. N. L. D. McLean, D.S.O.

the war and was to play a crucial part later on in my Arabian adventure.

Together we had walked across the frontier into Albania, where we had spent the following two years trying to organize resistance, first against the Italians and later against the Germans. We had worked with guerrillas of every political persuasion — Communists, Republicans, and Monarchists — only to see our efforts frustrated by a vicious civil war provoked by the Communists, which ended in the establishment of a regime intolerably oppressive to its own people and bitterly hostile to the West.

After this depressing but illuminating experience I had flown to the Far East and parachuted, in May, 1945, into the forests of north-east Thailand to work with the 'Free Thai' resistance against the Japanese. For a few months after the surrender of Japan I had remained in Thailand, on the frontier with French Indo-China, varying the monotony of disarming Japanese divisions with excursions into Laos to help the French against the Communist Viet-minh.

Even after the war I had done comparatively little regimental soldiering. A six months course at the Staff College in 1946 was followed by my appointment as Assistant Military Attaché in Warsaw during one of the worst periods of Stalinist tyranny and terror. For a short time afterwards I had served as Second-in-Command of my regiment in Germany, and later, at the age of 35, I had achieved command of it. But my next posting, in April, 1955, was to Stockholm as Military Attaché. Despite the rigours of social life and the complexities of Swedish etiquette it was a pleasant existence, not only for me but also for my wife and young family. I had married in April, 1947, a tall, slim and beautiful girl whose first husband had been killed in action in Germany in April, 1945. Moy was the daughter of Lord

Francis Scott, one of the early settlers in Kenya, a farmer, leader of the Legislative Council, and member of the Governor's Executive Council. We were planning to retire there at the end of my three years in Stockholm and we had already bought a farm when my Albanian past caught up with me in the form of a telephone call from my wartime friend, Julian Amery.

Amery had joined McLean and myself on our second mission to Albania in April, 1944, and the three of us had shared adventure, hardship and disappointment for close on seven months. Brought up from the cradle on politics and history, he already knew a great deal about the Balkans, and had proved a useful guide through the jungle of tribal jealousy, family intrigue and ideological hostility in which we had to carry out our work. I admired his urbanity and dry, sardonic wit, and we had kept in touch after the war, while we pursued our respective military and Parliamentary careers. Now he was Undersecretary of State for War. He telephoned me early in 1958, on my last home leave from Stockholm, and asked me to go and see him.

'Sit down, David. I have a job for you.' He handed me a bulging folder. 'You can read all about it in there.'

'What is the job?' I asked suspiciously, 'and where?'

'I want you to command the Sultan's Forces in Muscat.'

'The Sultanate of Muscat and Oman',[3] I read, 'is the largest state in the Persian Gulf. It has an area of over 82,000 square miles, and a population of more than half a million Arabs.' I also learned that it was a sovereign state, its Sultan an independent ruler, though linked to Britain by treaties of friendship and co-operation. 'In other words,' explained

---

[3] Strictly speaking, Muscat is the capital and port, Oman the hinterland.

Amery, 'we give him help; we sometimes give him advice. But' — he gave me a knowing smile — 'we do *not* give him orders.'

Independence, or rather turbulence, was a constantly recurring theme in the story of piracy and tribal feuding which forms so much of the history I now began to study of that harsh and hostile land. Settled some four or five thousand years ago by migrants from Egypt and in later times by tribes from the Yemen, this south-eastern corner of Arabia, between the great sands of the Empty Quarter and the sea, has suffered over the ages repeated foreign invasions and long periods of alien rule. Its strategic importance on the approaches to the Persian Gulf, and the piratical inclinations of its seamen, have excited the ambition or the anger of imperial powers from the time of Sennacherib.

Although Omani Dynasties have on occasion extended their territory as far afield as India and Zanzibar, Muscat itself has known a long succession of foreign overlords, from the Persians of Cyrus the Great to Albuquerque's Portuguese — who behaved atrociously, lopping off limbs, ears and noses to punish or even to prevent resistance. These and other invaders — the hosts of the Prophet, the Caliphs of Baghdad, Turks and Tartars, Wahabis from beyond the Empty Quarter — have swarmed over the country. But although some of them ruled, for longer or shorter periods, over Muscat and the coastal belt, none of them established firm control behind the mountains, in Oman, where the tribes continued in their old way of life, intriguing and fighting among themselves in rancorous isolation from the outside world and deeply resentful of all intruders, Arab or *nasrani* [Christian].

They followed the Sharia law of Islam, rigorously interpreted according to the doctrines of the Ibadhi sect brought to Oman by the Kharejites [Seceders] — survivors from mutinous

14

soldiers in the army of Ali, the Prophet's son-in-law — and proclaimed at Nizwa at the end of the seventh century by Abdullah bin Ibadh. Ibadhis may not drink or even smoke, and must not trim their beards — though they sometimes trim their moustaches. Their puritan creed regards the Koran as the sole source of authority and teaches that it must be read literally, without interpretation; and, more important for the political history of Oman, their tradition requires that the choice of their Imam should be by election among the Faithful.

For nearly a thousand years, until the early seventeenth century, the Imams of Oman, who held both spiritual and temporal jurisdiction over their subjects, were elected on personal merit or popularity; any attempt by a reigning Imam to ensure the succession for his eldest son was fiercely resisted by the fanatical Ibadhi *Qadhis* — the judges who administered the law. But early on in the seventeenth century there arose a dynasty of Imams, the Al Yaarabah (or Yariba), who from their capital in the ancient fortress town of Rostaq established firm control over the interior of Oman. They not only expelled the Portuguese from Muscat, built up a powerful navy, and extended their influence throughout the Persian Gulf and even to East Africa, but such was their prestige that they were able to modify the elective principle and ensure that the succession to the Imamate continued in the direct line for nearly a hundred years. This last achievement was to have profound significance for the future.

After 1720 the al Yaarabah dynasty began to collapse in a series of disputes over the succession. There followed nearly twenty-five years of civil war, with two rival Imams fighting for supremacy, one supported by a confederation of tribes under the leadership of the Beni Ghafir — the Ghafiri faction — the other by a confederation under the Beni Hina — the Hinawis;

these factions, whose rivalry has dominated most of the subsequent history of Oman, exist to this day and any Ruler, to be successful, must be able to control or hold the balance between them. The war ended with the victory of the Hinawi candidate, Ahmed bin Said, Governor of Sohar; this brave and energetic soldier expelled the Persians, who had taken advantage of the confusion to re-occupy Muscat, and founded the present ruling dynasty of Al bu Said.

After his death one of his sons proclaimed himself Imam, finally dispensing with the formality of election, which has never been revived in the ruling family. His defiance of Ibadhi tradition antagonized the more fanatical tribes of the interior at the same time as his removal of the capital from Rostaq to Muscat on the coast weakened his control over them. They disapproved, moreover, of his new relations with infidel powers such as the French and British, and they hated his agreements with them to suppress the traffic in slaves and arms; nor did they much care for the alien title of Sultan by which he allowed the British to address him. They elected an Imam of their own and, although he was overthrown in 1871, there were further outbreaks of revolt, culminating in a full scale rebellion in 1913, when the tribes of Oman — under another elected Imam — marched on Muscat and were bloodily repulsed by a British-Indian regiment sent to protect the Sultan.

Eventually in 1920 the Sultan and most of the leading Omani tribes came to an agreement, through British mediation, known as the Treaty of Sib — from the small coastal town northwest of Muscat where it was signed. While insisting on the paramountcy of the Sultan and his right to represent them in all external affairs, the treaty granted the tribal leaders a measure of autonomy, including their right to elect their own

Imam and his right to appoint *walis* (Governors) in the areas under his administration; the boundaries between these areas and those directly under the Sultan were, unfortunately, never precisely defined, but in general the Sultan's *walis* were in the towns on the coastal side of the mountains, and the Imam's were in the interior. In any case, the arrangement worked extremely well for more than thirty years, Sultan and Imam remaining on the best of terms until the Imam's death in 1954. Indeed, in 1952, when the Saudis suddenly occupied a part of the Buraimi oasis belonging to the Sultan, it was the Imam who rallied the tribesmen to the Sultan's banner to expel them; only the British Government's decision to put pressure on the Sultan at the last moment — calamitous 'advice' on our part, as it turned out — prevented him from doing so. The Treaty of Sib, therefore, gave the country a welcome interval of peace, but the causes of conflict remained beneath the surface, ready for exploitation by the unscrupulous; and so, at the first favourable moment, they were exploited.

The British connection with Muscat dates from the early days of the East India Company in the seventeenth century, though the first treaty between Britain and the Sultan was not signed until 1798. An agreement followed two years later for agents of the East India Company to reside at Muscat, but the appalling climate killed off so many of them that it lapsed.[4] Throughout the nineteenth century the British and the Sultan, who was then the most important ruler in the Gulf, collaborated closely in suppressing piracy, and the slave trade ceased in the Sultanate under a treaty of 1822.[5] By a treaty of 1852 Britain

---

[4] There is now a British Ambassador at Muscat.

[5] Although there were still African slaves in the country during my time there, they had all been born into slavery, not imported — as they were, for example, in Saudi Arabia — and were treated as members of the family.

(and France) recognized the independence of the Sultan, who still conducts his own foreign policy and maintains his own armed forces. Under subsequent agreements he may call on British help in time of trouble.[6]

The trouble came soon after the old Imam's death; the principal causes were Saudi ambition and, of course, oil. Ever since 1937 the Saudis had been trying to expand their territory beyond the edge of the *Rub al Khali* [the Empty Quarter], claiming frontiers with their neighbours — the States of the Aden Protectorate, the Sultanate, and the Trucial Sheikhdoms — which those neighbours refused to accept. After the Second World War the two superpowers, Russia and America, became increasingly involved in Arabia and the Gulf, the former pursuing an old imperial design, the latter attracted by fresh discoveries of oil: both with a common interest in reducing the influence of Britain. Encouraged by the new situation, the Saudis in 1952 suddenly occupied the strategic oasis of Buraimi, owned partly by the Sheikh of Abu Dhabi, a Trucial State, and partly by the Sultan of Muscat.

The Sultan gathered a force of between six and eight thousand tribesmen and, but for the ill-advised intervention of the British Government, would have expelled the intruders immediately, thus dealing a sharp blow to Saudi prestige and cementing the loyalty of the Omani tribes. When he failed to move, Saudi intrigue began to prosper.

The dispute went to international arbitration at Geneva, where the Saudi method, perfectly respectable in Arabia, of

---

[6] The Sultanate of Muscat and Oman had no political connection with the former 'Trucial Oman' (earlier known as the 'Pirate Coast'), a Protectorate of seven petty sheikhdoms extending from the base of the Qatar Peninsula eastward to the entrance of the Persian Gulf, whose defence and foreign relations were, until 1971, the responsibility of the British Government. Their defence was mainly in the hands of the Trucial Oman Scouts, a locally recruited force with British regular officers and NCOs.

reinforcing their arguments with offers of large sums in gold to the members of the Tribunal caused such scandal that the President and the British delegate resigned in protest. At the end of 1955 the seemingly inexhaustible patience of Her Britannic Majesty's Government ran out; in a sudden, bloodless *coup* the Trucial Oman Scouts descended on Buraimi, expelled the Saudi garrison, and established a garrison of their own and another of the Sultan's in the Oasis.

But the three year delay had been disastrous for the Sultan. The Saudis had made good use of the time to spread their influence in Oman, suborning the tribesmen with lavish gifts of money and arms. Moreover, a new Imam had arisen on the death of the Sultan's old friend: one Ghalib bin Ali. A weak and colourless personality appointed by a cabal of three sheikhs but never formally elected, he was virtually a Saudi puppet; he possessed, however, a valuable ally in his brother, Talib, the Wali of Rostaq, a brave, energetic and extremely ambitious leader with considerable military ability, who soon emerged as the driving force of the movement. Immediately after his election Ghalib, with his brother, toured his domain, setting up his own garrisons in his holy capital of Nizwa and in other strategically important towns and villages in the interior.

They soon attracted two powerful allies: Suleiman bin Himyar, Sheikh of the Beni Riyam, Lord of the Jebel Akhdar [Green Mountain] — even his writing paper carried the letterhead, 'Lord of the Green Mountain' — and descendant of the ancient Nebahina dynasty who, on their impregnable mountain, had for centuries preserved their independence from Sultan and Imam alike; and Sheikh Salih bin Isa of the southern province of the Sharqiya. An impressive, even venerable figure with his long white beard, Suleiman was in fact a harsh and vicious tyrant who exercised a master's rights not only over his subjects but over their wives; but if they hated him his people also respected him for the prestige he brought them. Moreover, through family alliances his following included, besides the villages of the Jebel Akhdar, the tribes of the old Ghafiri faction. Sheikh Salih's importance lay in his position as leader of all the Hinawi tribes. Between them these four controlled most of inland Oman.

Ghalib's tour was a gesture of defiance towards the Sultan, and thereafter a virtual state of war existed between the two, with Ghalib receiving increasing support from Saudi Arabia. An open breach soon occurred over the right to grant an oil concession. A British Company, a subsidiary of I.P.C., wanted to drill around the Jebel Fahud [The Mountain of the Leopards] in the west, on the fringe of the great desert. The Sultan claimed the sole right to negotiate with the company on the grounds that this was an external matter, reserved to him under the terms of the Treaty of Sib: the Imam, backed by the Saudis, by certain covetous American oil interests, and by the strident voice of Cairo radio, maintained that oil was essentially an internal affair and so reserved to him under the same Treaty.

The Sultan settled the matter by a show of force. In December, 1955, he sent one of his units, the Muscat and Oman Field Force, from Fahud, where they had been guarding the oil company's camp, to occupy Nizwa, Ibri and the other main centres of Oman. There was no fighting — indeed only one shot was fired in the campaign — and the Sultan, leaving his palace at Salalah on the Indian Ocean, drove across mountain and desert to Nizwa, where he received the formal submission of the rebel chiefs. Ghalib abdicated and was allowed to retire to his village; Talib escaped from Rostaq, where he had been under siege, and fled to Saudi Arabia; Sheikh Salih joined him there, after a visit to Cairo; and Suleiman made a brief, dignified, and totally insincere gesture of loyalty to the Sultan before withdrawing to the top of his mountain. The Sultan sealed his victory with a triumphal tour of Oman and Muscat, and the country was again at peace.

But not for very long. Throughout 1956 Talib was recruiting men from Omani labourers in Saudi Arabia and having them trained, under Saudi instructors, in the use of Bren and Browning, mortar and mine. His plan was for a simultaneous revolt in central Oman, led by himself and Ghalib, and in the Sharqiya under Ibrahim bin Isa, Salih's brother; it was to begin in May, 1957. Ibrahim, however, jumped the gun; having involved himself in a dispute with the Sultan's Governor, he began his revolt a day early. When the local population failed to respond, he went to Muscat to make his peace with the Sultan, who gave him peace of a kind — in the grim fortress prison of Jalali. The Sharqiya remained quiet under its civilian Governor.[7]

Talib, however, landed from a dhow on the Batinah Coast, north of Muscat, with a force of trained guerrillas; in small groups they made their way through the mountains to the interior, where Talib and his brother again raised the Imam's white standard in rebellion. At the same time Suleiman bin Himyar, whom the Sultan had enticed to Muscat and placed under House arrest, escaped to the Jebel Akhdar and rallied his tribesmen to the side of Ghalib. The Muscat and Oman Field Force, attacked on all sides, was caught in an ambush on its retreat and cut to pieces; its British officers brought a few

---

[7] It was lucky that Salih bin Isa stayed in exile; in his absence the leadership of the Hinawi tribes was split, and by skilful diplomacy the Sultan managed to prevent them from uniting against him.

survivors back to the safety of Fahud, but as a fighting force it was finished. The Imam was back in Nizwa. The Sultan called on Britain for aid.

The British Government sent it quickly, before the combined pressures of Cairo Radio, Saudi-American intrigue, and left wing protest at home could cause further embarrassment. A combined offensive by a company of the Cameronians, the Trucial Oman Scouts, and the remnants of the Sultan's army, supported by the RAF, recaptured Nizwa and drove the rebels with Ghalib, Talib and Suleiman up the Jebel Akhdar, from which it was impossible to dislodge them with the forces available. The Cameronians withdrew to Aden — most unfortunately, as it turned out, for the future peace of Oman — and the country settled down again, albeit uneasily, under the rule of the Sultan.

But there could be no hope of lasting peace as long as the rebels held the Jebel Akhdar, a sheer limestone massif between forty and fifty miles in length and twenty miles wide, with a fertile plateau at six thousand feet and peaks rising to nearly ten thousand feet at the summits; the approaches to the mountain led through narrow ravines which could be held by a few determined marksmen against an army. There were villages and crops on the plateau to house and feed the rebels, and caves where they could shelter from aerial bombardment; moreover they continued to receive arms and other supplies from Saudi Arabia, smuggled by friendly tribesmen. The Sultan's army was too weak and demoralized after the destruction of the Muscat and Oman Field Force to invest the Jebel and prevent the smuggling — let alone to mount an assault. Gradually the rebels built up their strength; they began to send patrols down to the plain, lay mines on the roads, and even ambush the Sultan's convoys.

In this grim situation a British mission led by Julian Amery visited Muscat in January, 1958, and in the following July, during the Sultan's visit to the UK, there was published an Exchange of Letters between HMG and the Sultan which covered the provision of assistance in the expansion and reorganization of the Sultan's Armed Forces and in financing a civil development programme under Colonel Hugh Boustead — a legendary figure in the Arab World, who was to be a great support and comfort to me during my service in Oman.

'The job I am asking you to accept,' concluded Amery after many hours of briefing, persuasion and discussion, 'is the command of the Sultan's Armed Forces. Your official title will be Chief of Staff, and you will hold the rank of full Colonel.'

'I'll discuss it with Moy when I get back to Stockholm,' I answered after a great deal of thought. 'But I've already bought my farm in Kenya. We were both looking forward to living there, and I don't want to disappoint her. If she likes your idea I'll accept. Otherwise not.'

Chapter II: Sun, Sand and Soldiers

As the little Heron aircraft of Gulf Airways lifted from the runway I pressed my face to the window and watched our shadow sweep across the sand flats that run out into the shallow water of the Persian Gulf. We banked steeply, gaining height, and I looked down on the airfield we had just left, the flat roofs of Muharraq, and the long, narrow causeway connecting the two main islands of Bahrain; beyond was the blur of Manama, the capital, with the naval base and — though I couldn't distinguish it in the haze — the white Residency, where I had spent the last five days and nights in air-conditioned comfort as the guest of Sir Bernard Burrows, the 'Political Resident, Persian Gulf', in whose hands were gathered the threads of British power along the shores of the Arabian Peninsula from Basra to the Indian Ocean.

We completed our circle and flew again over the sand flats and the lines of fish traps, made of stakes interlaced with palm fronds, that formed a pattern of arrowheads pointing out into the shallows. Travellers have commented on these fish traps, a frequent sight all along the coast ever since Nearchus the Cretan observed them in the fourth century BC when he sailed the fleet of Alexander the Great from the Indus to the Euphrates; and it is unlikely they have changed in construction or design to this day. I remembered as I looked down on them that it was on these waters that men are supposed to have first taken to the sea in ships; but this theory seemed to me only an archaeologist's fantasy, impossible of proof, and I had no time now for fantasies. I had to concentrate on the harsh reality waiting for me at the other end of the Gulf.

When I told her about Amery's offer, Moy had been so enthusiastic that I had cabled my acceptance at once. Although she wouldn't be able to fly out with me, she hoped to join me in Muscat in the autumn. And so we left Stockholm for the last time early in April, 1958, sailing home with our children and our dogs in a cargo boat preceded at first by an ice-breaker; I was due for six weeks' leave, but the problems of Oman were considered too pressing for me to take it, and after ten days of frantic preparation and last-minute briefing in London I found myself flying through the darkness on my way to Bahrain.

The Political Resident's car was waiting for me at the airport, and with it a thin, taciturn sapper with a sandy moustache, who introduced himself with a smart salute as John Goddard, my Brigade Major. Seconded, like myself, from the Regular Army, he turned out to be a most efficient and conscientious officer who knew his job thoroughly; despite his dour temperament and an overzealous regard for regulations which sometimes led him into difficulties with senior officers and subordinates alike, I found him invaluable.

Another visitor at the Residency was Colonel Stewart Carter, commanding the Trucial Oman Scouts, whose headquarters was at Sharjah. Described by one of my officers[8] as 'a ferociously-moustachioed, carnivorous-looking man,' he was tall and broad and dark, with a great hooked nose and a loud, infectious laugh; his flamboyant personality, indestructible sense of humour, and boundless enthusiasm made him an ideal leader for his unconventional little army. I remember him best in his grey shirt and flowing Arab head-dress — a red and white chequered *kaffia*, tied with the black *agal* that does double

---

[8] P. S. Allfree, *Warlords of Oman* (Robert Hale, London 1967). The most detailed — and the wittiest — account I have read of our operations.

service to tie the feet of the Bedouin's camel when at rest — with a falcon on his wrist.

I had first met Bernard Burrows when he was serving at the British Embassy in Cairo during the war. Now he was the most important figure in the Persian Gulf, directly responsible to the Foreign Office for the Defence and Foreign Policy of Bahrain, Kuwait, and the sheikhdoms of the Trucial Coast — but not, of course, of Muscat.

'Your master,' he explained to me, 'is the Sultan. But if he should give you any order you consider contrary to British interests, you have the right to appeal to me, and through me to the Foreign Office.' I only had to exercise that right on two occasions.

Burrows dwelt at some length upon the delicacy of the British position in the Gulf, and the pitfalls that lay in my path. No power is more vulnerable than that of an Empire in the process of dissolution; and now, after the Suez catastrophe, every move by Britain was subject to hostile scrutiny, particularly by the Russian-backed coalition of Egypt, Syria and the Yemen. Cairo Radio spewed out to the Arab world an unending stream of anti-British propaganda; and even the Americans, I knew, would vote against us in the United Nations, whose notorious double standards held us up to world obloquy for Suez, while leaving the Soviet Union uncondemned for the bloody suppression of Hungarian freedom, and the indiscriminate hanging of teenage boys and girls in the vengeful aftermath of the 1956 Revolution.[9]

I should have to tread most warily in Muscat, while my enemies would be under no such restraint. On the contrary, as

---

[9] Some of these children, it was revealed in Parliament, were under the legal age for the death penalty, and so were kept in prison until the law allowed them to be hanged.

I now learned from Military Intelligence, the rebels had become much bolder in their sorties from the Jebel Akhdar, minelaying was more frequent and arms smuggling more blatant by land and sea.

After we had crossed the low-lying Qatar Peninsula there was nothing below us but the burnished steely surface of the sea, until, after nearly two hours, I saw on the starboard side a line of bare sand dunes that marked the Arabian coast; we began to descend, circled an estuary and a mud town, and landed on the airstrip of Sharjah beside a gleaming white fort.

After lunch in the fort, which contained an air-conditioned restaurant, we flew on eastwards over the bare, black volcanic peninsula of Ras Musandum — the hottest place in the world, so I had read — before turning south-east to follow the Batinah Coast to Muscat. On our port side we passed almost every minute some giant tanker ploughing its way to or from the oil ports beyond the Straits of Hormuz; to starboard the white sails of dhows floated gently over the sea. The featureless dunes of the Gulf now gave place to mile upon mile of pale yellow sand fringed with the deep rich green of date plantations; fishing villages, brown clusters of reed or palm frond huts, dotted the shoreline, and sometimes the square outline of a stone fort revealed an old Portuguese or pirate stronghold. Inland from the date palms a scrub-covered plain, intersected by wide *wadis* [dry watercourses] stretched away to a line of haze-shrouded foothills; beyond towered the grim black peaks of the Hajar Range, their flanks scarred by a criss-cross of deep, precipitous clefts. Somewhere along that jagged crest-line lay the Jebel Akhdar, the rebel stronghold I must assault.

We crossed a headland with a fort on the top, and flew low over the bay of Mattrah, the Sultanate's commercial capital,

27

skimmed another steep promontory and circled above the mud roofs of Muscat, hemmed in a gleaming white crescent within its deep rock-bound cove. A great stone citadel crowned each flank of the narrow harbour — 'the hidden port,' the old Arab sailors called it, because it was almost invisible from the sea; we passed above it and headed inland to cross the mountains. My stomach contracted as we shaved the crest of a high ridge before descending steeply to land at the extreme end of a short dirt airstrip. This was Beit al Falaj — 'the house of the water channel' — the headquarters of the Sultan's Armed Forces.

Hugh Boustead, I remember, once quoted me an old Persian proverb: 'The sinner who goes to Muscat has a foretaste of what is coming to him in the other world.' As I stepped from the aircraft onto the floor of that dusty, sun-baked encampment, the heat of late afternoon enveloped me like a stifling blanket. I was sweating profusely, and even my dark glasses misted up.

'Welcome to Muscat, Smiley. I'm Waterfield.' A tall, broad-shouldered man of about fifty wearing a neat, grey tropical suit pushed through the crowd of Arabs thronging round our aircraft to shake my hand. I looked back with considerable interest, for I had already heard about Pat Waterfield, my predecessor as Chief of Staff. A retired Regular officer who had served for many years in India, he still stood high in the Sultan's confidence, despite the reverses his army had suffered the previous summer; indeed, when the British authorities in Bahrain had blamed Waterfield for that disaster, the Sultan, who valued his loyalty, had refused to dismiss him, and had promoted him instead to be his Defence Secretary.

'It is most important,' they had told me in Bahrain, 'that you should get on with Pat Waterfield.' Sensing now a certain reserve behind his bland expression, I felt the situation might hold complications for us both. Although he was not entitled to give me orders, he would inevitably overawe the Contract Officers, who knew he had the Sultan's ear.

He turned to introduce Goddard and me to a tubby lieutenant-colonel with a round, jovial, moon face and a dark military moustache, who wore the khaki balmoral of the Royal Scots Fusiliers. Colin Maxwell was the senior, as well as the most dedicated and competent, officer in the Sultan's Armed Forces. After Regular service with the British Army he had spent some years in the Palestine Police, and so had considerable experience of 'counter-insurgency'. He was a fluent Arabic speaker, whom the Bedouin respected and liked and the Sultan and his advisers trusted. Despite painful arthritis, which caused him to limp and to worry frequently about his health, his equable temperament, quiet confidence, and genial manner remained unruffled by frustration, crisis or adversity; officers and men alike, with no apparent urging, gave of their best when under his command, and I never encountered from him any of the suspicion — amounting to resentment — that sometimes created difficulties between his colleagues and those of us who arrived on secondment from the British Army.

A Land Rover took us over to the camp, which was enclosed within a barbed wire fence with the entrance on its eastern side. At one corner long, low whitewashed barracks, like those of an Indian Army cantonment, housed the troops; at another clustered the khaki tents of the officers and a large marquee that served as their Mess. The dominant feature was a white, crenellated fort, which, but for the little mosque beside it, might have been the centrepiece in a studio set for a film of *Beau Geste*; from its main turret flew the Sultan's scarlet flag.[10]

---

[10] It was also the flag of the Sultan of Zanzibar.

Waterfield's house was in the south-west corner of the camp, a white mud and plaster rectangle with a flat roof and a verandah on three sides.

'Your own house is over there.' He pointed to a smaller white bungalow, standing bleak and lonely on a mound beyond the southern perimeter fence, and separated from it by a *wadi*. 'It isn't quite ready for you yet, I'm afraid, but I'd be delighted to put you up for a few days.'

When, with some foreboding at its stark appearance from afar, I went to inspect my house at close quarters, I was quite appalled at the squalor of it. In London, knowing nothing about Muscat except that it was damnably hot, I had enquired about our future living conditions, in particular whether we should have air conditioning. A signal back from Waterfield had described the house as having '13 rooms *with* air conditioning'. The reality, as I now found, was 3 rooms and no air conditioning — and none likely for at least a year, Waterfield told me.

'It's really not necessary,' he calmly assured me. 'My wife and I manage very well without it, and we never had it in India. You've got electricity, after all, and electric fans.'

There was no running water either, but in a small space off the bedroom stood a tin hip bath, which the Baluch water coolie would fill from old four-gallon petrol drums, carried slung on a yoke across his shoulders from the *falaj* by the fort. The only sanitation was a huge wooden 'thunder-box' placed in the bedroom, to be emptied by the sweeper after use.

'It's all we ever had in India,' explained Waterfield defensively, as he intercepted my furious look.

I drew his attention to the streaks of grime running down the walls, where the rain had leaked in through the roof.

'I expect you had those too,' I muttered, 'in India.'

30

The furniture, I observed, had the merit of simplicity — no more than a camp bed, two wicker chairs, and a plain deal table. There were no cupboards.

I had, of course, often put up with varying combinations and degrees of heat, dirt and discomfort during the past twenty years; but I was damned if I would impose these on Moy. When I had been told, in London, that only the Air Force Commander and myself enjoyed the privilege of having our wives on station with us, I had assumed that there would be at least tolerable living conditions for a woman. Now I felt I had been tricked; I felt so even more when I found the War Office deducting a substantial portion of my salary 'in respect of rent for Colonel's accommodation' — especially since I knew the Sultan charged them no rent for the house. I resolved to take the first opportunity of telephoning Moy and warning her that I meant to resign. I would go into Muscat and do it tomorrow.

But when I spoke to her she reacted with her usual vigour. 'Nonsense!' she protested. 'You stick it out, and I'll join you there in the autumn. Just put up with it till then.'

Beit al Falaj sweltered in its shallow bowl among the hills. At night the scorched, volcanic rocks threw back the heat, giving no relief between sunset and dawn; the thermometer in my bedroom read 112° Fahrenheit. As I lay on my mattress in a pool of sweat I was cruelly reminded of the fact that just two weeks ago I had been driving my car across the Baltic, towing my children on skis over snow and ice twelve feet thick.

Strategically our headquarters was well sited, at a point where all the routes from the interior to Muscat converged. In the evenings and at daybreak I would often watch the laden caravans lumbering slowly past my verandah on their way to Mattrah; in one I counted well over a hundred camels strung out in single file across the plain. Notwithstanding its ugliness and its exposed situation outside the protection of the barbed wire perimeter, my house commanded a fine view of the camp across the *wadi*. On the far side, to the north, rose a ridge of grey basalt with a gap at its western end, through which wound the road to Mattrah and Muscat; hills hemmed us in on the west and on the south, where another basalt ridge climbed steeply from the back of the house in a succession of sharp rocky outcrops split by narrow, boulder-strewn ravines. The only splash of green to relieve the stark brown and grey of the landscape was an infant bougainvillea planted at the foot of the verandah by the previous occupant, Frank Haugh, a dapper ex-cavalryman who had commanded the Muscat Regiment before my arrival. When Moy came out we began work on a garden, and by the time we left the walls and columns of the verandah were clothed in mauve and purple, the top of the mound bright with frangipani and oleander.

On the eastern side a mile of flat, stony desert divided the camp from the encircling hills; across it wound the caravans, past a small and dirty village from which, day and night, I could hear the ceaseless creaking of well wheels turned slowly by plodding bullocks. On this plain was the narrow airstrip where stood the two single-engine Pioneers, used for communications and casualty evacuation and flown by RAF pilots, that made up the total strength of the Sultan's Air Force.

At five in the morning I would awake to the bugles of the Muscat Regiment sounding reveille from the fort. This unit, numbering about 250 officers and men, had no operational role and was employed on garrison and guard duties at Beit al Falaj and in Muscat, where it was under the command of Major Richard Anderson, a red-faced mountain of a man whose uniform seemed on the point of bursting at the seams, but who nevertheless had a flair — and a passion — for ceremonial drill; he was also a notable gourmet and, as President of our Mess Committee, spurred on our Goan cooks to achievements of Cordon Bleu standard. The teeth of the Sultan's Army was the Northern Frontier Regiment of some 450 men, including a depleted Company composed of survivors from the ill-starred Muscat and Oman Field Force; these troops were deployed in the interior, with their headquarters at Nizwa, under Colonel Colin Maxwell, who was also the area commander. They were reinforced by an Artillery Troop of two 5.5 inch guns, on loan from the British government, and two 75 mm gun-howitzers — the 'screw guns' of Rudyard Kipling's day. The Training Depot was some fifteen miles from Muscat, where a group of twenty-five instructors, under a British officer, looked after a varying number of between sixty and a hundred and twenty recruits.

The Fort at Beit al Falaj housed my headquarters, known officially as HQ, SAF[11] and controlled by my very capable Brigade Major, John Goddard, who was directly concerned with the drafting, distribution, and to some extent the implementation of my orders; he carried a heavy load of work, for he had also to co-ordinate the activities of the elaborate organization that comprised my staff: there was a detachment from the Royal Corps of Signals which kept me in wireless touch with my units throughout the Sultanate, and with Bahrain; the Administration Branch, which dealt with such matters as pay; the Quartermaster's department, whose duties involved not only supply, but also supervision of the repair and maintenance of our trucks and Land Rovers; and a small but highly efficient Intelligence Unit under an enthusiastic captain,

---

[11] Sultan's Armed Forces.

Malcolm Dennison — a quiet young man of gentle but persuasive charm and tireless persistence who spoke fluent Arabic. His office was in the main turret, next to my own and underneath the Interrogation Room, where he would exercise his talents, without violence but with the most gratifying results, on suspected enemy agents or mine-layers. On the ground floor was a store room where I found a huge hoard of ancient, silver-embossed muskets and old Martini-Henry rifles dating from the Franco-Prussian War. There were nearly four thousand of these antique weapons stacked round the walls; many of them, like the muzzle-loaders with their delicate silver chasing, were valuable museum pieces which I once suggested to the Sultan that he should sell abroad. He replied with — for him — unusual firmness and promptitude.

'No, Colonel Smiley. I am keeping those guns for a purpose. In the event of a rebellion I intend to use them to arm the friendly tribes.'

The Sultan maintained a small private army of his own, the 'Dhofar Force' of two hundred men under a British officer, which was based on Salalah and did not come under my jurisdiction. Altogether my command numbered a little over eight hundred men, of whom a bare half could be deployed as fighting infantry. It seemed a ludicrous figure when I considered all the tasks we had to undertake: containing a strong and wily enemy on the Jebel Akhdar, watching the many infiltration routes to and from it, garrisoning strategic points in the interior, aggressive patrolling, and guarding the roads from mine-layers — to name only a few of them. I was lucky, however, in having a few British troops attached to me from Bahrain and Aden: two squadrons of the Trucial Oman Scouts, one at Ibri, the other at Izki; one troop — later increased to two — of Ferret scout cars from the 13th/18th Hussars, based on Nizwa;[12] and one Royal Marine officer and eight sergeants attached to the Northern Frontier Regiment as 'junior leaders' — an outstandingly keen and efficient little party who proved their value over and over again in training and in battle. Together with the signallers I have mentioned and the RAF pilots and ground crews, they made up a total of under fifty British servicemen of all ranks — rather less than the ten to twenty thousand attributed to me by Cairo's 'Voice of the Arabs'.

With the exception of a few Pakistanis and Arabs in junior grades, the Sultan's officers were British — either mercenaries serving under contract or, like myself, Regulars seconded from the British Army. The Other Ranks were made up, when I arrived, of Arabs and Baluch in roughly equal numbers; the proportion of Baluch subsequently increased to seventy percent, for the Sultan never really trusted his Arabs — with good reason, as time was to show. I didn't have too much confidence in them myself; for, although they were intelligent and quick to learn — some of them, indeed, became very proficient signallers — they were far from natural soldiers. They were fish-eaters from the coast, not warriors from the fighting tribes of Oman — most of whom, when not neutral, were fighting on the other side.

Almost all the troops, Arabs and Baluch, were illiterate and had to sign for their pay with their thumb marks; but after I had been there two years we were able to start schools for them, and managed to overcome at least this initial disability.

The Baluchis came partly from the large colony in the Sultanate, but mostly from Gwadur, an enclave on the Baluchistan coast which belonged to the Sultan, who maintained there a resident of British nationality until 1958. In

---

[12] There were four scout cars to a troop.

the year of my arrival Gwadur was sold to the Pakistani government, but the Sultan retained by agreement his right to recruit in the territory. There were always plenty of volunteers — most of them signed on with the simple purpose of earning enough money to buy on their return a camel, a wife, and a transistor radio, in that order of priority.

Our principal difficulty with the Baluchis was that we didn't know their language and had no means of learning it, although Waterfield could talk to some of them in Urdu. They were not very bright either, and so misunderstandings were inevitable, leading on two occasions to mild outbreaks of mutiny. Yet despite — or perhaps because of — his abnormally stolid, often obtuse nature, the Baluchi had one formidable advantage as a soldier: in battle he was a sticker. Whether from courage or a simple inability to appreciate danger, he would hold his ground even under heavy fire or determined assault; in the attack he was effective only if well led. I can recall but one incident of desertion in the face of the enemy by a Baluch, and I prefer to attribute it — as the offender certainly did — to a misunderstanding. He had run away while Talib was mortaring one of our camps near Nizwa, but he returned a week later; when marched in front of me he defended himself vigorously.

'When I joined this army, Sahib, it was not explained to me,' he exploded angrily, 'that I should have to fight!'

Chapter III: The Viceroy and the Sultan

The track from Beit al Falaj to Muscat — it would be a distortion to call it a road — ran through a defile in a series of sharp corrugations over which we had to drive at high speed to avoid an agonizingly bumpy ride; the distance was about six miles, past Mattrah and thence along the coast. Outside the city wall of Mattrah was an enormous camel park, where the caravans unloaded their cargoes of dried fish and dates and packed them on to trucks or donkeys for the rest of the journey. An ancient law forbade camels to enter the town, and so when I passed that way I would see as many as a couple of hundred of them tethered there, kneeling or lying down, lazily champing their jaws and regarding the world with that look of supercilious resentment peculiar to camels. The air was heavy with their acrid smell, blending with the scent of wood or charcoal fires as their drivers prepared their meals or brewed coffee.

I had arrived during the Moslem festival of Id which celebrates the end of Ramadan and lasts three days; and so when I drove into Muscat for the first time I found all the shops and nearly all the offices closed, and had to confine myself to sightseeing. I watched the full dress parade outside the mosque at noon and admired the turn-out and bearing of Anderson's guardsmen in their carefully pressed and well-scrubbed shorts and red and khaki pill-box hats. All the Muscati dignitaries were there: the *walis* and *qadhis* in their black, gold-edged *abas* [robes] and cashmere turbans, together with their escorts of bodyguards and slaves; the venerable Minister of the Interior, Sayid Ahmed Ibrahim, radiating benevolence behind his luxuriant white whiskers; Sayid Shahab, Governor of Muscat and uncle of the Sultan, with his great black beard, harsh mouth and cold, pitiless eyes; and the ablest of them all, Sayid Tarik, the Sultan's half-brother, whom I was soon to meet directing operations against the rebels. I listened carefully as Waterfield whispered to me their names and rank, for I knew I should be working with all of them in the near future and their attitudes could either greatly simplify or wholly frustrate my work.

If Beit al Falaj had been a furnace, Muscat was a steam bath; closely encircled between sea and mountains, the city resembled a vast pressure cooker, simmering in the damp and suffocating heat. Within minutes my sodden uniform was clinging to me, stained with dark patches from the sweat that trickled in rivulets over my clammy, itching skin. Darkness would bring no relief, for the bare rocks behind held in the heat, which hung over the town in a heavy, sticky pall.

There were nearly as many foreigners as Arabs in Muscat, and probably more in Mattrah, which was the commercial capital: Hindu and Persian merchants and shopkeepers predominated in the *suks*, where each trade tended to monopolize a particular street or quarter of the bazaar; there would be a 'street of the silversmiths', a 'street of the spice-sellers', a weavers' and a shoemakers' quarter. Indian paper rupees were the currency in Muscat and Matrah, but in the interior only silver Maria Theresa dollars — in which we paid our troops — or gold were acceptable. Baluchis, too, were numerous in the town, their wives and daughters colourful in bright red, blue or green, with smiling, uncovered faces, in happy contrast to the veiled, black-draped Arab women.

Black features and colouring were not uncommon among the inhabitants, usually a legacy from the slave trade. Although, as

I have mentioned, there were still slaves in the bodyguards and households of the Sultan and nobility, they were well-treated — unless they ran away and were caught, in which case they might be whipped or put in shackles — and many were freed by their masters and rose to be rich, or even powerful; at least one of the Sultan's *walis* had started life as a slave. Under a curious survival from one of the earlier treaties, if a runaway slave could reach the British Consulate and clasp the flagpole in the courtyard, he became free. My most accomplished bugler was one of these; a bewildered Consul General had turned him over to me, and he served us well and cheerfully for several years until one day he deserted — to turn up later as the leading trumpeter in the Bahrain Police Band, at a much higher rate of pay.

Although both Muscat and Mattrah were good deep-water anchorages, neither had dock facilities or even a pier where ships could unload; liners and cargo boats had to stand out in the bay, while their passengers and freight came ashore in lighters. The little ports teemed with sailing craft of all sizes, from the hollowed-out tree trunks known as 'houris' to the ponderous 'booms' and 'sambuks' that plied up and down the coast; there were the fleets of dhows which traded with Zanzibar, waiting for the seasonal wind to blow them down to Africa, where they would remain until it changed to blow them back again. Once a week a big British India liner would call on its way between Karachi and Basra; this was an important social occasion, as were the visits we received from frigates of the Royal Navy, whose officers would come ashore in smart pinnaces to see the town and drive out to lunch with us at Beit al Falaj. The floor of the harbour at Muscat was littered with old Portuguese cannon, clearly visible through the crystal water — dumped there perhaps by the last garrison before they surrendered in 1660. Another chapter of history stared at us from a cliff face near the harbour entrance, on which were painted in huge white lettering the names of warships and merchantmen which had visited the port since the latter years of the eighteenth century. 'My visitors' book,' the Sultan would call it, boasting to the few Englishmen who were ever allowed to meet him that Mr Midshipman Nelson had commanded a painting party on that cliff when his ship, *Seahorse*, had called at Muscat in 1775.

Facing the waterfront, which was only a few hundred yards long, were the British Consulate, the Customs building, and the square palace of the Sultan, which he never visited in my time, preferring the cool ocean breezes of Salalah, some 600 miles down the coast — one of his gravest mistakes and probably his costliest. This palace, according to legend, was built on top of the old Portuguese cathedral, whose vaulted columns form part of its foundations. These fine buildings, gleaming white above the deep blue harbour, were overlooked on either side by two great stone forts — Mirani on the north, Jalali on the south — both built by the Portuguese in the sixteenth century.

Even from a distance Jalali looked a grim and evil place; its sheer granite walls, flanked by two formidable round towers, stood on the summit of a huge rock, accessible only across a narrow causeway and up a long, steep flight of steps cut in the cliff face. Inside, it was horrible. Here the Sultan kept his prisoners, nearly a hundred of them, criminals and political offenders or suspects. Although the political prisoners received slightly better treatment than the criminals — the more important ones had rooms to themselves and might receive visits from their servants with extra food — they were worse off in the long run; for the criminals at least had definite terms to serve, and knew they would then be free, whereas the political prisoners were there during the Sultan's pleasure — which might be for a year or a lifetime. Both categories were shackled, the fetters round their ankles connected by a heavy iron bar. When any of them had to go outside to relieve himself he lifted the bar by a piece of cord to take some of the weight off his feet; but most of the time they lay on the hard stone floors of their long barrack rooms, without mattresses or even straw to rest on. A silent, gloomy gaoler looked after them, and soldiers of the Muscat Regiment mounted a reluctant guard; the only Europeans allowed inside were the guard commander, Waterfield, and myself. Worse than the discomfort and the miserable diet was their lack of water, which the black-hearted Governor, Sayid Shahab, deliberately withheld from them; whenever I visited them — a regular part of my duties — they would crowd round me, trailing their shackles and gasping piteously, 'water, Sahib, water!' I did my best for them, pleading again and again with Sayid Shahab in the name of humanity to increase their ration; but he remained unmoved, his flinty eyes quite expressionless.

'They have done wrong, Colonel Smiley,' was all he ever said. 'They must be punished.' Eventually I managed to arrange extra rations of water for my soldier guards, which they passed on surreptitiously to the prisoners.

Shahab's son, Sayid Thuwainy, interpreted for us — a bright, bespectacled young man with an unusually alert intelligence. He was believed to sympathize with the rebels — and after talking with his father I could hardly blame him.

The two most important prisoners in the fortress were an uncle of the Sultan's who an alcoholic and was incarcerated there to keep him away from temptation, and Sheikh Ibrahim bin Isa who had led the abortive rising in the Sharqiya in 1957. These two were not manacled and had special privileges in the form of private cells and their own servants to cook for them. Among the other prisoners there was one at least who should never have been there — a harmless old lunatic. He would spring to attention, as smartly as his fetters allowed, whenever I appeared and shout, 'God save the King!' with a pathetic attempt at a salute. In any civilized country he would have been at large.

Fort Mirani was altogether a kindlier place, with brown humpy towers and mellow curving walls sprawling comfortably over the rocks. Above its gateway were carved the royal arms of Spain with the date 1588, a reminder of the period when the two crowns were united, and along the walls stood a line of old Portuguese cannon now used for firing salutes; in former times, I was told, they also fired prisoners from the barrels. In the magazine I discovered a store of explosive cannon balls, dating presumably from a period immediately before the introduction of the shell. John Goddard, a sapper, was horrified to see them, and assured me they were highly dangerous and might go up at any time, but when I asked permission to have them destroyed, the Sultan, who seemed to have an overdeveloped sense of property, obstinately refused.

Fort Mirani, garrisoned by a detachment of the Muscat police, was the scene of a curious ceremony known as 'Dum-Dum', which took place regularly every evening at sundown. At the precise moment when the sun disappeared, the policeman on guard would apply a match to the touch-hole of one of the old cannon, drummers on the ramparts would beat out a long, rolling tattoo, and the great gate of the city would be closed and barred. From then until sunrise anyone walking in the streets had to carry a hurricane lamp on pain of arrest — an electric torch wouldn't do. This law dated from the reign of the previous Sultan, when some visiting Chinese merchant was set upon by thugs and robbed. No one might enter or leave the city after Dum-Dum without a written permit from the Minister of the Interior; I was one of the very few exempted from this restriction, but whenever I invited any of my friends in Muscat to dine in our Mess, I had to make sure we gave them a particularly good dinner to compensate them for the trouble of getting a permit.

The Sharia Law was administered by the Sultan's *walis* throughout his thirty-six provinces, and interpreted in his courts by the *qadhis*, who enjoyed enormous prestige and influence. In Muscat the laws were harsh and punishments severe: for murder or adultery, death — although the murderer might escape with his life if the relatives of his victim agreed to accept blood money in compensation.[13] The method of execution was by shooting, which led to one of my two open breaches with the Sultan: when he ordered me to provide a firing party to execute a soldier guilty of murder, I appealed to the Political Resident at Bahrain, who supported me. Fortunately there were very few murders in Muscat — on average less than one in five years. An adulterous woman was unlikely to appear before the courts, because her dishonoured family would usually kill her themselves — and were never punished for it.

For drunkenness the punishment on first offence was thirty-six lashes, and double the second time; our Goan cooks were the most frequent sufferers, but they took their floggings philosophically and never dreamed of mending their ways. Reinforcing the Ibadhi prohibition, the Sultan punished smoking with imprisonment, although his father had tolerated it; I managed to obtain his permission for my officers to drink and smoke, but only in the Mess. Otherwise the law of the

---

[13] £300 was the sum fixed by the local courts.

country made no concession to the twentieth century; camels, for example, took precedence over motor vehicles, and in any collision between the two, whatever the circumstances, judgment was for the camel.

'Money,' said Waterfield emphatically. 'That is the root cause of all our difficulties. Money — or rather, the lack of it — is what's been holding up all my plans for improvements. You'll find the same, Smiley, when you've been around this place a bit. You simply can't run an army without money, and the Sultan just hasn't got any.'

It was the last day of the Id festival, during which all military as well as civilian activity had been at a standstill. Waterfield and I were sitting on his verandah overlooking the camp, sipping our evening gin and limes and watching the last orange-red glow of the sunset fade behind the western hills. I had been suggesting to him that the officers deserved better accommodation than the stifling tents in which they had to live at present, and wondering if we couldn't build them houses. Eventually we did, and before I left the country Waterfield, who was in charge of building operations, had put up stone houses for the officers and their Mess, laid on running water, and finally, much against his own inclination, given us air conditioning. But at this moment I was feeling a good deal of sympathy for him as he unburdened himself on the problems of finance and administration with which he had to struggle to keep the army on its feet.

'It's easy enough for people to call the Sultan an old skinflint,' he went on. 'Plenty do call him that. But they seem to forget that when his father, Sultan Taimur, abdicated in 1932 he left the country pretty well bankrupt. Oh, they had a high old time in Muscat in the old man's day, but he lived way beyond his means, and Sultan Said inherited an empty treasury. Up to now his only revenue has been from Customs dues and a tax on date palms. If he's miserly it's because he's damn well had to be. I sometimes wonder if even his puritanism doesn't spring from this driving need to keep down all expenditure — although of course his religious convictions play their part.'

'I see. But at least since last year he has been getting money from HMG.'

'The army share is not much these days, when you consider the cost of modern arms and equipment. And as for development, you could spend five times what he gets in this country and still have precious little to show for it. We're flying to Nizwa tomorrow, aren't we? Well, take a look around you at conditions in the interior, and you'll see what I mean.'

In fact I had little opportunity to study conditions in the interior on this particular journey — a brief visit of inspection to Colin Maxwell's headquarters. We took off early from Beit al Falaj to avoid the turbulence that developed with the heat of the day, and flew over the scrub and desert of the coastal plain before turning inland to follow the Wadi Sumail, which divides the mountains of the Sharqiya from the Jebel Akhdar. Looking down on that bleak, moon-like landscape of sheer precipices and deep, boulder strewn ravines, I wondered unhappily what chance we should stand if our single engine were to fail — our RAF pilot, a South African, had told me it had been known to happen, for these aircraft were notoriously unreliable. The answer, all too clearly, was no chance at all. For most of my service in Oman these Pioneers were the only aircraft available to me for communications, and neither I nor our pilots enjoyed flying in them over such inhospitable country.

On my right I could see the great rock slabs of the Jebel Akhdar thrusting up between eight and ten thousand feet into the sky, their smooth, almost perpendicular sides bare of any kind of vegetation, and I wondered how even the most resolute assaulting party could hope to scale them against opposition. Suleiman and his friends must have posted guards on all possible approaches, and unless we could discover some path they had overlooked we seemed to have little hope of dislodging them.

The journey, a hundred and twenty miles by road, took us only an hour. We passed over the sparse date palms and crumbling mud huts of Izki, an important junction of camel tracks between Nizwa, Muscat and the Arabian interior, where we had posted a company in a wired camp near the village along with one of the squadrons of the Trucial Oman Scouts, and soon afterwards circled the great round stone fort of Nizwa — the largest fort in Oman, famous throughout Arabia.

Nizwa was now the capital of the interior and a sizeable town by the standards of the country. Its flat-roofed mud houses spread outwards from the fort towards thick groves of date palms and a wide river that flowed with fresh water all the year round. On the far side of the river, about a mile east of the town, Colin Maxwell had set up his headquarters in a tented camp surrounded by a barbed wire fence; *sangars* built of rocks and sandbags provided strongpoints at intervals round the perimeter.

Maxwell met us at the small airstrip and took us to the Mess tent for a glass of beer before leading us on a tour of inspection of the camp. With him was his adjutant, Major Jasper Coates, formerly a Group Captain commanding the RAF in the Persian Gulf; on relinquishing his appointment he had come down in rank to sign on as a major in the Sultan's service. This was not his only eccentricity, for his appearance, even by the unconventional standards of the SAF, was extraordinary: under a battered and filthy old RAF cap he wore a pair of dirty, unpressed khaki shorts, open sandals, and a thick, untidy black beard. A likeable man with a heart of gold and a glint of humour in his eyes, he was a voluble talker and indefatigable raconteur, who also — and more seriously — regarded decisions from above not as orders to be implemented but as subjects for detailed and critical discussion with his fellow officers.

After my tour of the camp I decided to inspect the troop of 5.5" guns which the British government had loaned us, and which were deployed near the village of Kamah some five miles north of Nizwa; from positions at the base of the Jebel they kept up an intermittent bombardment of the rebels on the top. We set out in two Land Rovers with an escort of two Ferret scout cars; Maxwell and I led the convoy in his Land Rover, followed by Waterfield in the other, with the Ferrets bringing up the rear. Passing through the drab, sun-baked houses of Nizwa, each one a miniature fortress with its windowless mud walls pierced by narrow embrasures designed for marksmen rather than air or light, we paused a moment at the fort to pick up Sayid Tarik, the Sultan's half-brother and acting viceroy for the interior.

It was a bumpy, dusty ride to Kamah, for the road was no more than a camel track across the desert, and we were all hot and thirsty when we arrived. About three miles out of Nizwa we had passed one of the little round watch towers that dotted the interior of Oman; most of them were deserted, but this one had a small garrison of *askers*, or tribal levies, stationed there by Tarik to keep a lookout for mine-layers. They waved at us as we went by, and fired their rifles into the air in salute. At the gun position the officer commanding the troop — a Pakistani like his men — ordered a few rounds of fire for our benefit; it was an impressive display, although of course we couldn't see where the shells were landing. But the enemy had the last laugh.

We drove back towards Nizwa in the same order — Maxwell and myself in the lead, with Waterfield and the two Ferrets following — and after a couple of miles came in sight of the round watch tower. Suddenly there was a loud explosion behind and looking round I saw one of the Ferrets slewed over, with its near front wheel blown off by a mine. Nobody was hurt, for Ferrets are well enough armoured to withstand the blast of the small mines which at this stage of the war were all we encountered. But it was a lucky escape for the Land Rovers, and especially for me; Maxwell had removed all the sandbags, which were used to reinforce the floors of the Land Rovers against this eventuality, from his vehicle while he was having it repainted, and they hadn't been put back. I was sitting on the near side, and if we had detonated the mine — we must certainly have gone over it — I could hardly have survived. Maxwell was full of apologies.

'It never occurred to me we'd run into a mine in the middle of the morning,' he explained. 'The road was clear early today, and so that mine must have been laid in broad daylight, and probably just after we passed on our way to the guns — in full view of those damned *askers* on the watch tower,' he added explosively.

The *askers* had left their tower and were running towards us, screaming excitedly and firing their rifles in the air — a gesture both useless and extravagant in the circumstances, but always adopted by the tribesmen in moments of extreme emotion.

'Perhaps they're trying to let us know they've seen the mine go off,' I suggested to Maxwell. 'Trying to show Sayid Tarik how wide awake they are.'

If so, they failed. Sayid Tarik, who was nobody's fool, surmised that if they had seen the mine they had probably seen the mine-layer. Like all of us, he knew only too well that many of these tribal guards were of doubtful loyalty to the Sultan, while some of them were secret rebel sympathizers in Saudi pay. After snarling abuse at them for a few long minutes, he turned on his heel and we resumed our journey, leaving the damaged Ferret to be salvaged by a Scammel[14] from the camp.

Tarik had invited us to take coffee with him and so we drove up to the fort, whose huge circular bole of solid rock stood on a mound above the town, dominating the countryside, its mud-plastered sides gleaming a pinkish yellow in the strong sunlight — a monument to the strength and engineering skill of sixteenth century Portugal. Above the tower, on whose thick walls the rockets of RAF Venoms had made no more than a few dark splodges, were emplaced some enormous cannon of the same period, used for firing salutes and sometimes lethal to their gunners. Inside, a labyrinth of narrow, steep stairways and tunnel-like passages gave access to living and sleeping quarters, and two wells, driven through the rock, provided a plentiful supply of water for any besieged garrison. There were some hideous dungeons, too: deep holes covered by heavy trap doors, into which prisoners were lowered on the end of ropes and — in former times at least — left to rot.

While we were drinking our coffee we heard another explosion from the direction of Kamah. The Scammel had arrived and taken the disabled Ferret in tow, but after only five

---

[14] A breakdown truck, equipped with crane and winch for towing.

yards the Ferret had gone over another mine and lost a second wheel.

'I am giving orders to have those *asker* guards arrested,' Tarik told us when the news arrived soon afterwards. I wondered if they would end up in those dreadful dungeons and found I was shivering. All the same, they were luckier than another group of three *askers*, who were guarding a *sangar* a few months later when a mine went up on the road less than fifty yards from them, wrecking a 3-ton lorry at the head of a convoy. The Baluch driver pulled himself from the wreckage of his cabin, retrieved his submachine gun and walked over to the *sangar*, where he shot all three of its occupants dead.

This was my first meeting with Sayid Tarik, although I had seen him outside the mosque in Muscat during the Id celebrations. He was to become — and I like to think he still is — a close friend. A younger son of the previous Sultan by a Turkish mother, he was about the same age as myself; he had been educated at Heidelberg University and in Turkey, and spoke beautiful English as well as German. He was tall for an Omani, of portly build but truly impressive dignity, with a fine black beard which covered the lower part of his face from ear to ear and which he kept, contrary to Ibadhi custom, carefully trimmed. He was capable of the most strenuous physical exertion; indeed, he enjoyed nothing more than accompanying troops on arduous and hazardous operations, when he would be followed by two retainers carrying his personal Bren gun, which he would fire from the hip or shoulder at any likely target. He had passed through the military academy at Dehra Dun, and in the Second World War had served as an officer in both the Indian Police and Indian Army; he had in fact been Adjutant of a regiment on the Northwest Frontier. As well as great personal courage he had a lively sense of humour which, unlike that of most Arabs, did not depend for its nourishment on the misfortunes of others; and he was by far the most intelligent and able member of the Royal Family — a highly civilized and convivial person who loved classical music and played excellent Bridge, who had studied European history and political theory, and who suffered cruelly from the inner conflict between his genuine loyalty to his brother and his clear perception of the need for a greater degree of progress and freedom for his countrymen.

Sadly but inevitably he fell out of favour with the Sultan, who was both jealous and afraid of him: jealous of his popularity with the tribesmen, which he knew was far greater than his own, and afraid, however unjustly, because so many former Sultans had died violently at the hands of their kinsmen. And so Tarik's position as governor and viceroy, although of great importance, was really a form of exile, designed to keep him away from the centre of power in Muscat. The Sultan also kept him very short of money. Tarik had none of his own and every year, at Christmastime, he had to present himself at Salalah to receive his annual gift of cash, which was all he had to live on. When our war with Talib and Suleiman was over and the Sultan felt he could dispense with his services, he discontinued his pension. To keep himself and his family Tarik set up as a local contractor with a couple of broken-down old army lorries, but eventually — after I had gone — he left the country for Abu Dhabi and Turkey, taking his son with him to be educated abroad. Later he went to Germany, where he married a German girl and where he remained until the revolution that deposed his brother. I kept in touch with him during all this time, and was delighted to hear that the new Sultan, Qabus, had invited him back to Muscat.

On 28 April, just over a week after my arrival in Muscat, I flew to Salalah for my first audience with the Sultan; I was on my way to Aden to make my number with the military and civilian authorities there. The journey involved a flight by Pioneer to Sharjah, where I changed planes, thankfully, to fly on in an RAF Valetta. In Sharjah I had a meeting with my immediate superior, Brigadier Tinker, a tall, thin, studious-looking cavalryman with greying hair whose official title was Commander Land Forces Persian Gulf [CLFPG], and also with Group Captain Bufton, who, like Jasper Coates before him, now commanded the Royal Air Force in the same area.

Bufton was an exceptionally brilliant and daring pilot who took an enthusiastic personal interest in our war and was a valuable source of help and encouragement. Better than any other European he knew the layout of the plateau on top of the Jebel Akhdar, at that time quite inaccessible to us; he made a habit of flying sorties over it himself, cruising slowly at nought feet while he made sketch maps of the rebels' positions, impervious to the hail of fire that greeted him from their rifles and .5 Brownings. Sometimes he took a local informer with him to point out the caves of Suleiman and the other leaders, and sometimes he took me as well. At the end of each run across the plateau he would make a very tight turn, which usually caused the informer to throw up all over us, upsetting me almost as much as the sight of the tribesmen shooting at us from point blank range; but it never bothered Bufton.

Major St John Armitage, the Contract Officer commanding the Dhofar Force, met me on Salalah airfield and drove me to his bungalow outside the town, where I was staying the night. He was not a happy man, living in the shadow of the Sultan, with whom he didn't get on well, and sometime after the end of my tour of duty in Muscat he resigned his appointment. Meanwhile, he was spied on continuously, by his own servants and by the Arab waiters in the RAF mess, who reported his every word to the Sultan; he was not even allowed to visit the camp of the oil company nearby, where at least he might have enjoyed good food and drink. After he left, the Sultan advertised for officers who shared the Ibadhi prejudices against alcohol and tobacco — not that Armitage took either in quantity; he failed, not surprisingly, to find any from the British Army, and accepted Pakistanis instead, one of whom was to prove his loyalty with his life.

The Dhofar Force, recruited mostly from local Arabs and *Jibalis* from the mountains behind Salalah, with only a smattering of Baluch, fell prey in time to the many agitators who infested the Sultanate. In April, 1966, there was a ceremonial parade in front of the palace, attended by the Sultan. When ordered to present arms, some of the *Jibali* soldiers levelled their rifles instead at His Highness and fired. The gallant Pakistani saw the danger in time and threw himself between them and the Sultan, receiving the whole volley in his own body. He died immediately. The Sultan was unharmed. The mutineers absconded with their rifles to the hills.

On my first morning in Salalah I presented myself in full Service Dress at the Sultan's palace. It stood right on the sea shore — a well-designed, long, low building surrounded by high walls with crenellated battlements; a wide, palm-lined avenue led to a gate tower and a courtyard, where I dismounted from my car amid grave bows and murmured salaams from a group of waiting attendants. I walked across an inner courtyard to climb a long, wide staircase guarded by a double line of heavily armed retainers wearing turbans and

Arab robes and festooned with bandoliers full of cartridges; they were a fierce-looking body of men, who glared wolfishly at me as I passed.

The Sultan received me alone, a tiny figure standing in a large, thickly carpeted room comfortably furnished with deep armchairs and a sofa; through open lattice windows overlooking the Indian Ocean came a gentle cooling breeze. He was exquisitely dressed in a black *aba* edged with gold and a rich tasselled turban embroidered with the royal colours of purple, green and gold; in the middle of his belt gleamed the jewel-studded hilt of a splendid *khanja* — the great curved dagger carried by all Omanis. His bushy grey beard was untrimmed and liberally perfumed with frankincense, his eyes large and limpid, and his mouth, beneath a fleshy nose, at once arrogant and shrewd. Despite his small stature he had an air of unmistakeable authority, quiet dignity, and almost irresistible charm, and his voice was surprisingly gentle. He spoke an English so faultless that it could never have come from an Englishman — he had in fact learned it at Mayo College in Rajputhana, which used to be called 'the Eton of India'.

Born in 1910, he looked considerably older than his 48 years. He had succeeded his father at the age of 22, since when he had maintained a rule of narrow and puritanical autocracy, determined to preserve his country from the contamination of modern ideas. He would permit, in my time at least, no foreign journalists to enter the Sultanate, but would complain nevertheless when he received, inevitably, a very bad press. Suggestions for improvement would meet with a bland, noncommittal 'I will think about it'. But he seldom took any action. Poverty was his usual excuse.

'You may wonder, Colonel Smiley,' he once observed in a rare mood of expansion, 'why I never show myself in Muscat. I

54

will tell you. If I go to Muscat I will be surrounded by suppliants, all asking me for money. I have no money to give them, and so they will go away discontented. Therefore it is better if I stay here in Salalah.'

Some of his critics have pointed cynically to the luxurious style in which he lived during his visits to London, where he would stay at the Dorchester with a large retinue; he would probably reply that he owed it to the honour of his people to keep up appearances abroad. Certainly he had a profound distrust of innovation, which extended even to hygiene and education.

'We do not need hospitals here,' he told me on another occasion. 'This is a very poor country which can only support a small population. At present many children die in infancy and so the population does not increase. If we build clinics many more will survive — but for what? To starve?'

He was even more emphatic about schools. 'That is why you lost India,' he once said to Hugh Boustead. 'Because you educated the people.' When I broached the matter he brushed it aside. 'Where would the teachers come from? I cannot afford to pay good teachers from England, and so they would come from Cairo and spread Nasser's seditious ideas among their pupils. And what is there here for a young man with education? He would go to the university in Cairo or to the London School of Economics, finish in Moscow and come back here to foment trouble.'

He was fully aware of the threat posed by Cairo Radio, knowing how many of his subjects listened to it. Every Arab who could afford it, and many who couldn't, owned a transistor set, and the only clear reception came from Cairo or Moscow; Aden, despite our many protests, came over pathetically faint. The Sultan therefore suggested to me that we should set up a wireless station in Muscat to counteract Egyptian propaganda with news bulletins and commentaries of our own. I asked him how he proposed to fill up the programmes between the bulletins and commentaries, for I could hardly see him approving of the songs and dance music that made Cairo so appealing to its listeners. But he had thought of that, too. 'We can fill in the gaps,' he pronounced with evident satisfaction, 'with readings from the Koran.'

During this first audience, which lasted about two hours, our talk was confined to military matters. 'We shall begin,' he told me, 'by changing your appointment from Chief of Staff to Commander. After all, you are not my Chief of Staff, you are the Commander of all my forces — not only of my army but of my navy and air force as well, small though they may be. You will therefore be called *El Caid*, "the Commander."'

Having thus expanded my responsibilities to include the two Pioneers of his Air Force and the single motor launch that comprised his Navy, he asked me to reorganize the Muscat Army on the same lines as the British. When I asked him what was the maximum punishment I could impose — the War Office had told me two years' imprisonment — the Sultan promptly answered, 'Death — provided you consult me first'. I am thankful to say I never had to do so. For an officer, on the other hand, my ultimate sanction was to recommend his dismissal, and this I was obliged to do on two occasions.

As a first step in reorganization I suggested we put the army into a proper uniform. Hitherto there had been a wide variety, particularly in officers' headgear, and I asked the Sultan to approve a standard dress. After listening carefully he gave his standard response, in the two phrases I will always associate with him:

'I see, Colonel Smiley, I see. I will think about it.'

56

Inability, or refusal, to make up his mind was the most infuriating of the Sultan's defects. But this time he really did think about it, and soon after my return to Beit al Falaj he let me know his decision: khaki drill for all ranks; scarlet berets for me and my Headquarters staff, including the artillery troop; green berets for the Northern Frontier Regiment; and lastly, a most unhappy choice, scarlet balmorals, worn square on the head, for the Muscat Regiment. The cap badge for all units would be the same, a pair of crossed *khanjas*, in silver for officers, for myself in gold. A smart army is at least the beginning of an efficient army, and the Baluch in particular took enormous pride in their new uniforms, although the Arabs, with their bandy legs tended to look ill at ease in theirs.

I once suggested to the Sultan that he should let me groom some of his Arab officers for promotion to higher commands, up to the rank of lieutenant-colonel. He refused firmly.

'You must know, Colonel Smiley,' he said with his charming smile, 'that all revolutions in the Arab world are led by colonels. That is why I employ you. I am having no Arab colonels in my army.'

I should have liked to linger in Salalah, where the great rollers of the Indian Ocean beat incessantly on a palm-fringed shore, and fields of sugar cane and millet gleamed brightly in the sun. This province was part of the ancient 'Incense Coast' of Arabia, and frankincense still grew in the green, monsoon-drenched hills which enclosed the fertile coastal plain, and which reminded me vividly of the Kenya highlands where I had once planned to live. These hills between the Dhofar coast and the desert were the home of a strange, pre-Arab people, known as the Qara or, more commonly, *Jabalis*; their language bore no resemblance to Arabic. I saw a few of them in Salalah, where they sometimes came down to trade, easily recognizable by the blue dye with which they coloured both their clothes and their bodies and by their long hair worn in ringlets to their shoulders. The local inhabitants, too, were different from those of Oman proper, being generally black in features and much freer and more cheerful in manner than most Arabs; many of their women went unveiled.

In Aden I stayed with Air Vice-Marshal Maurice Heath, Commander-in-Chief, British Forces Arabian Peninsula; this had always been an RAF appointment, although it also involved command of military and naval units throughout the peninsula, including those in Bahrain and Sharjah. His HQ in Aden was also responsible for all operations throughout the Arabian Peninsula and East Africa in which any British forces were involved. I was not personally under his command, however; and any British troops serving in Oman came directly under me. But they were administered by BFAP, which conferred on Air Marshal Heath the right to visit them while they were there, though only with the Sultan's permission; the same situation applied to Brigadier Jim Hutton, who commanded Land Forces Arabian Peninsula under Heath. It was therefore important for me to maintain good relations with them both; fortunately, it wasn't difficult. They were sympathetic and anxious to help, and although they couldn't offer me any troop reinforcements, the Air Marshal hoped to be allowed to support me with strikes by Shackleton bombers. I was also fortunate in being able to talk with Sir William Luce, then Governor of Aden, a brilliant administrator and diplomat with unrivalled knowledge of the Arab world, whose wise counsel was to prove of the greatest value to me in the future.

My visit to Aden coincided with the opening of a serious campaign of agitation and subversion against British rule. A bomb exploded there during my stay, and on the very same night, I found out later, Waterfield and Sir Bernard Burrows were dining in Muscat at the house of Neil Innes, the Sultans' Foreign Minister, when a bomb went off outside the house, wrecking Innes's Land Rover; a few hours later another bomb caused some damage in the oil company's depot, five miles outside Muscat.

In my spare time I did some shopping to improve the amenities of the house at Beit al Falaj for Moy when she arrived; in particular I bought a bath, wash basin, a lavatory and two water tanks, which were flown up there after me in an RAF Valetta. They caused quite a sensation when they were installed, for they were the first of their kind to be seen in Beit al Falaj. While they were putting in the plumbing I made do with an Elsan which I set up in a small palm hut near the house; but I had to share this lavatory — and on several occasions nearly shared the seat — with a colony of scorpions.

Chapter IV: Mines and Missionaries

It was the beginning of May by the time I returned to Beit al Falaj and I quickly adapted my daily routine of work to the increasing severity of summer. Awakened at five, I would walk out on to my verandah to watch the first caravans lope by; this was the best time of the day, I felt, as I savoured the short-lived freshness and clarity of the early morning air and watched the mountains change from rose to gold in the splendour of the Arabian sunrise. Office work occupied me from six to nine, when I would return home for a breakfast of fruit and iced coffee. About ten o'clock I would drive into Muscat, where official business often kept me until lunch at one, when all officers would assemble in the Mess tent; the food was excellent, especially the shellfish — delicious little oysters, and succulent crawfish which we caught ourselves or bought in the market for a rupee each.[15] After lunch we slept until five — a sensible arrangement in temperatures well over 100° in the shade; even in the field both we and the rebels observed the siesta, and there was seldom any military activity on either side between 10 am and 4 pm, while rock and sand shimmered and glowed in the heavy heat haze.

Work, either in my office or in Muscat, occupied me from five till seven; we dined in Mess at half past eight and most of us were in bed by ten — not a very long working day, but quite exacting enough in such a climate. Even the Contract Officers, who were used to it, sometimes went down with heat exhaustion, and coming as I had straight from the ice-bound streets of Stockholm I found the days almost unendurable and

---

[15] About 7 ½ new pence.

the nights scarcely less hideous; usually I slept on the roof and I was lucky, also, in having a kind friend in Peter Mason, Manager of the British Bank of the Middle East in Muscat, who allowed me, when I could get away, to use his air-conditioned guest room.

Fortunately we were not short of water, thanks to the *falaj* from which our headquarters took its name. This ingenious system of irrigation was introduced by the Persians in ancient times — one of the few benefits of their many occupations; it is similar to the *qanat* system by which they brought water from the mountains to the plains, traces of which are still clearly visible from the air running across the plateau north of Tehran. The *falaj* channels, flowing mostly underground but at times on the surface, extend into the interior of Oman, where they provide essential water for the date plantations; the underground tunnels are pierced at intervals by air vents with stone steps, giving access for washing, bathing or drawing water. Our *falaj* gave us plenty of water for washing and, after we had boiled it, for drinking.

In this connection it is worth mentioning that, prior to the arrival of British troops in force, our soldiers, like the rest of the population, used to drink the local water straight from source, and suffered no ill effects from it. When British Army units were deployed in Muscat, RAMC officers insisted on adding sterilising tablets to our drinking water, with the result that many of our men went down with dysentery after returning from leave in their villages.

During my visits to Muscat I sometimes called on the American missionaries, Dr Wells Thoms and his wife, who had for many years run a hospital there under forbidding conditions of financial deprivation and official antipathy that would have made any less dedicated a couple give up long ago.

They did wonderful work among the people, treating cases of trachoma and other endemic ailments, particularly among the women and children. Their position in such a fanatically Moslem community could not be easy, but the Sultan tolerated them despite his strictures to me on hospitals; perhaps he had no objection to one that he didn't have to pay for. My early meetings with Wells Thoms were clouded by a certain reserve on both sides: he clearly disapproved of the Sultan and so, by derivation, of ourselves as his officers; while I had been warned that he was a subversive influence who sympathized strongly with the rebels. However, he was a man of such obvious sincerity, devotion, and genuine warmth of heart that it was impossible not to like and respect him. I was sorry for him too, because he had a pathetic faith in his ability ultimately to convert these intractable people to Christianity. According to the story I was told, he had actually made two converts in all his years in Muscat; but this pair, on emerging from their first church service, were arrested on the Sultan's orders and thrown into prison.

There were times, indeed, when I felt some sympathy myself with the rebels — and with Wells Thoms's views on the Sultan — although of course I concealed my feelings. Talib in particular, for all that he was a Saudi puppet, was a man of courage and ability, even of a certain integrity, far superior to either of his principal colleagues. If he had shown a little more initiative in his tactics, and made more use of ambushes to cover the mines he laid on our roads, he might well have forced us to withdraw our garrisons from around Nizwa — as at one moment he very nearly did. But, whatever my feelings about him, I could never forget that he was the servant of an aggressive and hostile foreign power, and it was my duty, as a

British officer as well as the Sultan's Commander, to destroy him.

All this time I was in daily wireless communication with Colin Maxwell, reinforced by occasional visits to him by air. I was again reminded of the risks of this form of transport by an incident that nearly put an end to me. About the middle of May I received a visit from Bufton and Tinker, who arrived from Sharjah in a Pembroke; we flew on together to Nizwa, where we spent most of the day, and took off towards evening on our return journey to Beit al Falaj.

We were flying down the Wadi Sumail at 5,000 feet, with the mountains rising high above us on both sides as we turned and twisted to follow the course of the road. Suddenly we were in thick darkness, unable even to see out wing tips. We had run into a sandstorm. The engines revved to a roar as we climbed at full throttle, striving to get above the murk, while my stomach contracted with fear as I waited for us to crash into the side of one of those imprisoning but invisible mountains.

At 10,000 feet we broke through into daylight; looking down we could see nothing but a thick brown blanket covering the earth in every direction as far as the horizon. We were now faced with another problem. The storm enveloped Beit al Falaj, and to attempt a landing there, on that narrow, mountain-girdled airstrip, was out of the question; we should have to make for Sharjah. Unfortunately we had omitted to refuel at Nizwa, now also blotted out by the weather, and Bufton, sitting with us at the back, calculated we had only enough petrol to take us about twenty minutes short of Sharjah. It looked as if our choice lay between a forced landing either among the mountains or in a shark-infested sea — in the middle of the sandstorm and with no radar or other navigational aid to blind flying. Nevertheless we should have to chance it.

We flew on, staring ahead with grim, set faces, each of us wrapped in his own sombre thoughts; I found myself looking back anxiously on all my past misdeeds and omissions and praying with a concentration I had never been able to achieve in church. Bufton's time limit expired, but still the petrol held out. It was cold inside the plane, but all of us were sweating with fear as we waited each moment for the cough and splutter of the engines that would announce our end. Another twenty minutes went by — they seemed a great deal longer — before the pilot called to us that we should be over Sharjah and he was going down; we could see nothing below but the thick cloud of sand. As we plunged through the gloom the tension rose unbearably inside the cabin and I scarcely dared glance at the strained faces of my companions, knowing how my own must look to them.

And then we were over the water — grey and foam-capped and only a few feet beneath us. The pilot made a smooth banking turn, we passed low over the coast and in five minutes I felt our wheels touchdown on a runway barely visible through the flying sand. We had enough petrol left, it turned out, for another ten minutes.

I had already made up my mind that Beit al Falaj was too far from the fighting to serve as our operational headquarters. Nizwa was obviously more suitable, and so I decided to spend a week or two with Colin Maxwell, making myself familiar with conditions in the battle area. I set out for his camp three weeks after my return from Aden, and found myself once again speculating gloomily about mines — for this was my first journey to Nizwa by road. I had already had one first-hand experience of mines, and had found it alarming; in the course of time I became used to them, like the rest of us, and apart from the initial shock as the mine went off, I soon got over my fright. Nevertheless, after spending a large part of my military career laying mines and teaching others to lay them on enemy roads, it was galling now to find myself at the receiving end. Mining remained our most formidable hazard all the time I was in Muscat, and we never managed to solve the problem. Of course, if we had been able to use the German — or Russian — methods of reprisals against the nearest villages whenever there was an incident, we should have had no trouble; but that solution was obviously unacceptable politically — as was the bright suggestion that we should place known rebel sympathizers in the leading vehicles of all our convoys.

I had known about the problem before I left England and had given it a good deal of study since. With our meagre resources and the great distances involved there was no effective way of preventing mine-laying; nor was it possible, for similar reasons, to prevent the smuggling of mines into the country. They came, all of them, from Saudi Arabia, where the mine-layers also received their instruction, and were brought into Oman either overland via the Trucial States — some of the Rulers there were happy to co-operate in the process — or by dhow to the Batinah Coast.

Even when we caught mine-layers, they only went to prison. I felt they should have been shot; but, apart from the international repercussions, it was very doubtful whether the Sharia courts, which would have had to try them, would impose the death penalty for this offence.

At this stage, as I have mentioned, we only had to contend with the light American Army mine — about 5 lbs of explosive which would blow off the wheel of a vehicle, but wouldn't cause serious injury to the occupants if the vehicle was armoured or sandbagged; but in the summer of the following year we began to have casualties, sometimes fatal, from the heavy American mine, although fortunately its bulk and weight made it harder to smuggle. The ideal answer, of course, would have been for us to stop the mines at source, in other words to persuade the Americans either to stop supplying them to the Saudi Army or to exercise some control over their use. I know we tried, but the Americans were brutally unsympathetic. Their reply was that they supplied the mines to Saudi Arabia under their Military Aid Programme, and it was not their concern how the Saudis chose to employ them.

Their attitude came as no surprise. After all, the Saudi seizure of Buraimi in 1952 would have been impossible without American co-operation — indeed the ARAMCO Oil Company had prepared refuelling dumps for the attacking column all the way across the desert, and lent them trucks for transport. Perhaps my friend the Swedish General Carl von Horn was right about American policy when he wrote:

'Basically, I had the impression that, under the cloak of a benefactor and supporter of national aspirations in the Middle East, there was the desire to cut the throat of British influence in the Persian Gulf.'[16]

Sitting beside my driver in the front of my Land Rover I mulled over our predicament as we bumped over the corrugated track from Beit al Falaj up the coast, kicking up a grey cloud of dust to smother our following convoy of Ferrets and trucks full of soldiers. I had little faith in mine detectors and similar devices; they could only operate at a snail's pace

---

[16] *Soldiering for Peace* (Cassell, 1966), p. 355. General von Horn commanded the UN Peace-keeping force in the Middle East until he resigned in disgust in 1965.

and would impose intolerable delays on our convoys. We might, I thought, impose fines on villages near to mine incidents; this would sometimes be unjust and would certainly incur resentment, but it would also make the mine layers unpopular. Conversely, we might try offering rewards for mines picked off the roads and returned to us, but could we match Talib's prices? He was said to be offering 1,000 Maria Theresa dollars for each mine successfully exploded. What about dogs? I would ask for them from Cyprus, where I knew they had been a help against the Eoka terrorists. Or trackers? Perhaps the War Office could send us a few from Kenya or Borneo, and they could train some of our own men. In the end I decided to try all of these remedies.

We halted for a glass of beer at Azaiba, where the P.D.O. (Petroleum Development, Oman) Oil Company had a camp. It was a transit post for cargo travelling by lorry or air between Muscat and the drillings at Fahud, and comprised an air strip suitable for much bigger aircraft than was ours at Beit al Falaj. The oil company employees were hospitable enough but their attitude to the SAF was bitter to the point of hostility; with Waterfield they were not on speaking terms. Their complaint, only partially justified, was that they paid us for protection and weren't getting it. In the course of time I managed to establish good working relations with most of them, especially their two senior officials at Muscat, who were both charming and reasonable people. But the man in charge here at Azaiba, an ex-RAF corporal, was of a very different calibre.

'What the hell do you lot think you're up to?' he snarled at me. 'We pay you idle sods good money to keep our road clear of mines and what do we get? One bloody truck blown up after another! I tell you, Smiley, our drivers are getting thoroughly pissed off and are saying they won't drive any more on the Nizwa road. When are you going to pull your fingers out?'

I kept my temper. 'You've been in this country long enough,' I replied quietly, 'to know the distances we have to guard, and the quite inadequate forces we have to guard them with. You also know we can't take the sort of reprisals that might put a stop to the mining. What do you suggest we do that we aren't doing already?'

'That's your ruddy problem, mate, not ours. We give you the money and it's up to you to earn it.'

The world is full of such little men, I reflected sadly, as we mounted our vehicles and turned inland for the long climb through the Wadi Sumail. The road wound up the mountainside in a series of curves and hairpin bends — ideal targets for guerrillas, I noted — past the little village of Bid-Bid with its clusters of date palms and a river below, which flowed all the year round; the valley was green with lucerne, and oleanders grew on the river banks. Then the hostile mountains hemmed us in on both sides, the fearsome bare granite slabs of the Jebel Akhdar rearing thousands of feet sheer above us on our right. We climbed on without halt or incident, past more dirty mud villages, until the valley widened and the road levelled out among the foothills of the Jebel — smooth, tawny-coloured outcrops cleft by narrow, twisting ravines sprouting a thin scrub and half blocked with falls of gigantic boulders. In that comfortless wilderness of rock we kept a small military outpost, supported by the company encamped near Izki.

Izki — unaccountably known to the troops as Ziki — stood on the plain in front of us. There the track divided: Oil company vehicles took the left fork and went across the desert to Fahud, while our route bore right towards Nizwa. I confess I began to breathe more easily once we were out of the Wadi

68

Sumail and trundling over the rough but comparatively straight road to Nizwa, another half-hour's driving, with the bleak wall of the Jebel all too close on the right but with gentle sandy slopes on the left, leading to the dunes of the Empty Quarter. The Wadi Sumail, our most vital road link, was a guerrilla's paradise, and to this day I have never understood why Talib let us go on using it. There were a dozen places where he could have laid mines — as indeed he often did — and then, from a prepared ambush among the rocks commanding the road, shot up our soft-skinned transport with virtual impunity; if he had done so, he would have denied us the use of the road. Perhaps he lacked the training, or perhaps his men just didn't have the guts. I should dearly have liked to take the matter up with him when I saw him, many years later, in Saudi Arabia, but I never had the chance. As it was, the rebels contented themselves with sniping at us from the distance — too great a distance, usually, to be effective — and sometimes mortaring the camp at Izki, wounding a few of the garrison.

Some of the villages on this last stage of our journey carried memories of the previous summer's disaster: Birket al Mauz with Suleiman's big fort standing derelict now, badly gashed and pitted by RAF rockets, and Firq, former headquarters of the Muscat and Oman Field Force, whence they had launched their ill-fated drive against Ghalib and Talib. Already we had passed, shortly before emerging from the Wadi Sumail, Suleiman's former home at Muti — a collection of dilapidated but still inhabited houses, some of them bearing the scars of RAF attacks, huddled on a small hilltop at the head of one of the narrow ravines leading up the Jebel. Sayid Tarik and the SAF had dynamited the houses of Suleiman's chief supporters and had destroyed all his date palms with paraffin. A date tree will normally continue to produce fruit without much tending;

but if someone climbs it and pours paraffin over the topmost part, the tree will die at once and never produce again. In time I came to recognize the sight of dead date palms as a sign of a hostile village which had already suffered retribution; in such villages, common among the Beni Riyam and the Beni Hina, we would find only women, children and very old men and we would know that all the young men were up on the mountain with the rebels.

The women would take food up to them at night — sometimes, perhaps, ammunition as well. We could not stop them, for it was an unwritten law of the country that we should never stop a woman, let alone search her. The custom had some advantages for us too. Once, when an RAF Venom crashed on the Jebel, we sent up a woman with a note to Talib asking for news of the pilot; she returned with his reply — typewritten — that the pilot had died in the crash. On another occasion one of our soldiers engaged in conversation with a woman returning, in daylight, from a visit to the mountain. She told him openly that she had been taking food to one of Talib's pickets.

'Which one?' he asked her casually. Unaware of the implications, she pointed out its exact position, and soon afterwards the Venoms swooped.

It was at Nizwa that I first became aware of the extent to which the rebels were still receiving supplies, not only from their sympathizers in the villages of the foothills but also through some of the Trucial States. The Ruler of Sharjah, in particular, was heavily implicated; he was an old enemy of our Sultan, but for political reasons which seemed to us both obscure and wrong-headed the British authorities were unwilling to put pressure on him.

If we could do nothing about the Trucial States, we could at least do something here to encourage our supporters in the villages and — rather less hopefully — discourage our enemies. I consulted with Sayid Tarik who, in addition to his position as viceroy, also controlled the complicated pattern of spies, informers and tribal levies that made up the Sultan's intelligence network in the area. We decided to make a tour together of the villages south and west of the Jebel to show the flag, to use a naval expression from the days of gunboat diplomacy, and for this purpose I formed a small battle group of scout cars, two sections of SAF in Land Rovers mounting Brens and a section of heavy mortars in case we bumped an ambush; Sayid Tarik brought his own Land Rover and his own guards.

We started from Nizwa early one morning, with scout cars at the head and tail of the column and Sayid Tarik leading the Land Rovers, followed by myself and my guards in my Land Rover; the Ferrets kept wireless contact with our base in case of trouble. We headed north-west, in the direction of Ibri, plunging across dried-up river beds, lurching among rocks and boulders, and finally ploughing through stretches of deep sand as we approached the fringe of the desert; a cloud of dust hung over the convoy, stinging our eyes, filling our mouths and nostrils, parching and half suffocating us. But we exploded no mines and not a shot was fired in our direction.

We halted at Jabrin, where Tarik showed me a seventeenth-century palace built by one of the great al Yaarabah Imams; it was still remarkably well preserved, with brightly painted ceilings whose colours of green and red and gold still gleamed fresh in the fierce light of noon. Our next stop was at Ghafat, a hostile village where there were no *feux-de-joie* to greet us — and no young men to fire them either. But the old Sheikh gave us a very good lunch, in accordance with the traditional code of Arab hospitality which dictates that even an enemy must be received with food and drink when he comes to visit — though he may be shot in the back after he has left.

At least there was no doubt of our popularity — or, more accurately, of Tarik's — when we arrived at Bahlah towards evening, on our way back from the desert. Entirely surrounded by a great battlemented mud wall, higher, longer, and in far better condition than the walls of Muscat or Mattrah, Bahlah disgorged a mob of tribesmen waving their old Martini Henry rifles and firing volley after volley into the sky in noisy greeting. Knowing that even an empty cartridge case cost one rupee in the Muscat market, I appreciated the extravagance of our welcome.

Surrounded by the villagers we followed Tarik to the residence of the Wali, a tall square stone building more like a border keep than a private house; it was typical of the more important Arab houses in the villages of the interior, indeed, throughout the Peninsula, and resembled many I had seen in Albania. A flight of stone steps led up to the first floor — the ground floor, open at the sides, was used as stabling for livestock — and to the guest room, which was the largest in the house. Its thick whitewashed walls were pierced with narrow, barred windows, the floor was spread with rugs and with cushions of vivid colours; there was no furniture except a large wooden chest and a low stool with a brass coffee tray.

The proceedings followed the ritual prescribed by Arab tradition, beginning with the conventional exchange of civilities with our host: '*Ahlan Wa Sahlan*' [Welcome], '*Salaam Elykum*' [Peace be with you]. We arranged ourselves in a circle on the cushions, contorting our limbs into attitudes that for me at least meant almost unendurable discomfort, and taking care to

ensure that the soles of our feet were never facing our host —
or any of the guests either. Even when there was business to
transact, it was very impolite to mention it for at least the first
five minutes, when talk was restricted to irrelevant pleasantries
and platitudes. It was also considered very bad manners to
speak to anyone during the course of a meal — an excellent
convention, in my view — and so all conversation took place
beforehand, while the party ate *mezze* — hors d'oeuvres of
bread and goat's cheese — and drank black coffee poured into
small cups by black slaves out of a huge coffee pot from a
great height and with unerring accuracy; when we had had
enough — it was usual to accept two or three helpings — a
guest would shake his coffee cup to show he wanted no more.

Then servants would bring in the meal, a single enormous
dish, usually a whole sheep or goat on a vast pile of rice. There
were no plates or cutlery, and everyone helped himself with his
fingers from the dish, using only the right hand, which he
would wash carefully after he had eaten. At the end of the meal
slaves would carry round an incense burner, from which the
guests would waft the smoke over their beards with their
hands; beardless Europeans would make the gestures of
wafting it over their chins. As a final ritual the slaves would
sprinkle rose water over the guests' heads. The guests would
then rise, shake hands all round, and depart. I must have
attended hundreds of these ceremonies, which we called
'fuddling', from the Arabic *fadal* meaning 'please'; the British
troops called them 'mutton grabs'.

After our dinner at Bahlah we drove on a few miles and
encamped for the night in the open, taking care to choose a
spot out of rifle range of the hills. I watched Sayid Tarik
tinkering with the engine of his Land Rover; wearing Arab
headdress, flowing robes and a cartridge belt crammed with

73

ammunition, with one hand resting on the jewelled hilt of his *khanja* and the other busy with a spanner, he presented a fascinating study of fusion between tradition and technology. When he had finished with the engine he called to his guards, and a black slave came forward carrying the viceroy's personal Bren gun; Tarik sited it carefully, changing the position several times until he was satisfied. Then he joined his bodyguard and, as the orange glow of sunset faded, they turned towards Mecca and began the recital of the evening prayer.

We breakfasted next day at Balat Sait, where we neither expected nor received a welcome, for this was Ghalib's own village, which had successfully resisted the attack of the Muscat and Oman Field Force the previous summer. But at Hamra, where we stopped for lunch some hours later, we had a very different reception. This was the principal village of the Abryeen tribe, friendly to the Sultan, on whom the Muscat and Oman Field Force had relied to protect their lines of communication with Nizwa during their unlucky thrust against Balat Sait and Ghalib. But the Abryeen, overawed by the rebels' strength, had failed to rally, leaving the Sultan's men to be cut to pieces on their retreat. They were particularly anxious now to re-establish themselves in our eyes. Enthusiastic villagers ran towards us, firing volleys of *feux-de-joie*, and somebody shattered my nerves by loosing off a cannon. Surfeited with rice and stringy chicken, we plunged into the water of a *falaj* before starting our final run back to base.

Our progress, however, had not gone unnoticed by the enemy and we very nearly ran into an ambush. A survey party of the Royal Engineers ran into it instead; their 3 tonner went up on a mine and for two hours they huddled in what shelter they could find, under fire from the surrounding hills. This was one of the few occasions when Talib's tactics were sound.

Luckily, they suffered no casualties, and by the time we arrived the heavy mortars had come up from Nizwa and the tribesmen were scattering under their bombardment. We drove on to Colin Maxwell's camp, feeling well satisfied with the results of our 180 mile tour, particularly with the way our vehicles had stood up to the arduous conditions of the journey.

I decided to take my 'battle group', during the course of the next week, up the *wadis* leading to the Jebel which I knew Talib's men must be using as supply routes, but which the SAF seemed to have designated as 'no go areas'. I was considerably perturbed by the low state of morale of our officers. Time and again I would point on the map to one or other of these ravines and suggest we should send a patrol along it or place an outpost to cover it, only to be told that it was impossible — that any patrol would assuredly be ambushed, any outpost destroyed. The only way to overcome this defeatism, it seemed to me, was to go myself. Sayid Tarik, who wasn't scared of anything, insisted on coming too.

Together we patrolled every one of these routes, penetrating on each occasion as far as the head of the gulley. Never once were we fired on, although almost invariably we would hear, on our return, stories of hordes of tribesmen descending on the place we had visited, two or three hours after we had left. Among the ravines we penetrated was the one dominated by Suleiman's former home, Muti — a village we had long suspected of hiding arms and harbouring mine-layers. A week or so later, when I was back at Beit al Falaj, it was to give us a very nasty shock.

I was in my office in the fort when a message came through to say that one of our Royal Marine sergeants who had taken a patrol up that same *wadi* had been ambushed and killed and three of our soldiers wounded; help was on the way from

Nizwa. I despatched my medical officer at once in the only available Pioneer; but there was no room for me to go with him and his orderly and their stretchers; and so I had to sit there all day waiting for news and knowing the patrol was trapped. The aircraft returned that night with the body and the wounded, and I flew up next morning, to arrive in the closing stages of the battle, when the opposition was melting away up the mountain. The relief force of Ferrets and SAF with mortars had held off the tribesmen and prevented them from rushing the survivors of the patrol, but the enemy fire was much too heavy for anybody to go near the sergeant, who was lying badly wounded in the open; although he managed to bandage his own wounds, he bled to death before the fight was over.

Men from Muti had laid the ambush, which took place in full view of the village. Sayid Tarik's face was black with anger. 'We will settle with Muti once and for all,' he growled. 'It shall be burned to the ground. Prepare your men, David, and come with me.'

We assembled a strong force of SAF and Tarik's *askers*, but needless to say, there wasn't a living soul in the place when we arrived, not even women or children. We went systematically from house to house, setting each one alight with paraffin until nothing remained but smouldering ruins. Muti would prepare no more ambushes and harbour no more mine-layers; and to close this supply route to Talib we stationed an outpost of SAF permanently on the hill commanding the ravine. Talib would receive no more supplies that way and perhaps that splendid marine sergeant would not have died in vain.

Chapter V: Reconnaissance

It was already clear to me that we could never hope to capture the Jebel Akhdar with the forces now at my disposal; they were barely enough to contain the rebels, and not enough to prevent them from mining the roads — as the oil company never ceased to remind me. To add to my difficulties, the squadron of Trucial Oman Scouts based on Izki were withdrawn from the country in June and I had to garrison the town with recruits from the Depot who had not even completed their basic training. Although the RAF were being very helpful, air attacks alone would not compel the enemy to surrender; in fact, as we discovered afterwards, they caused very few casualties.

The nature of RAF support was twofold: first, bombing of the plateau by Shackletons from Aden, which, we learned from our interrogation of prisoners, was largely ineffective. They had strict orders not to bomb villages, only caves and water systems; they came regularly at the same hour each day, and as soon as the rebels understood this pattern they took to their caves in good time. The second form of attack was by Venom fighters from Sharjah with cannon and machine guns seeking 'opportunity targets', and its effect was pretty terrifying; they flew very fast and low over the hills above the plateau, their speed preventing any warning of their approach, and often caught the enemy unprepared in the open. Although their speed also limited the duration and accuracy of their strafing — they were virtually useless for attacking caves — the very threat of their presence restricted rebel movements to the hours of darkness. Perhaps the most effective of all were the

Provosts recently added to the strength of the Sultan's Air Force; these piston-engined aircraft flew so slowly that they could spot the entrances to caves and put their rockets or cannon shells right inside.

The RAF suffered no casualties from enemy ground fire, although they took some hits; but they lost one Venom, which crashed on the Jebel when the pilot failed to pull out of his dive. The 'voice' Pembroke also had a very narrow escape when one of its twin engines was put out of action by a well directed shot, and the pilot made a very skilful landing on the strip at Firq with the other. This 'voice' aircraft was fitted with a loud-speaker through which we broadcast messages and propaganda to the rebels; after one of its flights they sent a message down to us complaining that the loud-speaker was faulty and they couldn't hear.

The only way I could see of ending the present stalemate was to ask for reinforcements of British troops to assault the Jebel. With this object I flew to Sharjah on 13 June to see Christopher Soames, the Secretary of State for War, who was passing through in the course of a visit to the Gulf; he was an old friend of mine from the days when we had been captains together in Cairo and he gave me a very sympathetic hearing, as also did General Firbank, the Director of Infantry, who was with him. They promised to do their best, but made it clear that the whole matter involved a political rather than a military decision, and that in any case the most I could hope for was two battalions. In these circumstances I asked if one of them could be either a Royal Marine Commando, parachutists, or a unit of the Special Air Service; I doubted whether a normal infantry battalion would be fit enough for the assault, at least without a great deal of extra training.

In any case, the heat was now so intense — it was 100° Fahrenheit in the shade, and at Nizwa it reached 125° — that there was no question of British troops operating in Oman before the cooler weather began in October. As a matter of fact, of the fifty British troops attached to me, forty-five had to be flown out to hospital suffering from heat exhaustion and two more died of it. The British medical authorities considered two months the maximum period for British troops to serve in the country without relief; but their ruling did not apply to British officers seconded to the SAF, with the result that all of us went down at one time or another with heat exhaustion, prickly heat, or both. A lesser aggravation, but one which the troops much resented, was that Arab convention forbade them to wear shorts in public, although some of the Sultan's Army wore them as uniform, or to go about stripped to the waist; even Moy, when she was outside the camp, had to wear trousers under her skirt, and long sleeves.

While I was in Sharjah Brigadier Tinker told me he was due to go home on leave and undertook to argue my case personally with the War Office. On my return I flew to see the Sultan, who was also about to visit London, and asked him to plead for us with the Foreign Office as well; I was hoping to go home myself on leave in July, when I would be able to follow up their lobbying. It was the Foreign Office who were objecting to the use of British troops because they feared repercussions at the United Nations, where both Saudis and Egyptians were denouncing British intervention in Oman, with grossly exaggerated accounts, such as I mentioned, of its scale.

In the meantime I decided to embark on a tour round the entire base of the Jebel Akhdar, a distance of over 700 miles, visiting as many towns and villages as possible. I set out towards the end of June, soon after my visit to the Sultan. As my guide for the journey the Minister of the Interior had given me one of the most endearing characters in the Sultanate, Sayid Salem bin Humaid al Saidi, the Wali of Buraimi. A figure of benign aspect and indulgent nature, he was known among my officers as Grock, for he had all that great clown's divine gift of eloquent pantomine; unable to talk intelligibly, even to our Arabic speakers, through his toothless gums, the old man had developed a vivid and hilarious vocabulary of signs by which, accompanied by whinnies of laughter, he conveyed his meaning almost more clearly, if more comically, than language. He sat beside me in my Land Rover, while his slave Mahmoud, a big, cheerful black man who spoke a few words of English, sat in the back, festooned with guns and belts of ammunition; beside Mahmoud sat my orderly, Ya Mohammed, also heavily armed and carrying my cartridge belt draped over his shoulder like a bandolier.

Soon after we entered the Wadi Sumail the leading Ferret, just ahead of me, hit a mine, and a wheel flew through the air to land a foot or so from my Land Rover; it would have done us no good if it had hit us, but Mahmoud gave a huge grin and Grock merely removed his cashmere turban and sat quietly scratching his shining bald pate while the Ferret was towed away. We drove on through Nizwa to a village with the charming name of Izz, where we stopped for coffee with the Wali, then headed straight across the desert to Fahud, where the oil company were drilling, as yet unsuccessfully, for oil. Both Grock and Mahmoud were keen back-seat drivers. Mahmoud in his broken English would urge me to go one way, while Grock pointed excitedly in the opposite direction; confused and irritated, I generally went my own way, which as often as not was the wrong one, with the result that our journey took longer than necessary.

Nevertheless, we reached Fahud on the best of terms, to lunch in the comfort of the oil company's mess. Next morning we headed north across gravel desert on the fringe of the Rub al Khali towards Ibri. One of my pleasanter memories of Oman is of emerging after long hours of driving in a cloud of grey dust into the greenness of an up-country village. Ibri was no village, with its big fort and battlemented walls, but its date palms were famous and the lush lucerne and flowing water were wonderfully refreshing to see after the arid harshness of the desert landscape. I stayed in the camp with the Trucial Oman Scouts and had a sumptuous dinner, laced with iced champagne, in the oil company's house. My host, Stewart Watt, the company's Personnel Manager, was a fluent Arabic speaker with an intimate knowledge of the country and the tribes; he was probably the best intelligence officer in the area as well, and I was delighted when he agreed to come with me on the rest of my tour as interpreter.

Next day we continued our journey, visiting Dhank and Yanqul, two hostile villages in the northern foothills of the Jebel Akhdar, which we suspected of concealing arms and providing, or sheltering, mine-layers; they received us with formal courtesy but divulged nothing. While I was sipping his coffee I reflected that the Wali of Dhank, like the Wali of Izz, must surely figure somewhere in the pages of Edward Lear — along with the Arond of Swat. We travelled on, across sandy desert, past the strange mountains of Hafit rising sharp and solitary from the plain, to the oasis of Buraimi, for so long a focal point of international quarrel and intrigue. Here again the Trucial Oman Scouts made me welcome in their fort.

Of the nine villages in the oasis, three belonged to the Sultan of Muscat and six to the Ruler of Abu Dhabi, in Trucial Oman; there was no conflict between the two about ownership —

only between them and the Saudis. But the contrast between the Sultan's villages and those of the Ruler was immediately and painfully obvious: the villages of Abu Dhabi looked prosperous, well-tended and clean, their people well dressed, well fed and happy; those of the Sultan were dilapidated and dirty, their inhabitants poor and surly. It was clear the Sultan had spent no money on his subjects here, and they were very jealous of their neighbours' good fortune. I believe that the Sultan realized that these poor people would much rather be under the lavish rule of Abu Dhabi and felt no loyalty towards himself, and so he took no care of them. Still, he had at least given them Grock for their Wali.

To send us on our way the old man gave us a superb banquet, one of the most lavish I ever had in Oman. Waving good-bye to him and Mahmoud, we turned eastwards towards the coast and plunged into the Wadi Jizzi (or Jeziz), a narrow twisting cleft that divides the Jebel Akhdar at its north-western end from the mountains of the Musandum peninsula. The journey took us two days, over a barely recognizable track in the river bed littered with rocks and enormous boulders, but we spent a refreshingly cool night on the top of the pass leading down to the coastal plain. A swift drive over flat stony desert and scrubland brought us to Sohar, the principal town of the Batinah Coast, where I installed myself for the night in a former palace of the Sultan.

Sohar was too hot and sticky even to bathe, but we soon had something more important to think about. A lorry with a cargo of mortars, heavy and light machine guns, and ammunition for Talib, carrying some forty tough new recruits for his army as well, had travelled from Saudi Arabia through Sharjah, certainly with the connivance of high officials in the Ruler's government, and had driven through the Muscati Customs

Post at Aswad; to be precise, the recruits had off-loaded the weapons and ammunition onto donkeys on the Sharjah side of the border and taken them over the frontier by inland routes unpoliced by the Sultan's guards, while the empty lorry had driven innocently through the Customs to pick up the recruits and their loads inside Oman. The whole consignment, I now heard, had passed through Sohar the day before I arrived. I decided to give chase.

The pursuit lasted two days, my own progress being hampered by the need to stop on the way to gather information from local sheikhs — a process which always involved a protracted discussion over coffee, if not a full meal. The trail led down the coast road at first, and to save time I took a chance and drove fast along the sand; it was a risk because there were not many ways off the shore, and if we had miscalculated the time of high tide, our vehicles might have been swamped, as in fact happened to two Ferrets of the Life Guards the following year.

We knew the rebels must be heading for the Jebel Akhdar and so we turned off the coast road to follow the route leading to the mountains, guarded by the old Portuguese castles of Rostaq, el Hazm and Nakl. All of them had garrisons of tribal *askers* because they commanded obvious approaches into the Jebel. At Rostaq, where Talib had been *wali* before his revolt and where the al Yaarabah dynasty had established their capital in former times, we learned that the lorry had passed through without pausing even to acknowledge the challenge of the guards. Most mortifying of all, when I asked Stewart Watt to find out why the *askers* hadn't fired when their challenge was ignored, he replied:

'They say the men in the truck were dressed as soldiers — as *your* soldiers!'

It was all too clear that some very skilful planning had gone into this operation; the genius behind it, I later discovered, was Sheikh Salih bin Isa, the old chieftain from the Sharqiya, who had fled via Cairo to Saudi Arabia after the abortive 1955 rebellion. I must stiffen these garrisons with some of our own troops, I decided, as soon as I have any to spare.

It was the same story at el Hazm and Nakl. Only at Awabi, where another castle overlooks the road at a point where it disappears in a steep wadi leading up into the mountains, was there any opposition. Here our guards had opened fire as the lorry sped past and wounded several of the occupants. But the driver only put his foot down harder and the truck hurtled on up the ravine, undeterred by bumps or boulders, until it was lost among the cliffs. Safe from pursuit at last, the rebels unloaded their stores onto waiting donkeys, another thoughtful piece of planning, and took them up to the top. Talib was now the richer by some forty stouthearted young men, three wireless sets, four Browning .5 machine guns with anti-aircraft mountings, thirteen Bren guns, nine heavy mortars, and plenty of ammunition for all of them — a remarkable load, incidentally, for one old British Army 3-ton lorry.

When I reached Awabi I thought there might still be a chance of catching up with the fugitives, and so I led a patrol of Land Rovers in pursuit. But the enemy was wily as well as tough. We had made about five miles up the gulley — its name was Wadi Beni Kharus — when there was an explosion behind me, and I heard the cries and groans of wounded men; the Land Rover immediately following me, carrying a section of soldiers, had gone up on a mine; I must have missed it myself by a matter of inches. I ran back to a horrid spectacle: among the stream of wreckage four men were lying, badly charred and covered in blood. I whipped my *kaffia* from my head and used it to improvise a bandage for the worst of the casualties; he was barely conscious and I was afraid he was going to die, and so I ordered the Ferret to call up Beit al Falaj and tell the M.O. to fly up immediately in a Pioneer; luckily there was a landing strip at Awabi. Then I called off the patrol and went back to await his arrival.

It was dark before he came, and so I stationed two Land Rovers, my own and another, at opposite ends of the strip to light it up. When I saw the Pioneer coming in to land, I got out of my car to get a better view, and it was lucky I did so. The aircraft overshot the runway and crashed into my Land Rover, crushing the bonnet and driving seat to pulp. The pilot and the doctor jumped out fast, bruised and shaken but otherwise unhurt; the aircraft, although it didn't catch fire, was a write-off, and so I sent off the wounded by road, with the doctor to look after them.

I returned to Beit al Falaj in easy stages, passing again by the pleasant town of el Hazm, where I paused to examine some Spanish cannon on the walls of the castle; they were in a fine state of preservation, the coat of arms on each clearly distinguishable, with the date 1607. Almost my first action on getting back was to strengthen the existing garrisons, and install some new ones, at the entrance to the Jebel. In this way I think I managed to cut down Talib's supplies, at least to the extent that vehicles and camels were no longer able to get to him, although donkeys still might. As a result of our recent experience I put a platoon of the Muscat Regiment in Awabi, and a section in the Customs Post at Aswad with orders to stop and search every lorry coming in from Trucial Oman.

At the end of my journey I had travelled more than 870 miles and personally visited all the approaches to the Jebel; I had also made a number of flights over the top, and so I was now able to appreciate clearly the nature of our problem. And what a problem it was! The Jebel was more extensive than the area in Cyprus where thousands of British troops were still trying, with the most modern weapons and aircraft but without success, to find and destroy Grivas; all the known tracks to the plateau led up narrow, steep defiles, easily held by Talib's men at their end but very hard for us to seal at ours. I decided our first objective must be to secure ourselves a foothold, somehow, on that plateau, from which we could harry the rebels. But how? The Persians had done it, I reflected, about 800 years ago, against equally determined opposition; they had carved steps up the rock — they were still there — and won a bloody battle at the top. If they could get up there, so could we. But — it all came back to the same thing — we must have more, and better trained, troops.

We were now seriously worried about the rapid increase in the scale of enemy mining. As recently as the middle of May I had written soothingly to Moy that in thirty-five mine incidents the only casualties, apart from damaged vehicles, had been two donkeys and a camel. By the beginning of July, it was a different story, and the vehicle losses were almost as big a problem as the casualties in men; not only the mines but the appalling roads, as well as a good deal of rank bad driving, were taking a heavy toll of our transport, and I was having nightmares that we might soon be unable to maintain supplies to our garrisons around Nizwa. If we had to withdraw them, the campaign was as good as lost. I even wrote to Moy on a gloomy note:

'I am seriously considering whether you should come out here in October. At the moment things are getting worse rather than better, and will go on getting worse until I can do some frank talking with Julian Amery and Christopher Soames.'

Every officer in the Northern Frontier Regiment had been blown up at least once, some of them several times. It was in the Land Rovers that injuries were most frequent and most serious; even with sandbags on the floors, their crews often sustained crippling wounds. After the incident in the Wadi Beni Kharus I was forced to ban their use in the interior. At this very critical juncture the British Army in Aden stepped in to rescue us with the loan of a fleet of Morris 1-ton trucks, enabling us to keep our Nizwa forces supplied. I took advantage of this respite to have the Land Rovers fitted with reinforced steel plates under the front mudguards, which made them much less vulnerable.

In the middle of July Waterfield returned from leave, and on the 25th I flew to Bahrain on the first stage of my own long-promised leave in England — or so I had supposed. But while I was waiting in Bahrain Bernard Burrows summoned me to say that the Foreign Office was insisting on my staying in Muscat until the Sultan's return, which would be about the 28th. There was another reason, too, for keeping me there: as a result of Kassem's successful *coup* in Iraq the situation in the Gulf was dangerously tense. I flew back to Beit al Falaj fuming.

I reached London about a fortnight later, suffering from dysentery and a good deal of resentment at losing two weeks of my leave. However, I cheered up as a result of my talks with Soames, Amery, and some very helpful generals at the War Office. The best news they gave me was that the 22nd SAS Regiment would be returning home from Malaya later in the year, and it might be possible for them to spare me a squadron for a few weeks' service in Oman. I also asked for a whole squadron of Life Guards Ferrets, instead of the two troops which were due to replace the 13th/18th Hussars, and my request was granted. I was particularly pleased because the Ferrets had proved to be the most useful of all our vehicles; with their armour, machine guns and wireless they were ideal for the protection of convoys. I also received permission to recruit more Arabs and Baluch into the SAF, which would give me the chance of bringing my garrisons up to full strength.

After my warm reception from the generals I received a distinctly chilly one from the diplomats. The Foreign Office over the last few years had viewed the British involvement in Muscat with increasing embarrassment and disapproval. Its officials were acutely sensitive to criticism at the United Nations, where the conference tables were groaning under the weight of Egyptian, Saudi and Soviet resolutions condemning British imperialism — regardless of the fact that Britain was the only country that paid UN resolutions the least respect. Now the very suggestion that regular British troops might again be committed to action in Oman made their well-groomed hair stand on end.

Nevertheless I returned to Beit al Falaj in late September in a much sunnier mood, to find that D Squadron, The Life Guards, under Major Kenneth Diacre, had already arrived and set up their headquarters alongside my own. Diacre was a perfect choice for this type of command; he was that rare kind of Regular officer who combined competence with imagination, a sense of humour, and a highly individual approach to every problem. Given a squadron with very young and inexperienced subalterns as troop leaders, he quickly transformed it, with the help of some first class NCOs, into an extremely efficient and happy fighting force.

We deployed a troop at Nizwa, another at Izki and a third to reinforce Awabi, and we kept two troops as a reserve and for convoy escort duties. I devoted the next two months to intensifying our blockade, which I could now make effective thanks to the influx of fresh recruits to the SAF. We sealed the last unguarded approaches to the Jebel when a company of the Northern Frontier Regiment occupied the village of Tanuf at the beginning of October and when, a month later, the Trucial Oman Scouts sent me a squadron to hold Yanqil at the extreme north-western end of the range; thereafter not even donkeys could reach Talib, and any supplies he received had to be carried up to him on foot. I also sent reconnaissance patrols up the tracks leading to his positions in order to locate his pickets, improve our miserably inadequate maps, and gather information on the most suitable points at which to launch the final assault. At the same time I sent out fighting patrols to engage the enemy in a series of small actions, in order to instil into the SAF the self-confidence and offensive spirit which they had so sadly lacked earlier in the year. We came off best in those engagements, and although we had a few casualties the sharp rise in our morale made them worthwhile.

The enemy's reaction was to launch a series of night attacks, accompanied by heavy mortaring, on our positions round Tanuf; we beat them off, though not without some sharp fighting in which we suffered some losses but inflicted many more. The capture of Tanuf had been a serious blow to Talib, whose headquarters had been in a cave nearby. After failing to dislodge us he kept up the mortaring for a while, and then, quite suddenly, made overtures of peace.

One day a woman arrived in Nizwa with a message from the Imam to Sayid Tarik suggesting a truce during which both sides would refrain from hostilities, including bombing and shelling on our part and mine-laying on theirs. The ostensible purpose was to allow time to work out an honourable agreement between the Sultan and the rebel leaders; the real reason, we suspected — and captured documents later proved us right — was that the enemy was hard pressed by our blockade and demoralized by our successes in action against him, and needed a breathing space to recover. Nevertheless we agreed, and for two weeks the skies were clear of Shackletons and Venoms, our guns were silent, and our transport — and the oil company's — passed freely along the roads. Not surprisingly, the terms proposed by the rebels proved unacceptable to the Sultan, and so we went back to war.

But the war was briefly interrupted soon afterwards by continuous deluges of rain, followed by floods. It seldom rained in Oman outside the monsoon areas of the south — in fact, it only did so three times during the three years I lived at Beit al Falaj, and always in October; but the effect was of a sustained cloudburst. For forty-eight hours I was isolated in my house at Beit al Falaj because the *wadi* separating it from the camp became a deep, impassable torrent. When it cleared I flew to Nizwa, where I arrived in time to witness another downpour. Within an hour there were huge waterfalls thundering down the steep mountainside; the river bed by our camp outside the town filled and swelled to an angry flood of tawny water six feet deep and several hundred yards wide, carrying along on its frothy surface the debris of uprooted palm trees and bushes and the carcases of sheep and goats.

On another occasion one of these sudden floods almost overwhelmed our company camp at Kamah; although the troops scrambled to safety they had no time to cut loose their pack animals, and thirty donkeys were drowned. We lost a few lorries too, because our vehicles often used tracks along the river beds, where the going was better; the drivers had orders to abandon their trucks if they were trapped in a *wadi*, and run for their lives to the high ground. The floods subsided very quickly after the rains, and within a few days the earth would be looking as dry and parched as ever.

In the meantime my widespread appeals for help had brought two responses, the first an unmixed blessing, the second an unmitigated nuisance. In the last week of October Lt.-Colonel Tony Deane-Drummond, commanding 22nd SAS Regiment, flew out from England to see for himself whether the proposed operation and the type of country were suitable for the use of SAS troops. A regular officer of the Royal Corps of Signals who had led his men with great skill and success against the Communist terrorists in Malaya, he had displayed no less remarkable qualities of resource and courage as a junior officer in the Second World War. Parachuted into Arnhem, he had escaped capture afterwards by hiding for a fortnight in a cupboard in a house full of Germans before making his way back to our own lines. I felt reasonably sure he would give his consent to my request, for he seemed the kind of man to whom difficulties and obstacles were a challenge rather than a deterrent. I took him on reconnaissance patrols around the base of the Jebel and on several low level flights over the top, which wholly convinced him. He returned home to put in a strong recommendation for the employment of one of his squadrons in the assault.

Much less welcome was the arrival, a little earlier, of two hundred little Somali donkeys from East Africa. They were supposed to carry our supplies up the Jebel during the attack, but the poor little brutes were much too small and much too weak for the job — despite glowing reports of their achievements in Somaliland. They didn't begin to measure up to the Omani jebel donkey, which could carry a load of 120 lbs. compared with the Somali's maximum of 50; moreover

91

they hadn't even been trained to a pack saddle, and we had neither the men nor the time to train them. We tried to use them during the final assault, but they proved more of a nuisance than a help — although, in a wholly unforeseen manner, their very failure brought us a bonus at the end. They remained in Oman after I left, but the tribesmen wouldn't even accept one as a gift.

On the whole, however, October had been a good month, the more so because it brought Moy out to join me with our young sons. Our house, though far from perfect, was at least habitable, and Moy soon improved it, and the garden, out of all recognition; there was wonderful bathing on the coast near Muscat for her and the children, though I could seldom spare the time to join them; and the cool season was upon us, banishing our prickly heat and restoring our good temper. From now until March the weather would be perfect for operations, and I had the promise of the British troops I needed. The frowning mass of the Jebel with its harsh and hostile slabs, its dark and sinister ravines no longer filled me with the frustration and despair of former months. Hope was high in our hearts.

Chapter VI: Assault

Hope rose even higher in the second week of November, when a small patrol of the Muscat Regiment led by a Contract Officer, Major Tony Hart, found an unguarded route to the top of the Jebel. The track, which led from the village of Hijar above our base at Awabi on the northern side of the mountains, was a good six hours' climb and involved negotiating more than eighty of those steps cut out in the rock by the Persians; but it was possible for donkeys as well as laden men. After reaching the top the patrol, which was too weak to withstand any attack, very wisely withdrew before it was discovered. A few days later I made a personal reconnaissance of the track to the top with Colonel Mike Reid, commanding the Muscat Regiment, and an escort; again we met no opposition. This was the first time we had reached the plateau, and I was determined to exploit our opportunity as soon as the SAS arrived.

A week later they came — some eighty officers and men comprising D Squadron, under Major John Watts; they were organized in four troops, or patrols, of sixteen men each, together with Squadron Headquarters. Despite their small number they wielded formidable fire-power, with their Browning machine guns, FN rifles and Energa grenades. We had built them a camp at Beit al Falaj, but Watts, a stocky, tough, and dedicated professional, sensibly decided to lose no time in making them familiar with their new conditions; for he realized that the steep bare rocks and sharp outlines of the Jebel would require tactics quite different from those they had learnt in the swamps and jungles of Malaya. We therefore split the squadron, sending two troops on fighting patrols among the giant slabs above Tanuf and Kamah, and the other two to join Tony Hart at Awabi. Men from the Sultan's Armed Forces accompanied the SAS on all their patrols, an arrangement which greatly improved the morale and fighting skill of my own soldiers, who in their turn provided the SAS with valuable local knowledge.

The need for different tactics struck the SAS forcefully and tragically on one of their first patrols in the Tanuf area. In a skirmish with the rebels one of their best NCOs incautiously showed himself on a skyline and was shot through the heart by a sniper. This sad incident at least gave them a healthy respect for the enemy, whom they had been inclined to underestimate.

The other two troops, with Hart and some of his men, climbed from Awabi by the Hijar track to the top of the jebel, which they reached undiscovered. They then pressed on across the plateau until they came under attack from some rebels entrenched among caves in a cliff known as the Aquabat al Dhafar; although held up, they inflicted severe punishment on the enemy without loss to themselves. While a platoon of the Muscat Regiment dug themselves in at the top of the Hijar track to establish a base for further operations, the SAS tried to work their way round the Aquabat al Dhafar. But the rebels had strengthened their positions, and as we were unwilling to commit the SAS to a full scale frontal assault, a role for which they were not intended, we contented ourselves with strengthening our new base on the plateau, in the hope of demoralizing the enemy and encouraging him to divert troops there from other sections of the Jebel. At least we were firmly on the top.

Action flared again at the end of November around Tanuf, where some forty rebels suddenly launched a determined attack, supported by heavy mortars, on a company of the Northern Frontier Regiment and our troop of 5.5s. At first the defenders wavered, and almost broke, but they rallied under the spirited leadership of the Royal Marine NCOs, until the timely arrival of a troop of Life Guards racing up from Nizwa turned the scales. After a fierce battle, in which the machine guns of the Life Guards' Ferrets took a heavy toll, the enemy withdrew; but the NFR had four men wounded, and we lost two of our gunners when one of their shells failed to clear their *sangar* and burst on the lip.

On 1 December the SAS troops in that area took the offensive. Eager to avenge their dead NCO and acting on the information they had gleaned on that unlucky patrol, they attacked one of the caves held by the rebels and, supported by a strike of Venoms, killed a number of the occupants; they claimed to have killed eight of them, but subsequent interrogation of prisoners revealed that only two had been killed and three wounded. All the same, it was a useful action, which raised their spirits as much as it must have depressed the enemy.

In the ensuing weeks we strengthened our positions on the other side of the Jebel. At the end of December the Trucial Oman Scouts put a squadron into the village of Hijar, out of which they maintained two troops at our new base on the top, to reinforce the existing garrison of the Muscat Regiment and SAS. A platoon from the Northern Frontier Regiment joined them, and to provide additional fire-power a dismounted party of twenty Life Guards under a Corporal of Horse carried up eight of their Browning machine guns. We never ceased to bless the authorities for giving us these Life Guards; they really entered into the spirit of our war and, when not engaged in a protective role with their Ferrets, were happy to turn themselves into infantry and carry out arduous and dangerous duties up the mountain.

The SAS now felt they had sufficient support to mount a strong night attack on the Aquabat al Dhafar. They excelled in night operations, and under a protective barrage from the Life Guards' Brownings and the heavy mortars of the Muscat Regiment, they scaled the steep cliffs with ropes and came to close quarters with the rebels in their caves. A wild melee ensued in the darkness, with bullets, grenades and insults flying between the combatants, but the rebels fought back stubbornly and held their ground until we called off the attack. Although once again they had inflicted casualties without loss to themselves, the SAS emerged from the battle with an even greater respect for the enemy.

Although our situation was immeasurably better than in the summer, we were still a long way from victory. John Watts and I agreed that our chances of storming the Jebel with a single squadron of SAS were pretty slim, but that with a second squadron we could be reasonably certain of pulling it off. We therefore sent a signal to Deane-Drummond asking if he was prepared to let us have another squadron; he not only agreed but added that he would come himself with a small headquarters to take over command of both squadrons.

Our next problem was to secure the approval of the War Office and the F.O. We put our case to the Political Resident on one of his visits to Muscat, and obtained his promise to forward it to the Foreign Office; and in Aden the military authorities agreed to back us with the War Office. With all this support we won our clearance but, needless to say, the F.O. modified it with a proviso of their own: all British troops must be out of Muscat by the first week in April. The significance of this deadline, apparently, was that the United Nations were to discuss the Middle East situation soon afterwards, with Oman featuring large on the agenda; British diplomacy must not be embarrassed by the presence there of British troops.

Deane-Drummond arrived on New Year's Day, 1959. Our first decision was to set up a joint headquarters to co-ordinate the operations of the Sultan's Armed Forces, the SAS, and the Royal Air Force, and we co-opted a senior RAF officer from Bahrain to serve as our Air Liaison Officer. We installed this 'Tac HQ', as we called it, in the Northern Frontier Regiment's camp near Nizwa, and I moved there from Beit al Falaj on 9 January with John Goddard and a small staff.

My next problem was the chain of command. Officially all British troops serving inside the country came under my orders, and hitherto my second-in-command had been Colin Maxwell. But Deane-Drummond had to be in a position where he could give orders to his own troops, and so, to avoid complications, I appointed him my Deputy Commander. From anyone less generous hearted and unselfish than Maxwell this arrangement might have aroused strong resentment; but he accepted my decision with his usual amiability, well understanding the reasons behind it.

On 12 January A Squadron, 22 SAS Regiment flew in from Malaya, under Major John Cooper, one of the longest-serving officers in the SAS. As a corporal, Cooper had been David Stirling's driver in the Western Desert in the earliest days of the regiment, and had taken part in some of its bloodiest actions in Sicily, Italy and France. Dark and thin, with strong, expressive features and a quick though short-lived temper, he was a brilliant soldier whose thirst for adventure and danger was to bring him under my command again in the Yemen.

We sent the new arrivals to relieve D Squadron, who came back to Beit al Falaj for a few days of rest and refit; the special SAS boots had lasted only a few days on the sharp rocks of the jebel — to the incredulous dismay of the experts in the Quartermaster General's department who had designed them — and so we replaced them with hockey boots, which were much more satisfactory. Fresh from the heat of Malaya, A Squadron needed time to adjust to conditions on the Aquabat al Dhafar, where it had turned very cold, with hail storms and even snow; water bottles froze at night and fires were a necessity, even at the risk of snipers' bullets; although, in fact, both sides took this risk and nobody ever shot at the fires.

Because of the imposition by the Foreign Office of an April deadline we had about three months in which to assault the Jebel. We had agreed that the attack must be launched at night and during a period of full moon — it would be impracticable in total darkness; the full moon period came at the end of each of the next three months, which meant that the last weeks in January, February and March were the vital ones. We would make our first attempt at the end of January, which would give us two more chances if we failed. We must therefore plan on a very tight schedule, for we had a bare three weeks before our first attempt in which to move all troops to their take-off positions, organize their reinforcement and supply, re-deploy our garrisons, find reliable guides and co-ordinate the support of loyal tribal irregulars — in close consultation, of course, with Sayid Tarik.

At the same time I was faced with a difficult problem in diplomacy. The O.C. Northern Frontier Regiment, a British Seconded Officer, had an unfortunate habit of quarrelling with everyone with whom he came in contact. Already his Contract Officers had formed up to me, one after the other, to tell me they would 'soldier no more' under him; I had to transfer them and replace them with seconded officers, which meant there were no Arabic-speaking officers in the regiment. Next he alienated the Life Guards at Nizwa, giving them orders which he was not empowered to give them but which, presented with even a minimum of tact, they would almost certainly have accepted; it is only fair to add that, in return, the Life Guards officers baited him unmercifully. The consequence for me was that I had to spend precious time smoothing ruffled feelings as well as preparing for war.

The primary object in all our planning was to gain a foothold as quickly as possible on the top of the Jebel, near the rebel headquarters, and hold it for the reception of air supply drops and as a firm base for further operations. Surprise was obviously essential in order to avoid the heavy casualties that we must expect if the assault were opposed. The Aquabat al Dhafar was too far away from the main rebel strongholds of Habib, Saiq and Sharaijah, and in any case the enemy was already well entrenched on the Aquabat, where he was expecting us to attack; we must encourage him in that expectation and hope he would concentrate the main body of his forces on the northern side of the plateau. On the other hand the shortest approaches to the rebel villages, the tracks leading from Tanuf and Kamah, were known to be guarded.

Deane-Drummond and I made several flights over the Jebel, cruising slowly just above the ground and scanning the smooth faces of rock to find a route that men and donkeys could climb. At length Deane-Drummond made his choice, a sloping buttress thrusting out above the Wadi Kamah on its eastern side. We sketched it, mapped it, studied photographs of it, and imprinted every detail of it on our minds; there appeared to be no track, but the slope looked feasible for the pack animals except in one place — a sharp ridge connecting the two main features — where we hoped the sappers would be able to improve the going.

This approach had two main advantages: first, it was unguarded, so far as we could see, and it was most unlikely the enemy would expect an attack by such a route; secondly, our men could climb it in one night — in about 9 ½ hours by our reckoning — and so by dawn the leading troops could be in position on the top, where they could receive supplies by air.

Following standard Army practice, we gave a code-name to each of the tactical features on the way up. Our principal objective, the top of the Jebel, we christened 'Beercan'; the first prominent peak on the approach to it became 'Pyramid', while the sharp ridge connecting the two, which we had already noticed from the air, received the name of 'Causeway'. There was a lesser crest about a third of the way up to Pyramid, which we called 'Vincent', and our final objective, a peak beyond Beercan overlooking the village of Habib, went down in our operations plan as 'Colin'.

The two SAS squadrons would lead the assault, for I had received strict instructions from Aden that all other troops — Life Guards, Trucial Oman Scouts, and Sultan's Armed Forces — were to be used only in support of the SAS. These orders caused some natural disappointment to the Sultan's forces, who had tried for so long to reach the top, and who had in fact been the first to get there — when Tony Hart had taken his platoon of the Muscat Regiment up the Hijar track. However, they accepted the situation philosophically, especially as they themselves had important roles to play: first, they would make diversionary attacks before the main assault; secondly, they would follow closely upon the heels of the SAS and take over successive features as they were captured; and thirdly, they would consolidate the top of the Jebel and hold it against attack while the SAS pressed forward.

'Once we're on the top,' I told Deane-Drummond, 'and the aircraft have made their supply drops, we'll have to play things off the cuff. It'll depend on a lot of factors we can't foresee at this stage, such as the rebels' reaction and the whereabouts of their leaders. Remember, from our point of view — that is, from the Sultan's — the capture of Talib, Ghalib, and Suleiman is very nearly as important as the capture of Beercan.'

We agreed that if there was no serious opposition Deane-Drummond would push his patrols on to Habib, Saiq and Sharaijah, while our supporting troops cleared the enemy from the Kamah track and opened it up for the donkey columns.

We planned to launch our attack on the night of 25 January, at the beginning of the full moon period, which would allow us to postpone the operation if the weather forecasts were unfavourable. It was vital for us to have at least twenty-four hours of good weather following the assault, to allow the RAF to drop their containers accurately; otherwise the leading troops would arrive on the plateau short of food, water and ammunition, for we couldn't expect the donkeys to get there in time.

Talib must by now have realized that an attack was imminent, but he had no idea from which direction it would come. In order to confuse him we mounted a series of diversions during the weeks before 25 January in different parts of the Jebel. Between 8 and 22 January D Squadron of the SAS and A Company of the Northern Frontier Regiment carried out offensive patrols from Tanuf, and drove the rebels from some high ground they were using as an observation post. From 18-22 January A Squadron of the SAS, supported by the squadron of Trucial Oman Scouts, made probing attacks against the Aquabat al Dhafar; but on the night of 23 January A Squadron disengaged all but one of its troops and, after a forced march across the mountain, came down to join D Squadron near Tanuf. The following night A Company of the Northern Frontier Regiment engaged the enemy again near Tanuf, while C Company put in an attack from Izki. On every occasion we met strong opposition — C Company had a particularly hard time, losing one soldier killed and several wounded — which showed us the enemy was reacting as we hoped.

But the most brilliant, and one of the most successful of our deceptions involved no fighting at all. 'I'm prepared to bet,' said Malcolm Dennison, my Intelligence Officer, 'that if we call leaders of the donkey men together on the night before the assault, and tell them in strictest confidence and under the most ferocious penalties that the following night they'll be leading their donkeys up the Tanuf track, Talib will have the news within twenty-four hours.' In fact, we learned afterwards, Talib received the news in twelve hours.

Our plan of attack was necessarily simple, even primitive. The operation was essentially a straight slog up the mountain face, and everything would depend on whether we achieved surprise; even when we postponed it for twenty-four hours because of a poor weather forecast — a wise decision, as it turned out — there was no need to alter the details. There were to be three phases: in the first A Squadron of the SAS would capture Vincent, and D Squadron would occupy Pyramid, Beercan, and Colin before first light. In the second C Company of the Northern Frontier Regiment would relieve A Squadron on Vincent, while the dismounted troop of Life Guards took over Pyramid; and lastly, A Squadron would consolidate their position on Beercan and D Squadron on Colin.

Two groups of irregulars would be taking part: on the southern side fifty Beni Ruawha tribesmen under Major John Clarke, a Sultan's Contract Officer, would accompany the SAS squadrons, while a force of two hundred Abryeen and a platoon of the Muscat Regiment, under the command of Jasper Coates, would create a diversion in the north and, if unopposed, would climb the Jebel by two tracks leading from Awabi. These two tribes were hereditary enemies of Suleiman and his Beni Riyam, and welcomed a chance to pay off old scores; the Abryeen, in particular, needed to restore their honour after their failure the previous summer to protect the lines of communication of the Muscat and Oman Field Force.

There would be air support the following morning: Venoms from Sharjah would strafe any pockets of resistance, while three Valettas from Bahrain would make a total of nine container drops on Beercan. We also had two helicopters ready at Nizwa to evacuate casualties to our Field Hospital there. If the weather was still bad we should be absolutely dependent for supplies on the donkey columns; the prospect worried me and my only consolation was that we had a few Omani jebel donkeys to supplement the poor little Somalis.

Just before the assault began, on the evening of 26 January, I drove in my Land Rover to the assembly points where our men were waiting. Unlike Deane-Drummond, who was going with his men up the mountain, I should have to spend the night in 'Tac HQ' glued to the wireless; as overall commander I had to be in a position where I could exercise control at every stage of the operation, and I could only do so from headquarters, where I should be receiving regular progress reports from all units throughout the assault. I found the SAS cheerful and relaxed, with the easy self-confidence of experienced professionals who knew their job and had no doubt that they could do it; my own SAF were more subdued but there was no mistaking their determination to do what was required of them. The tribesmen of the Beni Ruawah formed a picturesque if ragged group in their flowing robes, their only uniform a red armband to distinguish them from the enemy on the plateau. John Clarke was standing by himself surveying them with his habitual air of profound gloom; behind his melancholy manner, I knew, were efficiency and courage as well as a wry sense of humour.

'Do your boys know what they're supposed to do?' I asked him.

'Yes, they know what they're supposed to do.' He paused. 'God only knows if they'll feel like doing it.'

The assault was to begin at 8.30 pm. I returned to the camp in a mood of intense excitement, tinged with impatience as I awaited the first reports in our improvised operations room. I felt no apprehension about the result. We had done our planning with care and thoroughness, allowing for every possible contingency, providing for every conceivable mishap; the progress reports would give me an up-to-date picture of the battle and I could deal with any emergency over the wireless. I had the best possible men for the job, in first class condition and equipped with the most modern weapons, I never doubted the outcome.

Outside, the night was cool and clear and mostly very silent. Once I heard faint shots from the mountain as our leading troops brushed with an outpost, but it soon became evident that we had indeed taken the enemy by surprise. Our deception plans, as we discovered next day, had been completely successful. The rebels had reinforced their pickets on the

Aquabat al Dhafar — eight hours' march away, on the other side of the plateau — to more than a hundred strong, and both Talib and Suleiman had gone there to supervise the defence in person; their remaining strength was concentrated on the Tanuf track. There was only one outpost guarding our route — two men with a .5 Browning that was too heavy to move. They were half asleep in their cave, secure in the belief that no attack would come their way, when a soldier of the SAS stalked them and killed them both with a grenade.

In the half-light before dawn enemy mortars and machine guns opened fire on C Company of the Northern Frontier Regiment from the Kamah slab, but our 5.5" guns, thirsting for targets, quickly put them out of action. The SAS suffered the only casualties of the entire operation when a chance bullet hit and exploded an Energa grenade in a soldier's pack; he and the two men following him were badly wounded and two of them died within twenty-four hours. The only serious obstacle on the route was the ridge known as Causeway; here the donkeys were utterly defeated, but one of the SAS squadrons shed their packs and heavy equipment and scaled it with ropes in a couple of hours. Beercan, our objective on top of the plateau, was in our hands by dawn; the entire climb had taken 9 ½ hours.

While some of our troops consolidated on Beercan and others pushed forward to occupy Colin and the village of Habib, the three Valettas from Bahrain made their supply drops — nearly 30,000 lbs in all, including equipment, ammunition, food, and — most important — water. But the Venoms making their low level runs over the plateau found no targets for their guns and rockets; the opposition seemed to have melted away and the only signs of rebel activity to greet our men as they dug in on the heights they had captured were some twenty shamefaced Beni Riyam who came up to them in disconsolate little groups to surrender.

The total collapse of enemy resistance came as a surprise to us, and it was not until later in the morning that the mystery was solved. Prisoners told us that when they had seen the containers coming down on parachutes, the rebels had thought they were parachutists; without waiting to verify their first impression they had panicked and dispersed to their caves and villages. And so the little Somali donkeys had helped us after all, by their very uselessness; it was because of our total lack of confidence in them that we had originally asked for the supply drops. If only we could have told them of it, perhaps the irony would have consoled them in their long and lonely exile.

One of the 'Casevac' helicopters took off from the camp at dawn to fetch the two most seriously wounded of the SAS casualties. When it returned I watched while the orderlies gently offloaded the unconscious men, and went to the hospital with them myself before returning to greet Sayid Tarik, who had come to offer his congratulations on our victory. Although I was sad about the loss of two good soldiers from such an evil stroke of fortune, I had to admit that in every other respect we had been fantastically lucky.

Immediately afterwards Tarik and I climbed aboard the helicopter to be lifted to the top of the Jebel. As we flew up the mountain I could make out in the growing light the Life Guards pickets holding the heights which the SAS had captured; they had taken the Biza machine guns off their Ferrets and carried them for nine hours up the mountain — a remarkable effort on the part of men who weren't even trained as infantry. Around the crest of Vincent groups of Somali donkeys huddled miserably on the rock face, unable to climb any higher; they had been more of a hindrance than a help, the troops told me afterwards, although the big Omani jebel donkeys had carried on as far as Pyramid.

We landed at Pyramid, on a small pad the troops had marked out for the helicopters. As we hovered above it I saw in the distance a long column of SAS winding across the plateau towards Saiq; they might have been on an exercise, so peaceful was the scene. All the same, I came nearer to death a few minutes later than I had done in all the campaign — and a very stupid and messy death at that. I was anxious to photograph Tarik as he emerged from the helicopter, for I thought he would make a fine picture in his turban, robes, bandolier and assorted weaponry; and so I leaped out as soon as we touched down, clutching my ciné-camera and ducking low to keep well clear of the main rotor blade. As I ran round the back of the aircraft to catch Tarik climbing out on the other side, I forgot there was another rotor on the tail. I saw people in the crowd gesticulating frantically, and sensed they were shouting at me, but the noise of the engines drowned their voices and I paid no attention. It was only when I skirted the tail and felt the breath of the blade an inch or two from my ear that I realized how near I had come to extinction.

The Beni Riyam prisoners were standing in a silent little knot nearby, their eyes flickering nervously towards Sayid Tarik as he strode over to them. He shook each one warmly by the hand and they gathered round him, sitting on their haunches in a circle while he questioned them gently about our most immediate problem, the whereabouts of Talib, Ghalib and Suleiman. Although I doubt if they gave away anything, or even if they knew anything, they quickly shed their reserve and launched into animated and friendly conversation, obviously greatly relieved to find him so genial. After a few minutes he bade them farewell, telling them to return to their villages and persuade their fellow-tribesmen to come in and hand over their arms, with assurances that we would treat them well. They evidently obeyed him, for during the next two days parties of rebels began to drift in and surrender; no more than a trickle at first, the numbers increased over the next few days as it became known that we were taking no reprisals.

We flew on to Beercan to join Tony Deane-Drummond, who was in high spirits despite his exhausting climb. He had been talking on the wireless with his leading troops.

'They've just occupied Saiq,' he announced. 'Why don't we fly over there and take a look?'

During the short ten minute flight I looked down on the green, scrub-covered plateau bathed in the clear morning sunlight, a welcome contrast with the baking rock and sand among which I had been living for the last nine months; orchards and terraced vineyards covered the slopes below Saiq, and fields of millet and sorghum, interspersed with almond trees and apricots, spread their blend of colours over the fringes of the plain. In the village the SAS had just disarmed a small group of tribesmen, some of whom squatted on the ground in sullen and dejected silence while others protested loudly that they had been on our side all the time and cursed Suleiman for the trouble he had brought upon his people.

One of them went so far as to offer to show us Suleiman's cave. We accepted eagerly and followed him for about half an hour into the hills, walking warily with our rifles at the ready and accompanied by a small escort of soldiers. The entrance to Suleiman's cave was a large hole in the rock. We found nobody there, but a fire still burned inside, indicating that the occupants had left pretty recently. Leading off from this cavern was a veritable rabbit warren of smaller caves, into which we had to crawl on hands and knees by the light of electric torches which we had luckily remembered to bring. They were too numerous for us to explore in any detail, but we entered a few, where we found a rich treasury of loot: there were stores of arms, ammunition, and food as well as Suleiman's personal possessions, which included a new Singer sewing machine; also, to our astonishment and delight, there were boxes of documents and bundles of letters giving confidential details about the organization of the rebels and their secret sympathizers in the Sultanate. Under Tarik's direction we collected a few of the most important papers and posted SAS guards to keep watch on the caves until we could send for the rest. Before leaving we each took something of Suleiman's as a souvenir — mine was a fine round brass coffee tray, on which I still serve coffee to my guests at home in Spain.

Suleiman's documents, which included nearly a thousand letters, provided our intelligence officers with a complete picture of the enemy network throughout the country. They gave us the names of prominent citizens of Muscat who were deeply compromised; of Sheikhs and village headmen who, under a cloak of loyalty to the Sultan, were actively helping the Imam; of mine-layers and arms smugglers, and of *askers* who assisted them or let them pass. Some, no doubt, were merely re-insuring against the possibility of a rebel victory; but one *asker* leader, supposedly in charge of an important and troublesome stretch of road, was revealed as the principal mine-layer.

I could not understand why Suleiman, however hasty his flight, had been so criminally careless as to leave behind such damaging evidence; although not conspicuous for his loyalty to friends in time of trouble, he could hardly have meant to betray them in this manner. The most charitable explanation is that when he had left his headquarters for the Aqubat al

Dhafar to meet what he had believed to be our main attack, he had expected to return at leisure as a victor; but after the collapse of the rebels he had been forced to escape as best he could, and had no chance to revisit the cave. In that case the parachute scare had indeed served us well.

That same afternoon our troops entered Sharaijah unopposed. In the village they found only women and children, the elderly and the crippled; the young men were still hiding in the surrounding rocks and caves. With the capture of this village, the last on the plateau, the battle of the Jebel Akhdar was over; it only remained for us to establish our authority throughout the area we had just occupied. I detailed some of the troops to consolidate positions at strategic points against any possible counter-attack — although it was difficult to see where it could come from; others I sent out in strong patrols to track down the rebel leaders and search for arms. The task of making contact with the villagers still in hiding, and persuading them to surrender their weapons and return to their homes, I entrusted to our tribal irregulars.

Only fifteen out of the original fifty of John Clarke's Beni Ruawaha had made it to the top of the Jebel; the remainder, finding the climb too stiff for them, had turned back on the way. However, the fifteen survivors did useful work, visiting the villages and caves and promising the frightened rebels, in our name, that all who came in with their arms would receive a free pardon and be released immediately. As the word went round that we were keeping this promise, more and more tribesmen returned to their villages and their work.

Two days later Jasper Coates arrived at Saiq with his platoon of the Muscat Regiment and his horde of two hundred Abryeen under their Sheikh, Abdullah bin Henna. On their way up the mountain they had taken the surrender of some seventy of the Awalad Awaimer tribe, allies of Suleiman, and disarmed them; the Abryeen had then indulged in an orgy of pillage all over the plateau. The looting was bad enough; what I found intolerable was that they tried to blame it on my soldiers. At all events they made a rich haul; cavalcades of donkeys laden with rifles, and even one or two Brens, were seen making their way back to Hamra, and Sheikh Abdullah must have collected a sizeable armoury. There was nothing much I could do about it because almost certainly it was loot, not loyalty, that had impelled the Abryeen to join us in the first place; anyway, I reflected, the way things are in Oman it probably won't be long before the Beni Riyam revenge themselves on the Abryeen, swoop down on Hamra and take back their property — and maybe a bit more.

Intensive searches by our patrols in the villages and caves on and around the plateau uncovered a formidable stock of arms: there were .5 calibre Browning machine guns, mortars, and Brens, as well as ample supplies of American ammunition and American mines, all of which carried markings indicating that they came from Saudi Arabian army supplies; there were also Czech and Polish grenades. These patrols covered every track and visited every village, as well as all the known caves, and so impressed on the inhabitants beyond all doubt that the SAF were in firm control. The rebels, particularly the Beni Riyam, were loud in their denunciation of Suleiman. His rule had been paternal but scarcely benevolent, and they had hitherto accepted it for the increased prestige it had brought them; now, in their humiliation, they blamed him for all their misfortunes.

However bitterly they might blame him, none were willing to betray him. Although we followed up every rumour of their whereabouts — most of them doubtless spread deliberately to put us off the scent — we never found him or his two

111

associates. With a small band of picked followers they escaped down the mountain, passed through the cordon of *askers* we had thrown round it — almost certainly with the help of some of them — and made their way to the Sharqiya. There, but for bad luck and the stupidity of one of my officers, we might have caught them.

About a fortnight after the assault Malcolm Dennison received information, which he was able to check and confirm, that the three rebel leaders were lying up in a house in the Sharqiya. We knew the exact location of the house, and I worked out in careful detail a scheme to surround it and capture them. I was about to spring the trap when my plans were wrecked by the ill-considered zeal and insubordination of the Officer Commanding the Northern Frontier Regiment — the same officer who had caused me such headaches in diplomacy before the battle. After scaling the mountain with his men he had returned to Nizwa, where I had given him strict orders to remain. By some mischance, however, he also learned where Suleiman and his friends were hiding and decided to win for himself the credit of capturing them. Ignoring my orders, he gathered together a small party from the camp and went to the house where the rebels were hiding, knocked upon the door, and asked the owner outright if he was harbouring them. The owner naturally said he wasn't. According to later reports Talib, who was in a room upstairs, asked the others, 'Shall I shoot this stupid *nasrani*?' 'No,' replied Ghalib, 'He is not worth it. Let him be.' The officer returned to Nizwa, to be dismissed soon afterwards by request of the Sultan; the three rebel leaders slipped away to the coast and escaped in a dhow to Saudi Arabia.

Meanwhile the SAF and the SAS, together with the Life Guards and the Trucial Oman Scouts, continued to patrol the plateau and other parts of the Jebel, and made detailed and accurate maps of the whole area. I established a company of the Northern Frontier Regiment as a garrison at Saiq, in a tented camp at first, but later in permanent barracks, and we began to build a fort there to discourage any attempt by the rebel leaders, however unlikely, to use it again as a base. We also built a landing strip alongside the camp, which we soon enlarged to take twin-engined Pioneers, thus greatly simplifying our supply problem. Saiq became a very popular station, for at 6000 feet it remained delightfully cool even at the height of summer. Colin Maxwell received the official appointment of Military Governor of the Jebel Akhdar, but to all of us he was known henceforward as 'Lord of the Green Mountain'.

Chapter VII: Uneasy Peace

In accordance with the Foreign Office directive, the SAS returned to England in March for some well-earned leave; the Life Guards rejoined their regiment in Aden, but I wasn't entirely deprived of Ferrets because their A Squadron replaced them in Muscat for a further two months. We were deeply grateful to those units of the British Army and freely recognized that we couldn't have won our war without them — particularly the SAS, whose expert training and modern equipment proved decisive. But I confess I was a little piqued that in the accounts of our operations that appeared in the British Press the SAS received the entire credit for our success; the Life Guards were barely mentioned, and the Sultan's Armed Forces — who had, after all, borne the burden of the preliminary campaign and endured the appalling rigours of the heat and the hazards of mining throughout the summer — were totally ignored, although they had suffered the highest casualties.

The British Government even refused us a campaign medal — perhaps they were unwilling to admit there had ever been such a campaign; but when the Sultan awarded a Jebel Akhdar medal to all his troops and Contract Officers, the War Office forbade the British Seconded officers and attached British troops to accept it. For the next two years I struggled with the War Office to have a medal awarded to all troops who had taken part in our campaign, and even wrote letters to the British Press on the subject; all I achieved at the end was permission for them to wear a clasp to the General Service medal inscribed 'Arabian Peninsula' — a distinction they might share with every desk-bound clerk in Aden or Bahrain.

However, the SAS fully deserved their publicity, for their enthusiasm, courage and skill had put heart into us and enabled us to turn a dispiriting stalemate into an overwhelming victory. Our enemies were, for the time being at least, discomforted, the roads were free of mines, and the towering slabs of the Jebel, once a symbol to all of us of frustration and defeat, now served only to remind us of our triumph. It was in a mood of cautious optimism that I transferred my headquarters back from Nizwa to Beit al Falaj.

Having conquered the Jebel we now began a 'hearts and minds' campaign to pacify the inhabitants of the plateau. They seemed to feel little ill will towards us soldiers, although they resented having to surrender their firearms — a deep disgrace in a country where every man carries a rifle from an early age; eventually we handed them back a few rifles for the protection of their flocks and livestock from wolves. The first stage in our new campaign was to send up teams of sappers to restore the water channels and reservoirs and repair the houses that our bombing and shelling had damaged or destroyed. The Sultan did not approve.

'Those people', he protested to me, 'are my enemies. They have fought a long war against me and cost me a great deal. Why should I now spend money on them, simply in order that they should not suffer the consequences of their rebellion? I do not even have money with which to reward the tribes who stayed loyal.'

'The British Government, sir, attaches great importance to this work.'

He took my point: the British Government was paying him a sizeable amount each year for 'Development'. And so the work

115

on the plateau proceeded, under the inspired direction of Hugh Boustead, who had recently arrived to take charge of the new Development Department created by the Amery agreement of the previous year. Soon afterwards the Sultan presented me, as a token of gratitude for the successful conclusion of the campaign, with a signed photograph and a silver Muscati coffee pot — made in London by Mappin & Webb.

My work at this time involved me in close collaboration with Hugh Boustead; I found it an enriching experience. One of the last survivors of the British imperial tradition of great and eccentric proconsuls, Boustead had come to us from the Hadhramaut, where his energy and genius had breathed new life into the desert and new hope into its people. Since a very early age his career had been by any standards remarkable — from the moment, in 1915, when he had deserted from the Royal Navy as a midshipman in order to enlist in the South African army as a private. He thought he would see more action as a soldier than as a sailor, and he justified his belief by emerging from the war with several decorations for valour, a commission in the army, and a Royal pardon for his desertion from the Navy. Afterwards he fought with Denikin against the Bolsheviks; became first a soldier and then an administrator in the Sudan; took part in an attempt to climb Everest; helped to liberate Ethiopia from the Italians; and served as Resident Adviser in Mukalla from 1949 until some genius persuaded him to join us in Oman.

At the age of 65 he still glowed with vigour and enthusiasm, and set about his new duties with a resolution that not even the Sultan's indifference could stifle. He spent long periods on road surveys in the interior, sheltered from the fierce sun and blistering winds only by a small tent pitched among the rocks, in conditions of hardship that would have drawn indignant protests from even my youngest subalterns but never seemed to worry him. Although a fluent speaker of Arabic, the language he spoke — whether Sudanese or Hadhramauti — was wholly incomprehensible to the Omanis; yet by means of exuberant gesture, loud laughter, and sheer persistence he always made his meaning clear to them, and they loved him, laughed with him and did what he demanded.

During the time he spent at Beit al Falaj, Moy and I found him a most welcome neighbour; we were always glad to see his short, stocky figure approaching our house, a squat wide-brimmed soft hat covering his thin grey hair. He was an enlivening companion, with a fund of fascinating anecdotes laced with the idiom of an earlier age; conduct of which he disapproved, for instance, was 'a bit off-side, what?' or 'not quite cricket, old boy'. Driving with us through the countryside, he would insist on stopping to talk to passing tribesmen. 'Oh, you bloody *bedu*!' he would exclaim delightedly, his bright blue eyes flashing with excitement as he leaped out to shake their hands and pour out his strange Arabic until their bewilderment dissolved in broad smiles of friendship.

During the months of hot weather between March and October, when Moy was in England, I came to value his company even more, as a relief from the frustrations and worries of my work; there was almost no one of comparable age and experience to my own with whom I could discuss them and hope for sound advice as well as sympathy. Colin Maxwell, of course, was always helpful when he was there, but his duties on the Jebel gave him little opportunity to visit Beit al Falaj. With Waterfield I could never wholly relax — not, I think, through any fault on either side, but because of our different positions and often conflicting loyalties. Waterfield was first and solely a Sultan's man and his loyalty was entirely to the Sultan: I was an officer not only of the Sultan but of the Queen, and my first duty was to the Queen. The situation inevitably led to misunderstandings between us.

As I sweltered through those summers, plagued with worries and intrigues by day and unable to sleep more than a few hours at night — for the temperature seldom fell below 100° Fahrenheit — my earlier optimism literally melted away; indeed I only kept my mental balance by re-reading constantly Moy's letters from home, and looking forward to the two months' leave I would spend each August and September with my family in a cottage we had been lent in Aberdeenshire. I dare say each of those worries and irritations was petty enough, taken by itself, but their cumulative effect on me in that climate was overpowering. At one moment I even wrote a letter to the War Office saying I intended to resign at the end of two years' service instead of three; Amery persuaded me to withdraw it.

My principal task — and one of the most congenial — was to build up the strength of the Sultan's Armed Forces. Over the next two years we expanded the army from the original 800 to nearly 2,000, but we still had to maintain the balance of 70% Baluch to 30% Arabs. Victory had not lessened the Sultan's mistrust of his Arab subjects, notwithstanding the fact that he had some capable officers among them; and so our recruiting was limited to the tribes of the coast, to the exclusion of the better fighting material from the tribes inland.

Strangely enough, our only two mutinies were among the Baluch; both occurred during my last year, in 1960. The first, which took place at Izki, was a mild enough affair. On receiving the news over the wireless at Beit al Falaj I flew up at once, to find that all the Baluch in the garrison had marched themselves to the Guard Room, where they had solemnly taken off their belts — a symbolic gesture whose significance they alone understood. When I arrived they were squatting on the ground in silence, refusing to obey any orders but otherwise threatening no disturbance.

The routine procedure on these occasions — there had been other mutinies by the Baluch before my time — was to surround the offenders with Arab troops before making any other move; the Arabs never mutinied and had little liking for the Baluch. The garrison commander had already taken this step and so I simply harangued the mutineers through an interpreter for a few minutes, and finished by asking them to state their complaints to me. The ensuing chorus of shouting resembled a crowd scene from a Cecil B. de Mille film, so I left them alone for ten minutes to select three spokesmen, from whom I was able at last to disentangle their grievances. The two main causes were low pay and alleged ill-treatment by an officer. In a parting speech I promised them a full investigation, rebuked them for the undisciplined manner of their protest and ordered them to return to duty, which they did without further argument.

I kept my word and carried out the investigation promptly. I found that their Company Commander, a British Seconded Officer, had been knocking them about, and I had him removed. About their pay I could do little because the Sultan laid down the rates and I couldn't change them. Our men received substantially less than the Trucial Oman Scouts and resented the fact. Soon afterwards the Sultan granted them an increase, but unfortunately the Trucial Oman Scouts immediately put up their rates, thus maintaining the differential.

The second mutiny was at Nizwa, and a much more serious business. My first intimation of it was the arrival at my headquarters of a dusty and exhausted British subaltern in a

Land Rover, who gasped out that the mutineers had dismantled the wireless at the camp, to prevent our getting any warning, and had disarmed their officers and the Arab troops too.

'I'll fly up there right away,' I told Tom Batchelar, who had succeeded Goddard as my Brigade Major. He gave me a grin and ran out to warn the pilot.

'Be careful, Sir,' shouted the subaltern anxiously as I climbed into the cabin of the Pioneer. 'The men are in a dangerous mood.'

He was not exaggerating, as I saw immediately we entered the perimeter a few minutes after we landed. We had no escort, and the lowering faces and truculent gestures of the heavily armed Baluch and the dispirited aspect of the few Arab officers and NCOs, slinking around without even their side arms, were hardly encouraging. It took me nearly two hours of hard talking before I could detect a softening in the mutineers' attitude. Fortunately the Baluch were always susceptible to reason, and once I had convinced them that I would listen to their troubles and look into them without prejudice they calmed down. The issue once again was the low rate of pay, aggravated by the neglect of their junior officers to pass on their repeated complaints to us. One entire company had marched down from the top of the Jebel to state their grievances. The ringleaders of the mutiny, who had certainly inflamed the situation unnecessarily, were three NCOs with bad records. I thought it impolitic to dismiss them; instead I transferred them separately to other areas of the country, and discipline was restored.

My most satisfying achievement during this time was to persuade the Sultan to provide compensation for SAF soldiers wounded or killed on active service. Previously they had received no disability payments whatever, and their dependants had received nothing if they were killed — hardly an encouragement to stick their necks out in battle. After the Jebel Akhdar campaign, however, we instituted a fixed scale of payments, rising to 1200 Maria Theresa dollars [£300] to the families of soldiers killed in action; this sum was the same as the blood money paid in murder cases. I also contrived to send some of the wounded to Bahrain for artificial limbs; and, as a final boost to morale, I prevailed on Douglas Bader to come to Muscat and give a talk to the men who had lost legs in mine incidents — a most generous action on his part which did an immense amount of good.

For nearly six months after their defeat on the Jebel Akhdar the rebels lay low, and we could move about the country undisturbed; indeed for the rest of my time in Oman they confined their activities to occasional and ineffective sniping of our camps and to laying mines on the roads. But in the summer of 1959 the mining became once more a serious problem, with the introduction of heavier mines, American and Egyptian, which could destroy a Land Rover and sometimes caused fatal casualties. The methods of smuggling them were the same as before, but because these mines were heavier and bulkier than the earlier types it was the rebels' practice to smuggle them in without their detonators and store them in 'safe houses' to be collected by the mine-layers, who would enter the country separately with the detonators. The mine-layers were carefully selected by Talib from his 'hardcore' followers; many of them were his personal slaves, of black heritage, and were in my opinion the best soldiers on the rebel side. Their devotion to Talib was unshakeable.

The purpose of the mine-laying, apart from its mere nuisance value, was to provide material evidence for the claims of Cairo Radio that there was still a full scale war in Oman. Naturally these claims, and the figures of British casualties quoted in support of them, were wildly exaggerated; according to them at least one British vehicle was blown up every week, with the death of at least seven of its occupants and always including two or three officers. As a matter of statistical fact, during the entire period between the beginning of 1958 and the end of March, 1961, when I left, our casualties from mines were six killed and seventy-six wounded, of which one of the dead and eleven of the wounded were officers; civilian casualties were six killed and twenty-one injured.

To combat this smuggling I proposed to the British Government and the Sultan that we should raise a special paramilitary force, to be known as the Gendarmerie, to patrol the Batinah Coast and the northern frontier. Almost all the mines came into the country by one or other of these routes — either by dhow to the Batinah Coast, where the waters were too shallow for pursuit by the frigates of the Royal Navy, or overland from Abu Dhabi and Buraimi, through the Wadi Jizzi. The Sultan's army was too weak in numbers to guard both routes effectively, and so I suggested that we should form the Gendarmerie, recruited from men in that area who knew the country and could identify the people engaged in the smuggling trade. I wanted the force equipped partly with Land Rovers but mainly with camels, particularly the famous Batinah racing she-camels.

Both the Sultan and the British Government fully approved my plan from the start, but each insisted the other should pay for it, and the ensuing wrangle lasted nearly a year. However, in the summer of 1960 the Gendarmerie was established, with its base at Sohar; its initial strength was 36, but numbers soon rose to 72 and finally to 120, with their complement of Land Rovers and camels. Unlike the civil police they came directly under my command and they wore their own distinctive uniform. At first I put Jasper Coates in charge of them, but later on, when I sent him to command the Sultan's navy, four ex-Colonial Policemen arrived as officers; the most successful of them was a tough and trigger-happy Texan, Carl Seton-Brown, whose rough interrogation methods produced several large hauls of mines.

Vigorous patrolling by the Gendarmerie, the SAF and the Royal Navy, supported by an extensive intelligence network, considerably reduced the volume of this traffic but could not hope to stop it. Of the other countermeasures we tried, the most successful by far was the offer of a reward to anyone who handed in a mine to us or gave us information that led to its discovery; the reward varied from £125, in Maria Theresa dollars, for a light mine to £200 for one of the heavies. This was an expensive method, but nowhere near as expensive as losing an £800 Land Rover or a 3 tonner worth over £1800, not to mention the cost in lives and injuries. It also led, predictably, to a profitable racket, in which people smuggled in mines for the express purpose of bringing them to us and claiming the reward; but it was still worth our while.

We started a system in 1959 of imposing a fine of £250 on the village nearest to a mine incident. Although it made us unpopular with the villagers it made the mine-layers even more unwelcome, and sometimes led to our receiving information about their movements. But it also provided, in those conditions of inter-tribal rivalry and blood feud, an easy way of paying off old scores, and people would often lay mines near an enemy's village. I was reminded of a similar situation in

Albania, where Communists and anti-Communists would lay ambushes near each other's villages to provoke German reprisals on them.

In the same year two Kenya-born British officers arrived with six African trackers to help us. They did once manage to follow a mine-layer's tracks from the road as far as a village, where they lost them; but they were more successful in training our *bedu* and Baluch in their craft. In fact, the *bedu* proved better trackers than the Africans, and we allotted two of them to each of our infantry companies. They were particularly useful in guarding airfields; patrolling the perimeter at dawn, they could easily tell if anyone had crossed the airfield in the night, and detect the spot where he had laid a mine.

We also tried dogs. Two Alsatians came to us from Cyprus early in 1959. Unfortunately they turned out to be guard dogs, and by the time they had been re-trained as trackers the hot weather had begun; according to the vets, they would be unable to withstand the summer heat and so we sent them back to Cyprus. However, they gave rise to a very useful rumour to the effect that we had imported lions from Kenya to eat the mine-layers.

During the two years following the defeat of Talib I spent a great deal of my time touring different parts of the country, partly to visit our garrisons and partly to make myself thoroughly familiar with the terrain and the people, in case of another rebellion. I passed long hours 'fuddling' with *walis*, sheikhs and villagers. They could be valuable sources of intelligence to us, but first I had to break down the suspicion with which many of them regarded the army, and show them they had nothing to fear from us. We had to show them also that we could protect them, and so we would usually give a display of strength on our arrival, parading our mortars and machine guns in front of them, and sometimes firing a practice shoot — a spectacle that never failed to please and, we hoped, impress. Sometimes I spent the night in an old Portuguese fort; but more often I would camp in the open country outside a village, watching the bright stars and sniffing the clean tang of the desert air until I fell asleep, to be awakened soon after sunrise by the women coming to draw water from the wells or gather firewood from the river bank.

The women in Oman seemed to lead a wretched existence, and I used to pity them as they staggered under their heavy loads of faggots or goat-skins of water. They had to bear innumerable children, few of whom survived beyond infancy. In Muscat and the larger towns they had to wear hideous black, beaked masks over their faces when they walked abroad, despite the stifling heat; in the countryside they wore simple veils. The *bedu* women, who seemed much freer, often went with their faces uncovered. The Arabs demanded of their women strict chastity before marriage and absolute fidelity afterwards; any breach, or even suspected breach, of either brought dishonour on the woman's house, which her menfolk would punish with death. On one of my visits to Sohar I had to bring back in my aeroplane a fourteen-year-old girl with the face of an angel, who had been shot in the stomach by her brother for 'looking at a man'! She lay silent and uncomplaining on her stretcher, and died before we landed; her brother went unpunished.

Everywhere I travelled in the interior I was horrified by the poverty and disease of the inhabitants — although the situation improved dramatically after Hugh Boustead had persuaded the Sultan to let him build dispensaries and health centres throughout the country. One of the most sickening spectacles in up-country villages was the treatment of lunatics. Stark naked and shackled hand and foot, they squatted on the ground in their own filth, frothing at the mouth or emitting weird animal grunts while the villagers jeered as they passed by; nobody seemed to feed or care for them. I could do nothing to help them, and felt they might after all have been better off in Jalali.

In June, 1959, I visited the Musandum peninsula in the extreme north of Oman on the Strait of Hormuz. Although part of the Sultan's territory, it is cut off from the rest of Oman by the Trucial State of Fujairah, and so I had to make the journey by sea, flying to Bahrain and embarking there in HMS *Loch Fada*, a frigate of the Persian Gulf Squadron. Ras Musandum is the wildest, least explored, and most inhospitable part of the all the Sultanate; it has no coastal plain, and forbidding black volcanic mountains rise sheer from the sea to a height of six thousand feet. The Elphinstone Inlet, where we called — mercifully only for a brief inspection — is reputed to be the hottest place in the world, and I could well believe it; the great perpendicular cliffs rising on every side deflected the heat of high summer onto the narrow fjord, turning it into a giant oven. I heard that a scientific expedition once landed there for a few days; when their ship returned for them they were all either dead from the heat or mad.

There were very few tracks inland, and those were only suitable for donkeys. This was the country of the Shihuh, one of the oldest, most primitive of tribes in Arabia; according to legend they are descended from Sinbad the Sailor, but their true historical origin is unknown and their language, a form of Arabic, is not easily understood by other Arabs. Those I saw, in coastal villages we visited, wore beards and tattered Arab dress, but were taller than other Omanis. They had the strange habit, shared by Dinkas I had seen in the Sudan, of standing on one leg, and they carried tomahawks with a slender two foot shaft and a small metal head with a point on one side and a cutting edge on the other, which they used both for hunting and fighting — for they were very pugnacious. Most of them lived in caves in the mountains and had no love for strangers; in fact they once surrounded a party of prospectors from an oil company, stripped them of all their belongings, including their clothes, and sent them back stark naked whence they had come.

Later travels took me to the east of Oman, to Sur and Ras el Hadd. We had to blast a road through to Sur with explosives, and I took the first motor convoy to make the journey, in the autumn of 1960. Twice we were fired on, fortunately without casualties; the ambushes, it turned out, were the work of camel caravan owners, who feared a road for vehicles would deprive them of their trade, and hoped to scare us away.

Ras el Hadd, the most easterly tip of Oman, is the point where the waters of the Indian Ocean meet the Gulf of Oman and the approaches to the Persian Gulf. Brushed by the monsoon rains, it is refreshingly cool and green after the heat and dust of the northern and western regions; if I had to live in Oman, Ras el Hadd is the place I would choose to build my house. From the rocks on the shore I could see an astonishing variety of marine life: there were schools of porpoises and sharks, and once I saw a whale. Most spectacular were the giant manta rays, weighing over five tons and spanning thirty feet, that leaped clear out of the water, to come down with a thunderous clap as they tried to dislodge the parasites from their bodies; there were tales of them landing on top of fishing boats. In the evening the turtles would waddle up from the shore to scoop out holes in the sand and drop their eggs.

There was superb underwater fishing at Ras el Hadd, even better than at Muscat; crawfish abounded, as they did all along the coast, and small oysters clung to the rocks in clusters. Spearfishing was my favourite relaxation; I found it wonderfully soothing to glide through the clear water and look down on the sea bed with its graceful, flower-like coral, alive with small, brightly coloured fish. There was no danger from sharks, because the aggressive hammerheads and other man-eaters kept well out to sea and those we found inshore were docile; but there was danger from barracuda, moray eels, and a species of stingray, almost invisible against the sand, which could kill. Once I caught an electric ray, which knocked me flat on my back on the rocks with a charge of 250 volts.

Early in 1961, when my three-year contract was nearing its end, the Sultan asked me to stay on for a further year. I declined because I was planning to settle in Kenya. I took my leave of him in April, when he thanked me courteously for my services and presented me with a fine Muscati incense burner — manufactured, like the coffee pot, by Messrs Mappin & Webb.

My three years in Muscat had been an interesting and enriching experience for which I am grateful now, as I am grateful for the many good friends I made there. But at the time I left I was so demoralized by the accumulated load of worry and frustration inseparable from my work that I was happy to think I should never see Arabia again. I could not know that in a little more than two years I should be there again, on the other side of the peninsula, in the service of my former enemies, the Saudis.

Part II: Yemen

Chapter VIII: Imams and Incense

I left the army with a chip on my shoulder. When I returned to England from Muscat at the beginning of April 1961 I was offered the overall command of the three existing SAS regiments. Although the responsibilities were those of a brigadier, the appointment was to be in my present rank of full colonel. I declined it for reasons which I explained to General Bob Laycock, the Colonel-in-Chief of the SAS.

'For the last fifteen out of my twenty-five years in the army I've been a colonel — either a full colonel or a half — and if they're not prepared to promote me now, it's obvious that I've reached my ceiling. It's funny,' I added wryly, 'to think that a few years ago I was turned down for promotion to brigadier on the grounds that I was too young for the rank. Now I'm forty-five and I'd better get out before I'm too old to do another job.'

Laycock was sympathetic but he couldn't help.

'I know how you feel, David, but in fact the War Office simply isn't willing to pay a brigadier.'

And so, after a skiing holiday with my family in Switzerland, the most complete contrast I could think of to Muscat, I took one of the 'demob courses' the army provided for retiring soldiers. It was at the factories of Land Rovers and of Perkins diesels, and I chose it as a preparation for farming in Kenya. But we sold our farm without ever living there: in the first place, we both wanted our children to be educated in Britain, and if we had lived in Kenya the air fares alone would have ruined us; secondly, we weren't too optimistic about our prospects under *Uhuru.*

We spent the summer of 1962 at a cottage in Aberdeenshire, enjoying the superb country and the grouse shooting. But it was no place to stay in winter, and we accepted gratefully when Moy's cousin offered us the tenancy of his attractive old house, Branxholm Castle in Roxburghshire. As soon as we were installed I set about trying to find a job.

I soon realized I had made two bad mistakes. The first was in omitting to follow the example of most retiring officers, who made their arrangements for civilian employment before they left the army. That was something I could hardly do in Muscat. My second and graver error was to have found myself a home before I had found a job. After unsuccessful attempts to find employment within commuting distance of Branxholm, I finally accepted a part-time job as an itinerant inspector for Raymond Postgate's *Good Food Guide*; at the same time I tried, with indifferent success, to grow mushrooms.

I enjoyed my work for the *Good Food Guide*, although in my travels around Scotland I ate more bad meals than good, and thought it a pity that a country producing some of the best meat and fish in the world should cook it so atrociously. I was certainly happy at Branxholm, which my family loved as much as I did, but in time I might well have begun to fret at such a placid existence. However, it came suddenly to an end in May 1963, with a telephone call from my old wartime friend, Billy McLean, in London. He sounded excited.

'David? How would you like to come with me to the Yemen?'

In September, 1962, while I was shooting grouse on the Aberdeenshire moors, a revolution had broken out in southwestern Arabia, in the ancient Imamate of the Yemen. Planned as a short, decisive *coup d'état*, it developed quickly into a bitter civil war which was to plunge that primitive, little-known country into five years of suffering and bloodshed more devastating than any it had undergone in the previous three thousand.

According to Wilfrid Thesiger[17] the Bedouin believe that the *Arab al Araba*, the purest strain of their race, originated in the Yemen, and T. E. Lawrence[18] describes it as the cradle of the Semitic peoples. Certainly its mountains and deserts have bred some of the best of Arab fighting men — including, so Yemenis assert, the elite of the armies of Tarik[19] and Musa, who conquered Spain from the Visigoths. But for 1500 years before the birth of Mohammed there had been rich and powerful kingdoms in this part of Arabia — Arabia Felix, as the Romans called it. Minaean, Sabaean, and Himyarite dynasties guarded and prospered from the Incense Trail that led from Dhofar to Mesopotamia and Persia, Egypt and the Mediterranean; and it was from her capital at Marib in eastern Yemen that the Queen of Sheba came to visit Solomon.

Frankincense and myrrh were highly prized in the ancient world. The frankincense came from Dhofar, the myrrh from the hills of eastern Yemen; in Yemen therefore lay the key to both. For centuries before the rise of Islam the empires of the Middle East — Assyrian and Egyptian, Roman and Greek — had struggled for control of the incense route; in later years Abyssinians, Egyptians, Persians and Turks had occupied the Yemen at different periods, but their rule was seldom effective outside a few garrison towns. The Zeidi sheikhs and tribesmen of the northern and central mountains, the toughest Yemeni fighting stock, acknowledged loyalty only to their hereditary

---

[17] *Arabian Sands* (Longmans, Green, 1959), p. 91.
[18] *Seven Pillars of Wisdom* Ch. 2.
[19] Tarik gave his name to Gibraltar (Jebel Tarik, the mountain of Tarik).

Imams, who traced their descent from Ali, the Prophet's son-in-law, and to the Paramount Sheikhs of their two tribal confederations, the Bakil and the Hashid.

These tribesmen, who comprise about forty percent of the four million inhabitants of the Yemen, belong to the Zeidi sect of the Shia branch of Islam — the branch which regards Ali as the true successor to Mohammed and the Caliphate; Ali, in fact, was for a time governor of the Yemen, sent there by the Prophet to restore order. The Zeidi sect, founded in the eighth century by a great-grandson of Ali named Zeid, is less strict in religious matters and in the enforcement of Koranic law than, for instance, the Sunni Wahabis of Saudi Arabia; but its followers are utterly devoted to their Imam, whom they regard as their spiritual as well as their temporal ruler. The Imams of Yemen, originating with one of Zeid's followers who also claimed direct descent from Ali, broke away from Caliphate authority at a very early date. Their capital from the ninth to the seventeenth centuries was at Sada in the north; but the great national hero, Imam Qasim al Mansur, transferred the seat of government to Sana in central Yemen after expelling the Turks in 1629. Qasim al Mansur, or Qasim the Great, was the founder of the Hamid ud Din dynasty, to which the present Imam belongs.

The more numerous section of the Yemeni population, the city-dwellers and the plainsmen of the south and west, are Sunnis of a sect known as Shaffei, and do not acknowledge the religious authority of the Imam. Although more sophisticated than the Zeidis, they have little of their fighting quality.

When the Second World War ended, Yemen was a small, independent country of little commercial interest but with a considerable strategic importance based not on incense but on oil. The tanker route from the Persian Gulf to the Suez Canal passed through the Straits of Bab al Mandab into the Red Sea within artillery range of the Yemen coast, and so a hostile power controlling Yemen could threaten oil supplies to the West; it could also threaten Aden, the gateway to the Gulf. Moreover Aden, in the passionately held view of all Yemenis, was Yemeni territory and had been so for a thousand years; no Imam could afford to abandon this claim or recognize the British occupation as legal. The great Imam Yahya, grandfather of the present Imam, had signed a treaty with the British Government in 1934, giving *de facto* recognition to the *status quo*; but differences of interpretation gave rise to continual disputes and frontier disturbances after his death.

Imam Yahya, who ruled from 1904-1948, was a national hero scarcely less illustrious than Qasim al Mansur. For the first seven years of his reign he carried on a brilliant and successful guerrilla war against the Turks, who left the country for good in 1918. Although he lost a war with Ibn Saud, which obliged him to cede territory in the north, he governed his country with skill, authority, and, by Yemeni standards, lenience, and gave it a fair measure of prosperity. He was frugal to the point of meanness, and as a matter of policy kept his kingdom strictly isolated from outside influences; apart from a very few Italians, he admitted no foreigners within its borders.

His long reign came to an end in 1948 with his assassination in an attempted *coup* that also cost the lives of three of his sons. Of the fourteen sons of Imam Yahya, only two are alive today; seven met violent deaths and four of those were executed on the orders of their brother Ahmed, who succeeded Yahya as Imam. Ahmed was an obese and pop-eyed tyrant who maintained his rule, with considerable success, by terror; but his courage and resolution and the speed of his reactions, combined with the loyalty of the Zeidi tribes and a fair measure of luck, enabled him to survive three attempts to murder and overthrow him — in 1948, 1955, and 1961. He died in his bed in September, 1962, a week before the revolution which ended the Imamate — and which was to take me back to Arabia.

Ahmed moved his capital from Sana to Taiz in the Shaffei country of the south. He also began, reluctantly, to establish contact between Yemen and the twentieth century. He was conscious, especially after the 1955 rebellion, of the need to conciliate the more progressive among his discontented subjects; and he wanted help against the British in his feud over Aden. In 1956 he travelled in person to Jedda, where he signed a treaty of mutual assistance with King Saud, son of Ibn Saud, and with President Nasser. He also sent his son, the Crown Prince Mohamed al Badr, with a plentiful supply of Saudi money on a visit to Cairo, western Europe, Prague, Moscow and Peking. In Cairo the young prince conceived an uncritical admiration for Nasser and his policies and arranged for an Egyptian military mission to train the Yemeni armed forces; in western Europe he acquired a taste for alcohol, which has remained a problem with him ever since. In Prague and Moscow he bought aircraft and tanks and gave the Russians a contract for building a deep water port at Hodeidah; and in Peking he gave another contract to the Chinese, to lay a motor road from Hodeidah to Sana.

It can fairly be said of the Crown Prince's tour that all its results proved disastrous to himself. In the words of Dana Adam Schmidt, an American journalist who covered the subsequent civil war from both sides,

> Nasser's military mission became the vehicle through which Egypt introduced the agents who were later to organize Yemen's revolution. The tanks were used against the Imam in

the *coup d'état* of 26 September, 1962. The port and the road were absolutely essential to the introduction of the Egyptian army which supported the revolution. The alcohol which al Badr began to absorb undoubtedly reduced his ability to cope with the problems that beset him as soon as his father died.[20]

Another result of the Crown Prince's visit to Cairo was the alignment of Yemen with Egypt and Syria in a Federation of Arab States — an arrangement which lasted until 1961, when the Imam Ahmed quarrelled openly with Nasser and was expelled from the Federation. In addition to the Egyptians, Russians and Chinese, Ahmed allowed the Americans to look for oil and to begin work on a second motor road — from the old port of Mocha to Sana, via Taiz. A cynic might have observed that the Yemen was filling up with enemies of Britain.

Nasser, with his eyes on the oil of Arabia and the Gulf, had never concealed his determination to expel the British from Aden; control of the Yemen was a necessary step towards this end. Ahmed was too tough a ruler for him to dominate, but the moment he died the Egyptians were ready to implement their own plans for revolution, or to exploit those already prepared by others.

When Mohamed al Badr was installed as the new Imam in Sana on 19 September, 1962, immediately after his father's death, there were no less than four plots hatching against him. Of the two most important — both of them inspired and supported by the Egyptians through their *chargé d'affaires* in Sana — one involved a group of young Yemeni army officers

---

[20] *Yemen: the Unknown War* (The Bodley Head, 1968), p. 41. I have drawn extensively on this work for my account of events in Yemen before the revolution.

136

under the leadership of the Egyptian-trained Lieutenant al Moghny; the other was the work of al Badr's Chief of Staff, close friend and principal confidant, Brigadier-General Abdullah Sallal. Born the son of a blacksmith and trained in Iraq, Sallal owed a great deal to al Badr, including his position and even his liberty; for al Badr, who shared his enthusiasm for Nasser, had persuaded the Imam Ahmed to release Sallal from the dungeons of Hajjah, where he had lain for seven years, accused of conspiracy. In return, Sallal was about to overthrow and try to kill his benefactor.

Although the new Imam had received three separate warnings about the various plots against him, he chose to ignore them all. Unlike his father, he had an amiable and trusting nature; also, unfortunately, a weak one. He had shown courage and determination during the 1955 revolt, rallying the Bakil tribes to march to the relief of his father besieged in Taiz. But Ahmed had always despised him, although he was willing to use him on missions abroad, and never bothered to hide his contempt. As a result al Badr relapsed into long periods of depression, which he tried to alleviate with drink; although only thirty-five years old he was already flabby and overweight. For his part he hated his father's cruelty and was determined not to begin his reign with bloodshed. Had he but known it, his scruples were to cause far greater bloodshed than ever occurred under his father.

For a brief period in 1959, when Ahmed was having medical treatment in Italy, al Badr had governed the country in his name, and had tried to put into practice some of the theories he had absorbed in Cairo; he had freed some slaves and initiated reforms in the government. Unhappily, his good intentions were taken for weakness, and his promises only whetted the appetite while exciting the contempt of potential revolutionaries. Ahmed had to return hurriedly and restore the situation with the executioner's sword. Now, in a speech to mark his installation as Imam, al Badr repeated the promises and the good intentions of 1959, and specified a number of reforms he meant to introduce immediately in the interests of justice and good government. While he was speaking, the plotters were already preparing to destroy him.

When warned about the plans of al Moghny and Sallal, al Badr reacted predictably. Instead of arresting the conspirators, as his father would have done, he consulted Sallal, who easily reassured him. On the pretext of ensuring the Imam's safety, Sallal concentrated the army's few tanks and armoured cars around the capital, where they were taken over secretly by al Moghny and his supporters. Sallal, who was not personally involved in al Moghny's plot, intended nevertheless to use it as a vehicle to power; but Nasser, through his *chargé d'affaires*, controlled them both.

On the night of 26 September the conspirators struck.[21] That evening al Badr held a cabinet meeting in the Basha'ir Palace, which he had occupied as Crown Prince and where he still preferred to live. Sallal was present as a matter of course, but excused himself when the meeting ended at 10.30 pm, and went home. The Imam went upstairs to his private apartments, accompanied only by his father-in-law, Yahya al Hirsi, and two servants. As he went down a corridor towards his room, a soldier of the Palace Guard stepped from behind a pillar with a tommy-gun and tried to shoot him in the back. Luckily the weapon misfired, and the Imam, hearing the click — a sound

---

[21] The following account of events is abridged from the story told me later by the Imam himself. For fuller details see Dana Adam Schmidt, op. cit. pp. 26-35.

he easily recognized — plunged into his room, while al Hirsi and his servants overpowered the guard.

Soon after they had finished questioning the man, who seemed to them to be crazy, there was a violent explosion as a shell smashed through the wall of the palace and burst on the floor above; the tanks which Sallal had concentrated around Sana, and which al Moghny had just deployed to encircle the palace, were beginning their bombardment. As the building began to collapse under the impact of the shells, the Royal Bodyguard melted away; but the Imam seized a tommy-gun and fired a few bursts through a window in the direction of his attackers — a significant if ineffective gesture of defiance. Then he and al Hirsi made their way to the ground floor, accompanied by two loyal guards, a servant and two black slaves. At the same time the Imam managed to send a messenger with a desperate appeal for help — to Sallal. The Chief of Staff sent him back with an assurance of support.

But the rebels had also sent a message to Sallal, asking him to join them. He agreed, but demanded in return that he should be President of the new republic — a condition al Moghny readily accepted. That was the end of al Moghny; as soon as Sallal had no further use for him he sent him to fight the tribes in the Khowlan, where he was almost immediately killed.

In the first hours of the *coup* the rebels seized the arsenal, though not without a bloody battle, and the radio station, from which they broadcast news of their success, adding that the Imam was dead beneath the ruins of his palace. Al Badr heard the broadcast and realized that he must flee at once; if he could reach the safety of the mountains and rally the Zeidi tribes in person, the Imamate might yet be saved. He would have to leave behind his two wives and his daughter, but he knew that the rebels, who were also Arabs, would not dare to harm them.[22]

139

His small party left the palace, one by one, through a back street which the rebels had omitted to guard. They spent the hours of daylight hiding in friends' houses, where they changed their clothes and disguised themselves, and on the following night they made their way out of the city and headed on foot towards the north-west. They knew the Republicans were out looking for them, and so they avoided the towns and made for the mountain villages, where the people were loyal to the Imam. It was a gruelling journey for a man of al Badr's physique, softened by years of idleness and luxury; but anger gave him strength and resolution. He had been betrayed, as he now realized, by the two men he had most admired and trusted — Sallal and Nasser — and with that knowledge he shed his old lethargy, at least for a while, and his old illusions probably for ever.

As he travelled northwards through tribal territory his following grew; even his Palace guards, those of them who could get away, drifted back to join him. By the time he reached the Saudi border in the extreme northwest, three weeks after the *coup*, he commanded a force of several thousand men, whose numbers were increasing every day. After a brief visit across the frontier, to Jizan, where he received a warm welcome from the governor and messages of support from King Saud and King Hussein of Jordan, he returned to north-west Yemen and set up his headquarters in some caves in the Jebel Qara, north-east of the town of Haradh. There he was to remain for the next three years.

Meanwhile the Hamid ud Din princes were organizing resistance in the north and east of the country. Most of them

---

22 They were, in fact, interned for a year, before being exchanged for Republican prisoners of the Royalists.

had been in exile, in diplomatic posts in Europe or America, but as soon as they heard of the *coup* they flew to Saudi Arabia and held a council in the frontier town of Najran. Believing al Badr to be dead, they elected his uncle, the fifty-six-year-old Amir Hassan ibn Yahya,[23] as Imam in his place. Al Hassan, as he was usually known, was serving as the Yemen delegate to the United Nations in New York when the revolution broke out. He enjoyed enormous prestige and popularity among the tribesmen, and some of the princes would probably have preferred him to his nephew; but as soon as he learned that al Badr was alive he renounced his new title and offered his services to the rightful Imam, who appointed him his Prime Minister and designated him as Crown Prince to succeed to the Imamate in the event of his death.

The Egyptian occupation began almost simultaneously with the *coup*. Within a few hours of the rebels' broadcast an advance guard of the Egyptian Army flew into Sana while other troops, who must have sailed from Egypt before the revolt broke out, were landing with artillery and armour at the port of Hodeidah and driving up the motor road to the capital. The initial invasion force numbered about 3,000, and increased rapidly to 12,000; by the following April there were some 30,000 Egyptian troops in the Yemen. They were supported by a powerful air force, which began immediately to bomb villages in Royalist areas — at first with high explosive and later with gas.

To counter the Egyptian invasion, and the threat it posed to their own positions, the Kings of Saudi Arabia and Jordan gave their support to the Imam. King Saud provided money, arms

---

[23] Amir, meaning Prince, is the title of members of the Saudi and Yemeni Royal Families. *Ibn* 'son of', is more usual in this part of Arabia than *bin*. In speech it was generally omitted: for example, Amir Mohamed *ibn* Hussein was spoken of as Amir Mohamed Hussein.

and supplies; King Hussein sent military instructors — until warned by the American Ambassador in Amman that unless he withdrew his assistance to the Royalists, all US aid to Jordan would cease.

Both the United Nations and the United States were quick to recognize the Republican government. The UN decision was the result of a motion proposed by Egypt and supported by the Communist powers and *les Affreuses* — the Afro-Asian bloc; US recognition came on 19 December, 1962, and the motives behind it are still obscure. The new regime scarcely qualified under international law. It had come to power by a *coup d'état*; it controlled barely half the population and much less than half the area of the country; and the legitimate government it claimed to replace was fighting back strongly. The United States Government maintained it was a logical decision — perhaps because the Republicans were in possession of the centres of communications — but its reasons sounded unconvincing. They certainly did not convince the Swedish General von Horn, who later on commanded the UN observer mission in the Yemen. 'I have always thought,' he wrote, 'and I still do, that beneath this apparently logical decision by the Americans lay a baser policy aimed at embarrassing the British in southern Arabia, linked with a desire to further their own oil interests in the Arabian peninsula.'[24]

Stranger still, the US put the strongest pressure on the British Government to follow their example in a move so plainly contrary to British interests that it is surprising the Foreign Office even considered it. Nevertheless, they did consider it very seriously. In fact, there is little doubt that the British

---

[24] *Soldiering for Peace* (Cassel, 1966), p. 294.

would have recognized the Republican government soon after the Americans but for the happy intervention of Billy McLean.

By chance McLean, at that time Member of Parliament for Inverness, was visiting Saudi Arabia when the Yemen revolution broke out; while he was there he received an invitation from the Royalists, through his Saudi contacts, to come to the Yemen and observe the situation for himself. He went immediately, saw the Imam, and travelled extensively in Royalist territory. As a result, he sent a cable to the Prime Minister, Sir Alec Douglas-Home, followed by a personal interview on his return to England, in which he pointed out that the Imam was by no means dead — as the Republicans were still insisting; on the contrary, he enjoyed widespread support among the tribes, controlled a very large part of the country, and commanded a formidable and tenacious resistance movement which the Republicans showed no signs of overcoming, even with massive Egyptian military support. To the vexation of the Americans, HMG decided not to recognize Sallal.

McLean made further visits to the Yemen during the succeeding months at the invitation of the Royalists, who wanted to show him the full extent of popular support behind them, and the murderous bombing of civilians by the Egyptians in their efforts to suppress it. The Royalists hoped to attract support, or at least sympathy, from some Western country now that the United Nations had abandoned them to Egyptian aggression. Between his trips McLean discussed with Colonel David Stirling, founder of the SAS, the possibility of recruiting ex-officers and men of the SAS as mercenaries for the Royalists. The outcome was that a former CO of one of the SAS regiments, Colonel Jim Johnson, was persuaded to leave his insurance job at Lloyds and set up an office in

London to deal with the enrolment of volunteers, their administration and their equipment for the field. It was about this time that McLean telephoned me and suggested I should accompany him to the Yemen, at the expense of the Saudis, to write a report for Crown Prince Feisal on the military situation.

Meanwhile in Sana the new Republic, following the pattern of regimes that seize power by revolution, began its reign with a bloody purge of the opposition. Sallal himself presided over the early trials. There were twenty executions in the first two days, fifty in the following fortnight, including three princes of the Royal Family; they continued to grow until the Republican government, which claimed to have overthrown tyranny and oppression, had been responsible for more executions than any of the Imams.[25]

---

[25] These figures are taken from Dana Adam Schmidt, op. cit. pp. 73 and 77.

Chapter IX: Into the Yemen

'Let's have another bottle of wine,' said Billy McLean. 'It's the last you'll be drinking for the next month or so. Make the most of this meal, David. The food in the Yemen is even rougher than in Muscat.'

We had twenty-four hours to spend in Beirut between planes, because there was no direct air link from London to Jedda, in Saudi Arabia, where we were to see the Crown Prince Feisal; we were giving ourselves a gastronomic treat in anticipation of future deprivation. It was now a month since McLean had telephoned me at Branxholm. I had hastened to London immediately afterwards, for I was frankly thrilled at the idea of some action again; I was tired of earning my living eating indifferent meals in grubby hotels. In London McLean had briefed me on his recent visits to Yemen, and on the situation in the country.

'Militarily,' he explained, 'the Royalists are fighting back pretty well, although they had a hard time in February and March holding off the Egyptian "Ramadan offensive", as they call it, which was designed to cut their communications with the Saudis and also with the Aden Protectorate.'

'Were they getting arms from Aden too?' I asked with some surprise.

'Just a few. Sherif Hussein, the Ruler of Beihan State, is a sympathizer, and he was smuggling the odd consignment over the border to Harib — for as long as the Royalists held the town. But now the Egyptians have taken Harib, and Marib too — that's in the east, on the edge of the Rub al Khali, where the Saudis used to send in convoys. This last offensive also took the Egyptians into the Jauf, and so they have cut almost all road communication between Saudi Arabia and the Royalist armies to the north and east of Sana.'

'How are the Royalists getting their supplies now?'

'Trucks can go some of the way from the frontier — by night, of course, to avoid the bombing. After that it's donkeys and camels. The Saudis channel their supplies through the two border towns of Jizan, on the coast, and Najran further inland; Jizan feeds the Royalists' western front, and Najran the eastern. Or they did until the other day. But this month the Saudis and Egyptians signed an agreement under UN sponsorship, whereby the Saudis would suspend their supply operations in exchange for an Egyptian withdrawal from Yemen. But the Egyptians won't withdraw, that's certain, and so the Saudis will have to recommence supplies soon. Meanwhile the Royalists aren't too badly off for small arms; almost every tribesman has a rifle, as you probably know, though some are pretty ancient. And they're absolutely superb shots with them; they can hit a Maria Theresa dollar at fifty yards. But they're low on ammunition. And they need automatic weapons and mortars, and bazookas for the enemy tanks. The trouble is, hardly any of them know how to use those weapons. A few of the princes have military training of some kind, but the sheikhs and tribesmen have none at all. That's why I'm so anxious to get Jim Johnson's men in quickly to train them. There are a few French and Belgians there now, ex-Congo mercenaries, but we badly need more.'

'Are the Imam and his commanders planning any military operations at the moment, do you know?'

'Oh, they all talk grandly, especially the younger princes, about capturing Sana and scotching the rebellion at one blow. But they haven't the heavy weapons, or the training or the discipline, to stand up to a modern army in the open, not even the Egyptian army. They're going to try and take Haradh soon; that's a biggish town between the Imam's headquarters and the Saudi frontier. But, as you and I learned in Albania, the most effective action for a guerrilla army is to attack the enemy's communications — and the Egyptians are absolutely dependent on the roads.'

'Haven't the Royalists been doing that?'

'Oh yes, they have — and doing it bloody well. They've ambushed and shot up a lot of convoys and actually annihilated one or two, and they've taken a number of prisoners. They've even knocked out a few tanks and armoured cars. But they still have this obsession with capturing towns. Anyway, you can form your own opinions soon. Let's go and get your Saudi and Yemeni visas.'

We went first to the Dorchester Hotel to see Sheikh Hafiz Wahba, the Saudi Ambassador, or rather Ambassador designate, to London. He was an old friend of McLean's and had been Ambassador here at the time of the Buraimi dispute, when Britain and Saudi Arabia broke off diplomatic relations. Now that they were being resumed, he was waiting to present his Letters of Credence, while living at the Dorchester. An Egyptian by birth, he had joined Ibn Saud at the beginning of his rise to power, and had fought alongside him in his desert campaigns. Afterwards he became, and remained for many years, the King's adviser on foreign affairs and continued after their father's death to serve his sons in the role of Elder Statesman; before his return to London he had represented his country at the United Nations. King Saud and his half-brothers, Crown Prince Feisal, the Prime Minister, and Amir Sultan, the Defence Minister, held him in the highest regard.

He was a magnificent old man of impressive dignity and enormous charm, who gave us an effusive welcome, an excellent dinner, and, within a surprisingly short time — considering the usual difficulties in obtaining them — our Saudi visas. In this and all my subsequent meetings with him — he invited me to approach him at any time for advice or help on any matter concerning Arabia — I found him a most sympathetic, wise, and sincere friend.

Next we went to the Yemeni Legation in South Street, where McLean introduced me to the Royalist Foreign Minister, Seyyid Ahmed al Shami, who luckily happened to be in London, and his brother, Abdul Wahab, the Ambassador. Here again we met with a cordial welcome, and I received not only my visa but letters from Seyyid Ahmed showing that I was going to the Yemen on the invitation of the Royalist government.

I needed one thing more: a journalist's cover to give respectability to my trip. To this end I wrote to an old friend and former brother-officer in my regiment, Colonel Julian Berry, who was Chairman of the Household Brigade Magazine, and suggested I should be Special Correspondent to the Magazine in the Yemen; he accepted, on condition that I wrote an article for it on my return. More realistically, perhaps, I went to see the Foreign Editor of the *Daily Telegraph*, who agreed to take articles from me on the war in the Yemen and gave me a Press Card to enable me to cable news from Jedda.

On 14 June, 1963, McLean and I flew out of London. As the plane headed southwards over the Channel my thoughts went back to a similar night, just twenty years ago, when he and I had sat in an aircraft flying through the darkness, about to launch ourselves into a guerrilla war in another unknown country.

As the Caravelle came to rest on the tarmac at Jedda a large American saloon drew up alongside, it's smooth coachwork gleaming even in the dim reflection from the airport lights. An official of the Royal Protocol department of the Saudi Ministry of Foreign Affairs stepped aboard and motioned us to follow him. For a moment the damp heat smothered us like a blanket, and then we were driving off in air-conditioned comfort towards the town; we had seen neither Customs nor Immigration. The car left us at the Jedda Palace Hotel, a flamboyant new building with every modern luxury, where we were to stay for the next two nights.

Coming down next morning, I noticed a familiar figure sitting in the hall, reading a newspaper; at least, he was familiar from photographs.

'Billy', I whispered. 'There is my old enemy Talib bin Ali! You remember — the brother of Ghalib, the Imam of Muscat. I fought against him for three years. I must go over and talk to him.'

'You'll do nothing of the kind,' said McLean firmly. 'That would be very bad security and could lead to all sorts of complications.'

I knew he was right, but I hated to lose such an opportunity. I never had another.

Jedda typified the collision between the two existing cultures of Arabia: the world of the Arabian Nights and the world of oil; the garish, air-conditioned ostentation of the Jedda Palace Hotel and the tall, flat-roofed white houses of the old town with their beautifully carved balconies and latticed windows. In the old city we saw the house where T. E. Lawrence had lived — already condemned for demolition and by now certainly pulled down. The legendary Lawrence, McLean told me, is no longer a legend in Arabia; if ever he asked some old man who

149

could recall the 1914-1918 War if he had known Lawrence, he would answer, if he remembered him at all, 'Oh, yes, he was the Englishman who came with all the gold.' But St John Philby — Abdullah Philby, to use his Moslem name — was still well known, even in the Yemen.

Saudi Arabia has no less than three capitals: Jedda on the Red Sea, which is also the principal port; Taif, about 100 miles inland, in the mountains south of Mecca; and Riyadh, Ibn Saud's original capital, almost in the centre of the country. The King and his Court alternated between the three, spending an equal number of months in each — a political arrangement to preserve the loyalties of the various tribes. But the government Ministries were in Riyadh, except for the Ministry of Foreign Affairs, which was at Jedda; the unfortunate diplomatic colony therefore had to stay permanently in the hottest and most humid capital of all.

During our brief stay there we had audiences with the Prime Minister, Amir Feisal, and his half-brother, Amir Sultan, the Minister of Defence. We were lucky to have as our interpreter Seyyid Ahmed al Shami, the Yemeni Foreign Minister who had helped us with our visas in London and who was now back in Jedda. Seyyid Ahmed, who had an excellent command of English, was probably the most astute politician among the Royalist leaders. At the end of the war in the Yemen the government of the new Republic, a coalition of former Royalists and Republicans, sent him as their ambassador to London.

Our meeting with Amir Feisal took place in a large modern building which was probably one of the palaces of his brother, the King. McLean and Seyyid Ahmed left me in an outer room while they conferred with the Amir for half an hour. When he returned with them I was immediately impressed not only by the dignity of his bearing but by the natural simplicity and courtesy of his manner, which was without any trace of arrogance. He had the lean features and prominent hawk nose of the Bedu warrior, and I remembered that he had personally led camel charges in his father's campaigns. After presenting me, McLean opened the conversation, speaking through Seyyid Ahmed, with some words that took me aback.

'You know, Sir, Colonel Smiley commanded the Sultan of Muscat's army, and was fighting against your people?'

'Yes, I know,' he answered, the humourous mouth above the small, jutting beard curling in a smile that held no malice. 'Colonel Smiley was only doing his duty. And he did it very well.'

I had already been warned that, although he never used English in public and always conducted his interviews through an interpreter, he did in fact understand it well; he had been a long time in the United States. I had my own confirmation in a later interview, after one of my visits to the Yemen, when I was criticizing the Royalists for wasting their efforts in attacking towns rather than communications; before the interpreter could translate, Amir Feisal interposed in English, 'I agree with you one hundred per cent.'

He explained to us that although he himself had made the decision to send us to report on the Yemen situation, his half-brother Amir Sultan would arrange the details of our journey and plan our itinerary. Amir Sultan, scarcely less distinguished in appearance than his brother, though somewhat rounder and plumper in the face, told us he had already made arrangements, through his ADC, Zeid Sudairi, for us to fly south next day to Jizan. From there we would go by truck across the frontier to the Imam's Rear Headquarters at the village of Mabda, and thence by donkey up the Jebel Qara to the caves where we

151

would find the Imam. He had already prepared letters for us to take to the Governor of Jizan, Amir Mohamed Sudairi, the father of his ADC, who would organize our onward journey and our reception by the Royalists. Letters of introduction, I soon learned, played an essential part in all journeys in this part of Arabia. For one thing, it was impossible to buy an airline ticket without a permit, and the issue of these permits, as well as exit visas to leave the country, were the perquisites of the Saudi princes.

We lunched and dined that day with Zeid Sudairi, a good-looking young man with a trim military moustache, who had learned his English while training at Sandhurst. He had a beautiful blonde English wife, Jean; two sweet little daughters of 3 and 4; and a Palestinian orderly named Said who had served in the RASC during the war and was in the Middle East Commandos at the same time as myself. Zeid's first job on returning to Saudi Arabia from Sandhurst, he told me, was to train Omanis fighting against me in Muscat.

'What were they like?' I asked him.

'Hopeless.'

As it turned out, McLean had to leave me in Jedda because he was summoned back to London to vote in an important Parliamentary debate; but he would join me as soon as possible at the Imam's headquarters. Early on the morning of 16 June Zeid Sudairi called for me at the hotel with my air ticket, took me to the airport, and saw me aboard an old Dakota aircraft of Saudi Arabian Airlines, bound for Jizan.

On arrival there I was taken to his father, Amir Mohamed Sudairi, the Governor, who was in charge of all supply operations from Jizan into the Yemen. A burly, almost portly figure with a thick black moustache and small imperial beard, who was always dressed in spotless Arab robes, he received me at this first meeting with some reserve, though with perfect courtesy; he had beautiful manners and was always a generous host, and he became in time a very good friend. He spoke no English, but explained through an interpreter that he would arrange for me to leave for Mabda by truck that same afternoon. I must be ready by 4 pm, Greenwich time — it was necessary to clarify this last point because the Arab day starts at sunrise; many people in Jedda kept two watches, one set for Greenwich, the other for Arab time. Meanwhile, he sent me to rest and refresh myself at his guest house on a hill near the sea, where a faint breeze gave some relief from the sticky heat, and where his own servants looked after me.

From the house I had a fine view of the town to the north. Modern white houses in the Arab style, squat and square and flat-roofed, were interspersed with beehive huts of mud and thatch and the slim white minarets of mosques; westwards, a narrow jetty, still under construction, jutted out half a mile into a vivid blue sea, giving shelter to a cluster of dhows anchored on its southern side. A quiet, sleepy little port in normal times, it was now a point of assembly for material destined for the Yemen to supply the Imam's headquarters and the Royalists' western front.

As such it had already attracted the attention of the Egyptian air force, which had not hesitated on several occasions to bomb Saudi territory. There had been a bad air raid three days previously, when a squadron of twelve four-engined Tupolev bombers, flying from Aswan with mixed Russian and Egyptian crews,[26] had dropped over a hundred bombs on the town from about 40,000 feet. They had badly damaged several government buildings, as well as the hospital, killed 33 civilians,

---

[26] The composition of the crews was not known until later.

but no soldiers, seriously wounded a further 47, and injured about 250 more. Thousands of people had fled in terror to the countryside.

Amir Mohamed took me to see the bomb damage.

'A few days ago,' he told me, 'General von Horn, who commands the United Nations Observer Mission, came to see me, and promised that an observer team would visit Jizan every two days. He saw the damage from the air raid and was very angry.'

Nevertheless, there was no mention at the United Nations of the bombing of Jizan or of a raid on Najran either, although the Egyptians bombed it while foreign journalists were there. This was no fault of von Horn's, who reported both, but was one example among many of the hypocrisy and double standards that governed the deliberations of that august Assembly. When the RAF bombed Harib fort, after dropping warning pamphlets, in an attempt to stop attacks on British-protected tribes in Aden by Egyptian aircraft based on Harib, the UN categorically condemned Britain; yet, as will be apparent, they allowed no mention, let alone criticism, of Egyptian air attacks on Saudi Arabia, or of their use of poison gas against Royalist villages in the Yemen, although the evidence was incontrovertible.

I was ready, as instructed, at 4 pm, but we didn't leave till 6, when only two hours remained of daylight. I settled myself in the cabin of an open Dodge truck with four-wheel drive, between my guide, a certain Sheikh Ahmed, and Faiz, the driver. In the back with my luggage rode two Yemeni men and a boy.

We travelled north across mud flats and desert until 10, when we halted at a village for food — a delicious draught of warm *leban*, or camel milk — and a rest. I slept on a charpoy till 4 am when we resumed our journey, changing our direction gradually until we were heading east.

We halted several times at villages of 'beehive' huts like those I had seen in Jizan, conical structures of sticks and straw tied together with string, where we drank coffee or mint tea and exchanged gossip. Nobody in our party spoke English, and my limited Arabic hardly extended to conversation; but at Mabda I was expecting to meet the Imam's uncle the Deputy Prime Minister, Amir Abdurrahman ibn Yahya, who had interpreters. About three in the afternoon we left the plain and began to climb among rocky foothills, some of them crowned by watch towers such as I used to see in Oman. Our general direction changed to south-west and my spirits rose when Sheikh Ahmed indicated to me that the watch towers marked the frontier of Yemen.

The road was no more than a widened camel track, but the Dodge negotiated it easily; as we climbed steadily the air grew cool and clear. The hills, unlike those of Oman, were green with trees and shrubs; I noticed euphorbias on the banks, and aloes sprouting on wayside graveyards. Streams of water glistened in the *wadis* and along the mountain sides above them wound a delicate tracery of neat, rock-walled terraces mellow with the gold of ripening millet. These terraces of the High Yemen and the stone conduits that irrigate them are among the oldest agricultural systems in the world; they were devised by the earliest settlers in southern Arabia at least a thousand years before the birth of Christ. There were hump-backed oxen, like those I had seen in Africa, pulling primitive wooden ploughs; there was wild life in plenty — a pack of six red-bottomed baboons, a fox, and several hares; there were birds of every species and colour — bright blue rollers, a vivid blue kingfisher and clouds of doves. That night I even saw a mongoose at a water hole.

About five in the evening we stopped at a small village which must have been a rear supply dump; there were sacks of flour and dates and crates of ammunition piled everywhere, and a lorry left soon after we arrived, towing a 47 mm gun. After a meal and a short sleep we drove on to another supply base in a *wadi*, where I saw many more crates of .303 ammunition, boxes of mortar bombs, and the large plastic mines which had worried us so much in Muscat. It was dark by the time we left, and we had difficulty in keeping to the track, which ran mostly along the sides of the *wadis*; we had to drive much of the way without lights because the Egyptian artillery had already registered the road; from time to time a shell came over to burst among the rocks above us.

Inevitably we ran off the track; with a sudden sickening lurch a front wheel dropped three feet into a ditch and the truck keeled over on its side. Luckily we carried a winch in the front, which we attached to a conveniently handy camel-thorn tree, and after an hour's hard work we had winched ourselves back onto the road. At intervals a shell would land fifty or a hundred yards away, to spur us on; from the north-west came the sound of rifle and machine gun fire and the thud of bombs, and the sky was bright with parachute flares and the flash of bursting high explosive. I gathered the fighting was around the town of Haradh, where the Imam's men had encircled the Egyptian garrison.

About 10 pm, to my great relief, we halted for the night. We bivouacked in a *wadi* bed and ate a large meal of hare — shot during the journey by one of our passengers — rice, chupattis and tinned pineapple. For a long time I lay awake, listening to the explosions of shells and mortar bombs and suffering the assault of an army of mosquitoes. At last I dozed off, to be awakened around five by the crowing of a cock which had travelled, along with four unhappy hens, all the way from Jizan, in the back of the truck, hanging upside down with their feet tied.

We now began the last lap of our drive — by far the most terrifying two hours of the whole journey. The rough track wound up the steepest gradients and round hairpin corners which we had to negotiate in several stages, advancing and backing to and fro before we could get round them; my anxiety was increased by the knowledge that our handbrake didn't work at all, and our footbrake only with frequent pumping of the pedal. However, Faiz drove with superb skill and the engine performed magnificently. Once we stopped while I photographed a wrecked Egyptian tank.

For the last fifteen minutes, in the early light of dawn, we drove up a narrow *wadi* with pink oleanders growing thickly up its banks; among the trees on either side were clustered hundreds of tribesmen. All of them carried rifles — either .303 Lee Enfields or American Springfields — gaily decorated bandoliers stuffed with shiny cartridges, and large curved daggers, called *jembias* — like the Muscati *khanjas* — thrust into their belts, encased in silver or green corded scabbards. They wore thin jackets of blue or brown cloth, khaki shirts tucked into khaki *iz-zars* [Yemeni skirts] and a variety of head dresses: colourful turbans made of cashmere shawls, white skull caps, called *ma-arraga*, resembling those worn in northern Albania, or brown straw caps shaped like an inverted flower pot.

Most of them were squatting round fires, brewing coffee or chewing *qat*, an almost universal habit among the tribesmen. *Qat* is a bushy green tree extensively cultivated in the Yemen; the branches are picked and the leaves placed in the mouth and

157

chewed for hours on end, the cud forming an unsightly bulge in the cheek. The juice is spat out at intervals, and the cud itself eventually. Doctors say its only effect is to cause constipation; the Yemenis claim it is a stimulant, but in my experience it only made them lethargic. It is very expensive and wasteful too because the land it grows on could produce good coffee. But although the Republican government prohibited it, and its use was banned in Saudi Arabia on pain of flogging, I seldom saw a Royalist tribesman without a bulge of *qat* in his cheek. I tried it myself once or twice and didn't care for it at all.

At the head of the *wadi* the track ended and we drove our truck under the shelter of some bushes to screen it from the air; this was a wise precaution because jet bombers flew over us throughout the morning, although at a great height. We were now at Mabda, the roadhead for the northern front. Here supplies from Saudi Arabia were unloaded from the lorries to be carried up the mountains on donkeys and camels. Yemen was the only country where I have seen camels used as pack animals in mountain country; the poor creatures hated it, for their loads were invariably too heavy and the sharp rocks cut their feet to ribbons. I would often hear them moaning with the pain of trying to walk.

After breakfast with the crew of our truck Sheikh Ahmed and I walked up the *wadi* for about fifteen minutes, until we came upon a tented camp and headquarters among the oleanders, where we expected to find the Imam's uncle, Amir Abdurrahman. But he had already left for Jedda, presumably by a different route to the one I had taken. I was lucky, however, in finding there two young men who spoke English; they were cousins from the well-known Yemeni family of al Khibsi and had been educated at the American University in Beirut. Abdullah was secretary to Amir Abdurrahman, and Ibrahim, who had just returned from hospital in Jedda after a wound from bomb splinters, was usually employed as secretary to the Amir's brother, the Crown Prince al Hassan. They received me cordially and promised to arrange donkeys with a guide and escort to take me up to the Imam the following morning.

They gave me an excellent second breakfast of eggs, chupattis, tinned fruit and cheese, and showed me to a bed where I dozed for an hour or two. After a very refreshing bathe in a stream I changed into Yemeni dress. I put a white *ma-arraga* on my head and swapped my trousers for a khaki *iz-zar*, which I found much more comfortable, although I missed the pockets; only the Egyptians wore trousers in the Yemen, and I was taking no chances. For a similar reason I had to accustom myself to another Yemeni habit — to squat while passing water; according to the tribesmen, 'only dogs and Egyptians pee standing up,' and I had no wish to be shot in mistake for either.

Ibrahim Khibsi told me they had radio-telephone communication with Jizan, but were dependent on couriers to get word to and from the Imam's caves at Qara. However, I noticed a profusion of transistor radios among the tribesmen and heard over one of them that the Conservative Government had received a large majority in the debate McLean had flown home to attend; he should therefore be with us within a week.

A sharp rainstorm in the afternoon and a torrential downpour in the evening reminded me that Yemen is in the monsoon area and thus enjoys a fertile soil unknown elsewhere in the peninsula except in the Dhofar province of Muscat. In between the storms I stood outside my tent, breathing in the clear, cool air and watching the eagles circling overhead; I looked up at the great mountain ranges that towered above us, and at the fierce, bearded tribesmen around me, chanting ancient battle songs and feinting at one another with their naked *jembias* in a weird war dance.

I went inside, but had barely fallen asleep when the al Khibsis woke me for my first full Yemeni meal. There was a whole roasted sheep in a very hot sauce, with unleavened bread, beans, peas, and rice; then bananas, mangoes and grapes, and finally the local brew of coffee — highly spiced with something like very strong pepper. Outside, the rain came pelting down again, thunder echoed across the valley and the lightning crackled and flickered viciously through the darkening mist.

Chapter X: The Caves of Qara

We had arranged to leave at four in the morning, because it was a seven-hour climb up to Qara and we hoped to avoid travelling in the heat of the day. Having forgotten about the Arab attitude to time, I was ready at four and so were the donkeys; but there was no sign of guide or escort, whom I eventually found placidly cooking their breakfast. They were in no hurry to start, and it was 8 am before we were on our way. I realized that my journey was going to be arduous as well as hot when Sheikh Ahmed loaded all his kit — considerably more than the 50 lb I was bringing — on to one of our two donkeys, and rode it himself as well; I wasn't prepared to do the same with mine, and so I put my kit on it and walked all the way. It was lucky that my years in Muscat had taught me not to lose my temper with Arabs.

Nevertheless I found it hard to restrain my anger at the brutal treatment given to donkeys in this country; they were always cruelly overloaded and overworked, they were covered with huge, untended sores, which their drivers would poke with the sharp ends of sticks to urge them forward, and they were mercilessly beaten when too tired to carry on. But that was the normal practice with animals here; no one would have understood my protests and so I kept silent.

The journey took nine hours — seven hours of walking and about two of rest at intervals on the way — and during that time we climbed from 1,000 feet above sea level, at Mabda, to nearly 7,000. But it was easier walking than, for example, the Jebel Akhdar, and not nearly so steep. The villages on the mountain tops were grander by far than those of Oman; these

161

were high buildings of solid grey stone perched on rocky crags overlooking green and gold terraces of millet, maize and sorghum. Sometimes a belt of cedar trees crowned the summit of a ridge. I found the climb much less tiring than I had expected, but by the end of it I was suffering severely from sunburn, especially on my face and neck and the backs of my arms and legs, and I had a splitting headache from the heat and glare.

As we approached the Imam's headquarters every ridge and spur was lined with tribesmen in brightly coloured jackets and turbans, singing and waving to us as we passed. Standing in the open, without camouflage or cover of any kind, they violated every rule in the military textbook, and I could only pray no aeroplanes were near enough to swoop down and teach them a lesson.

On the top of a mountain stood the houses of Qara, tall stone rectangles like border keeps. In caves in the rock cliffs below them lived the Imam, his staff and retainers, and his bodyguard. Nearly every mountain I saw in the Yemen was honeycombed with such caves, or with overhangs of rock which could be made habitable by the erection of stone walls across the open sides. The tribesmen took full advantage of these natural shelters. Across the mouths of their caves the Royalists at Qara had built stout, high walls of boulders as protection from rocket attacks by aircraft. Passing through one of them, I followed my escort into my sleeping quarters — a hollow about eight feet in breadth and fifteen in depth, with four feet of head-room; the only furnishings were a rush mat on the floor and a camp bed. I was to share this accommodation with my guide and five servants, including my escort.

I lay down on the bed and rested until sunset, but when it was time for the call to evening prayer I went outside to watch. All around me, on cliff top, ledge and terrace, wherever there was a piece of level ground, hundreds of tribesmen were standing in silence. As the sun fell behind the western mountains the priest raised his voice in the traditional chant: '*Allah akbar, Allah akbar. Ashad an la ilah illallah we — Mohamed rasul Allah.*'[27]

The tribesmen, either singly or in small groups, turned to face north, towards Mecca, laid their rifles on the ground, and prostrated themselves in prayer. It stirred me deeply to see these savage, bearded men, bathed in the crimson glow of sunset, bearing witness to their faith among the cliffs and crags of the High Yemen.

Inside my cave my five companions were sitting round a pressure lamp, whose light was attracting such a cloud of winged and crawling insects that I soon withdrew to the open. Among the drawbacks to cave life, I soon discovered, were the creatures who shared it with us. Scorpions were too plentiful for comfort — the Imam had recently suffered a sting from one as he slept — and a large, black, hairy spider, reputedly dangerous, was another visitor; there were poisonous snakes, too, although I never saw one. And so I sat on a rock outside and looked over the valley, attracting in my turn the frankly curious though not unfriendly stares of the tribesmen.

About 9.30 I was summoned to the presence of the Imam. Stumbling in the darkness, I made my way over the rocks and pushed through the throng of guards at the entrance to his quarters. Inside was a labyrinth of caves, in the furthest of which the Imam was seated on a carpet with a single

---

[27] God is greatest. I testify that there is no god save God and that Mohamed is the apostle of God.

163

companion; around them were piles of letters, a thermos and a spittoon. The roof was a mere three feet high and, doubled up as I was already, I found it hard to make the bow protocol demanded as we shook hands.

The Imam, it was clear, spent far too much of his time in this restricted space. He was taller and more heavily built than most of his countrymen, with a fleshy face, full lips, and large, staring eyes; his moustache and beard were well trimmed, his hair long, thick and very curly. But although well-groomed and carefully dressed, he had the puffy cheeks and sallow complexion of someone who has led for too long a confined and sedentary existence; dark circles under his eyes told of constant strain and unhealthy diet. But his sombre manner dissolved in a charming and friendly welcome as he greeted me and took the letters I had brought him from Ahmed al Shami, McLean, and Ibrahim al Khibsi.

His companion was his father-in-law and confidential secretary, Yahya al Hirsi, who had been with him in Sana on the night of the *coup* and had shared the hardships and hazards of his journey to the north. A very small, slight figure with shrewd eyes and a ready smile, al Hirsi had an unusual, not to say chequered, past. Trained at Sandhurst he had been Commandant of the Lahej State Forces in the Aden Protectorate until the sudden defection of his master, the Sultan, to Cairo during the time I was in Muscat; al Hirsi defected too, taking most of the army with him, and found refuge in the Yemen, where one of his daughters married al Badr, the Crown Prince. Now he shared al Badr's quarters in this tiny cave, acted as his interpreter in Press conferences and dealings with foreigners — for in spite of all his travels the Iman spoke only Arabic — handled his correspondence, and issued his orders. This arrangement, I discovered, was highly unpopular with the princes commanding the fighting fronts, who disliked al Hirsi and distrusted his ambitions.

During the two hours of our meeting, while both men chewed *qat* incessantly, ejecting the juice at intervals into the spittoon, al Hirsi and the Imam gave me an optimistic and, I later found out, a far from accurate account of the Royalist situation. They quoted me inflated figures to illustrate the strength of their supporters, and greatly exaggerated their successes against the Egyptians, whose difficulties and setbacks they tended to overestimate. Nevertheless I was able to check for myself that there was a basis of fact behind some of their claims; the morale of the tribes was indeed high, and they were holding their own against the Egyptians, on whom they had inflicted some sharp reverses. But the air attacks on Royalist villages and his inability to prevent them were a serious worry to the Imam, as he himself admitted; and I also suspected that, however strong his support among the Zeidi tribes of the north, it was still slender among the southerners.

Somewhat to my surprise he said he was satisfied with the supplies he had; apparently he had received a large consignment just before the Saudi-Egyptian agreement of the previous month, and it had included field and anti-aircraft guns, machine guns and mines. His satisfaction was not shared, I soon discovered, by his commanders. Now he asked me to remain at Qara for the next two days before going on to visit his cousin, Amir Hassan ibn Hassan further east, on the Jebel Ahanoum; he promised to find me an interpreter to go with me.

At his headquarters they worked all night and slept by day. The routine was imposed by the Imam himself after a bad air raid which caused heavy casualties among the tribesmen gathered in hundreds around his headquarters. He received a constant flow of visitors, mostly sheikhs with their followers, who came to swear allegiance to him or ask him favours, and the crowds provided obvious targets for aircraft during the day.

I spent the next morning drawing maps and strolling about the rabbit-warren of caves that formed the camp; in the afternoon I slept. While waiting to see the Imam that evening I sat outside in a throng of more than a thousand tribesmen watching a colourful *jembia* dance by two men to the music of a flute accompanied by a boy beating an old petrol tin. Eventually the Imam sent for me, and I went in to find him and al Hirsi stolidly chewing *qat* exactly as on the previous night, while the Imam wrote me letters of introduction and safe conduct for my journey to his cousin, Amir Hassan ibn Hassan; in the intervals of writing he held his fountain pen between his toes. It was at this meeting that he told me the story of his escape from Sana.

Our talks revealed one vital weakness in the Royalist command structure — their communications system. Apart from the radio telephone between Mabda and Jizan, all orders and messages from headquarters had to go by runner. As a result the Imam was not in control of the Royalist forces and each field commander had of necessity to fight his own independent campaign. Only a sufficient number of wireless sets, and trained operators, could remedy this situation, and I made a note to report accordingly to Amir Sultan. The Royalist intelligence system, though often remarkably accurate, suffered from the same delay; it took three days for couriers from Qara to reach Sana, although they went there frequently to buy food and to spy.

The following afternoon the sky darkened and the temperature fell sharply as a great sandstorm blew up from the Rub al Khali and blanketed the camp. I sat on my bed with a

166

transistor radio which al Hirsi had lent me for the duration of my stay in the country, and listened to the news from England. I was interrupted by the arrival of a small, thickset, young man with thin receding hair and a serious but friendly manner.

'I am Mohamed Zabara,' he introduced himself in slow, hesitant English, 'and I come to you as interpreter. Please forgive me if I am not very good. I have not spoken English for six years.'

He explained to me that he had come here straight from the University at Florence, where he had been studying political science; his father, a former Prime Minister under the Imamate, was in prison in Sana. Although his English was poor, Mohamed spoke fluent Italian, and had already acquired European tastes and a western attitude towards his own country. For instance, he inveighed strongly against the practice of chewing *qat* and praised the Saudi government for having outlawed it; and, though clearly no friend of Sallal and the Egyptians, I sensed he had reservations towards the Royal Family.

We were to leave next day for the headquarters of Amir Hassan Hassan, and so I sent Zabara off at 6 pm to arrange an interview when I could take my leave of the Imam; I waited up for him but he didn't come back till four in the morning, when he announced that we must be on our way within the hour. Perhaps to console me for my lost night's sleep, the Imam lent me one of his riding mules and al Hirsi loaned me not only his transistor set but also a boy to carry it for me; there was another mule for Zabara, a good donkey for our baggage, with a donkey boy who was also our guide, and a bodyguard of four tribesmen.

We set out at five in the morning of 22 June, as dawn was breaking.

'It's only six hours to Hassan's headquarters,' al Hirsi called after us. 'So you will be there for lunch.' I remembered how often I had heard that kind of forecast in Albania, and wondered if it would be different here. It wasn't.

For the first three hours I went on foot, enjoying the cool morning air as we dropped down towards the plain, past terraces green with millet or *qat* trees and little turreted villages of stone. The last part of our descent was by a narrow zig-zag track across the face of a steep mountain with a horrifying abyss at the edge; I hated to think of the climb on our return journey. At the bottom, nearly six thousand feet below Qara according to the altimeter I carried, we found ourselves in a great *wadi*, where we mounted our mules. They were in good condition, though I didn't like the savage bit which the Yemenis attach to the bridles of riding mules, and often those of donkeys too.

Having covered three of our alleged six hours' journey, we were shaken when our donkey boy-guide told us our destination was another eight hours away. By now the sun was well up and it was getting hot; I noticed that Zabara, who was no mountaineer, looked as depressed as I felt. We followed the *wadi* for a while, and then rode over undulating country for seven hours, stopping at intervals to drink from a well or a water hole. We were both beginning to feel really exhausted when our guide pointed out an immense mountain ahead of us, much higher than the Jebel Akhdar, and cheerfully informed us that we must climb it because Amir Hassan's headquarters lay on the other side. This was the Jebel Ahanoum, and the thought of climbing it in our present state, and in the increasing heat, was too much for us. We decided to stop at the next village for food and rest.

At two in the afternoon we came to a village at the foot of the mountain, where, after some bargaining, we rented a room. As in Oman, the only acceptable currency was the Maria Theresa thaler or the British gold sovereign, both of which I carried. Our room was on the first floor of a two-storey stone house, whose ground floor, as in the mountains of Albania and Oman, was used as stabling; there was a threadbare carpet on the mud floor and a fireplace stacked with logs, but the blankets which the owner brought us housed colonies of fleas. While we waited for food my escort unloaded the animals and filled the room with their own accoutrements — rugs, bunches of qat, a kettle and a huge hubble-bubble.

After we had eaten I slept for a couple of hours and then, leaving Zabara still asleep, climbed up to the roof, where it was cooler, and listened to the Test Match on my transistor. We left as the light was failing, and I rode until it became quite dark; then the track became so steep that I decided to walk. It grew steadily worse until it became no more than a giant rock staircase with steps a foot high. For three hours and a half we laboured up it in the darkness, our only light a flickering hurricane lamp, until I was soaked through with sweat and my legs felt like jelly.

At the top we rested and swallowed some water, then mounted and rode for half an hour along a frighteningly narrow traverse on the mountain face, with a sheer drop below; there followed another hour of scrambling up steps in the rock the worst part of the whole journey, until at last we came to level ground and a village of very tall stone houses, some of them perched upon the edge of cliffs. We passed plenty of huge craters, and our escort told me this village had suffered repeated air attacks, and more than a thousand bombs had fallen on it.

At 11 pm we entered the massive keep of el Hazm — the Arabic for 'castle' — which was the headquarters of Amir Hassan ibn Hassan; we had been eighteen hours on the road, fourteen of them on the march, instead of the six hours predicted by al Hirsi, and I was almost unconscious with fatigue. Guards answered our summons and opened the gate of the great outer wall, and we led our mules through a courtyard to the main door. Here we learned that the Amir was awaiting us in a room at the top of the castle, and so we gathered our last remaining strength and climbed ten storeys to be shown into his presence.

Although only in his late twenties, Amir Hassan had scored some spectacular if short-lived successes against the Egyptians at the beginning of the campaign, including the temporary occupation of Harib and the capture there of a Russian helicopter with its Soviet crew. Although he possessed great personal courage he suffered from ill health and had only recently returned from a visit to London for medical treatment; he was now commanding some 2,500 Royalist troops and tribesmen in operations against the Egyptian-held town of al Qaflah, about five miles from his headquarters. He was a good-looking young man with a large nose, well-trimmed moustache and close-cropped beard who wore a brown 'flower-pot' hat over his thick curling hair and a dark cardigan on top of a white shirt; like many of the princes — and myself — he wore light desert boots. He greeted me warmly in English — I learned later that he had been educated in Germany and spoke both English and German — and gave me a sweet, fizzy drink, followed by an excellent meal. He had good manners too; for, seeing how tired I was, he didn't detain me in conversation but let me go to bed as soon as I had eaten.

I was shown into a small room over the main doorway, with a mud floor and a carpet, whitewashed walls, and stained glass windows. Adjoining it on the same floor was the *hammam*, the wash room and lavatory, which measured some three feet by six, with a hole in one corner and a large earthenware pot of water in the other; after making use of both I felt a great deal better. Then I spread my sleeping bag on the floor and climbed inside, for it was very cold; within minutes I was asleep.

El Hazm al Ahanoum, to give the castle its full name, was a tall, square bastion, centuries old and partially ruined at the top; it stood on the edge of a great cliff and commanded a superb view across a scrub-covered plain, whose far side rose in cultivated terraces to another great range of mountains. Inside, each of its storeys contained numerous small rooms like my own, which housed the Amir's headquarters staff, bodyguard, and servants — including, I reflected after lunch, an outstandingly gifted cook. At Qara we hadn't eaten nearly so well.

I spent much of the day sleeping or taking photographs, but in the evening the Amir came to my room for a long discussion, which we held in private. I found him, on this and later occasions, both frank and friendly, and he was always helpful to me. But that evening I could give him no answer — I had none myself — when he asked me, 'Why can not the British help the Imam? It is in your interest to do so, as well as ours.'

And I could only sympathize with him when he remarked on the absurdity of both the Russians and the Americans giving help simultaneously to Sallal. As he left the room he said with a note of apology:

'I fear you may have a disturbed night because I have given orders to my men to fire upon al Qaflah.'

Sure enough, my sleep was punctuated with the rattle of machine guns and the explosions of mortar bombs.

We left for Qara the next afternoon at 4.30; I had planned to start at 3. Although rested by my stay at el Hazm, I was suffering from 'gippy tummy', brought on either by contaminated water or the rich concoctions of Amir Hassan's gifted chef, and after two hours of walking down the big rock steps my legs were giving under me; I could at least be thankful that these mountains were of sandstone, which is much kinder to the feet than the unyielding rock of Oman. At the base of the Jebel Ahanoum I mounted my mule and rode for the rest of the way. I had discarded my skirt and put on trousers for the journey, ignoring the risk of being taken for an Egyptian; not only was it difficult to ride in a skirt, but my legs and knees had been lacerated by camel-thorn and blistered by sunburn.

We travelled all night, stopping only briefly for water; it was certainly far cooler, and quicker, than travelling by day, and it took us a mere twelve hours to reach Qara. One of our little baggage donkeys was in the lead and, to my amazement, only lost the way once. About midnight we heard the sound of a battle in the distance, with heavy machine gun and mortar fire; but I had tuned in to the BBC on my transistor and listened instead to the Test Match.

Chapter XI: Bombs and Bandits

I was disconcerted to receive no news of McLean at Qara, and so I arranged with al Hirsi that if he didn't appear within thirty-six hours I would depart on another tour. With the Imam's approval we arranged for me to go south to visit the Royalists in the al Mahabisha and Hajjah sectors, where there had been considerable activity; the whole journey would take between ten and fourteen days. I wrote a note for McLean in case he should arrive while I was away.

Throughout the morning of my arrival from Jebel Ahanoum we heard the sound of heavy bombing from the directions of al Qaflah and Mabda; I inspected the two .5 Brownings that constituted our only anti-aircraft defence, and found they had plenty of ammunition. The following morning, 27 June, several jet aircraft flew over us at such a height that I couldn't see them; nor, I am sure, could the gunners on our Brownings, but they and some of the riflemen opened up with wild enthusiasm — a waste of our ammunition but probably good for morale. Later on an Ilyushin flew over and dropped a large bomb about half a mile away; fragments fell in the camp, but did no harm.

That afternoon, with no word yet from McLean, I decided to leave for the south. Before going I had another interview with the Imam and al Hirsi. So far I had travelled unarmed, but now I asked if I could have a weapon for my personal protection; I had been hoping for a pistol but instead they gave me an American Springfield .30 calibre rifle with a hundred rounds of ammunition. It was much heavier than the British Lee-Enfield, and after carrying it for two hours I was regretting I had asked for anything.

Whenever I went to see the Imam my guards had to force a way for me through a crowd of petitioners waiting at the entrance of his cave to present their *warragas* to him. *Warragas* were pieces of paper with requests for favours or complaints of injustice written on them; there was always a pile of them beside the Imam and beside each of the Royal Princes when I saw them. Whenever I went in for an audience, people in the crowd would try to press their *warragas* on me to present for them; much as I hated to do so, I had to refuse.

I noticed that when they greeted the Imam, or one of the Royal Princes, the tribesmen would attempt to kiss his feet, his knee or his arms. Although Yemenis often shook hands with each other, and invariably with me, it was traditional that when two men exchanged greetings, the one of lesser rank would take the hand of his superior and kiss the back of it three times, finally bringing his own hand to his lips and kissing its back. I have sometimes observed two men of apparently equal status engage in quite a tussle, each trying to kiss the hand of the other in an excess of courtesy.

Mohamed Zabara and I left Qara soon after 6 in the evening, with an escort of four soldiers, a donkey boy, and our guide Sheikh Ahmed,[28] who was chief of a small tribe in the region of al Mahabisha. After four hours of very rough going we found ourselves riding on a track along the top of a range of hills, with the beautiful clear light of a quarter moon to guide us and a cool breeze to fan us; my only worry was a nasty precipice a foot from the edge of the track and the fact that my mule, which may have been a bit lame, kept stumbling.

---

[28] Not to be confused with the Sheik Ahmed mentioned earlier.

174

From here we descended into a valley to cross a motor road, where we saw a wrecked Russian 75 mm gun and an abandoned armoured personnel carrier, the results of a Royalist ambush. In the next valley I noticed a delicious smell and found we were riding past a plantation of coffee shrubs — the first I had seen in the Yemen. Finally, after a gruelling hour's climb, we reached a house — it was more like a hovel, being dirty, hot, and full of flies — on a hilltop, where we stopped to eat and sleep. But the heat and the flies and the noise of our escort's hubble-bubble kept me awake and when I finally dozed off it was the flies and the hubble-bubble that woke me at 6 in the morning.

I saw now that our house was one of many perched on the top of cliffs and crags in the usual manner of villages in the High Yemen. While I was brewing Nescafe — I always carried my own kettle as well as my own aluminium wash-basin — the donkey boy came in to tell me that his animals were unfit for further work and we must wait while he found us fresh ones. Confined in the small, stuffy room with our escort, I spent the morning making notes on their style of dress, which was typical of all the tribesmen; it was more elaborate than it appeared at first glance.

On their heads, which were often shaven, perched skull-caps, or white embroidered pill-box caps called *kofias*, or the hand-woven basketwork 'flower pots' I have already described; they wound cashmere shawls or lengths of khaki cotton round their caps or hats, in the form of turbans. Tattered jackets of European design hung from their shoulders over shirts and vests, and over the jackets ran crossed bandoliers, each carrying about fifty bullets. Every man wore a long cummerbund, which served the double purpose of belt and pockets. Thrust into this belt, behind the *jembia*, which is a

175

defensive weapon, was a long, straight knife used in the attack, and behind it reposed an assortment of articles, allegedly nine in number and all beginning with the Arabic letter for M: there was a pair of scissors, a needle, tweezers for extracting thorns, a bunch of keys, a pen — usually with ball point — writing paper, a purse, and sometimes a watch strapped round a knife. Everyone wore an *iz-zar*, with underpants of cotton, and some men wore the baggy Moslem trousers under the *iz-zar*. Most of the tribesmen went barefoot, but some favoured Japanese 'flipflops', and others a type of plastic sandal with studs, such as I used to see displayed in West End London stores at extravagant prices for wear on the beaches of the Mediterranean.

All morning there was heavy gunfire and the sound of bombing from the direction of al Qaflah, and several Ilyushins flew over us at a fair height; according to rumour, Amir Hassan Hassan was attacking the Egyptian garrison. When we set out at 3 in the afternoon the sky had clouded over, and we had a cool and easy ride for the first four hours until it was dark. Although we were about 7,000 feet up, just below the clouds, the countryside was rich in crops, with terraces of maize and millet, coffee and *qat*, bushes of pepper, and banana and mango trees. At 8.30 pm, after a final hour of steep climbing, we reached the town of Kuchar, the capital of the province; here we stayed the night in the castle palace of the Governor, who turned out to be a cousin of Ahmed al Shami, the Foreign Minister.

We left at 6.30 in the morning after I had photographed a pair of hoopoes nesting in the palace wall. The first part of our journey, after the descent from Kuchar, lay through a green valley, where we stopped at a village and breakfasted off bananas and a honeycomb, which we ate in our fingers; I saw many strange and beautiful birds on the way, and reflected that this whole country would be a paradise for ornithologists and botanists. An hour's climb out of the valley brought us onto a plateau, among fields of maize and potatoes, bounded by hills with hamlets perched on their tops. As we came nearer to al Mahabisha the sound of bombs and gunfire grew louder.

In the afternoon we marched along the top of a mountain range parallel to a ridge lower down where the Egyptians were dug in, and from which they shelled and called down air strikes on the Royalist villages almost every day. All the villages we passed bore signs of bomb or shell damage, which the inhabitants insisted on showing me. At dusk we reached the hamlet of Meharnaf and stopped for the night; it was only two hours from our destination, but clouds obscured the moon and if we used lights the Egyptian machine guns would fire on us. I had a good night's sleep on the roof of a house, scarcely disturbed by the intermittent firing of the Egyptian batteries and the whistle of their shells overhead; they were shelling the Royalist headquarters at al Mahabisha, where we would be going in the morning.

We left after breakfast and climbed for three hours up the Jebel Raheyah. On the way two MiG fighters swooped over us to attack al Mahabisha. We saw them coming, and I was able to get off half-a-dozen shots at them from my Springfield semiautomatic rifle; I don't think I scored a hit, but I remember thinking at the time that this was good practice for the moors of Aberdeenshire. In a cave on the top of the Jebel we met Sayid Hamoud al Harshib, formerly the Governor of Amran and now commander of the Royalist forces on the al Mahabisha front; he was a cheerful old man with a bushy white beard jutting from his chin and a bulging paunch.

I had a long discussion with him and his deputy commander, who pointed out to me the Egyptian positions half a mile across the valley. Much as I liked Sayid Hamoud, I was not very impressed with his command, which included about a thousand tribesmen and a 75 mm gun; I was horrified to learn that he had only ten rounds for the gun, and no bombs for his 81 mm mortars, especially since I had seen plenty of ammunition in supply dumps near Mabda.

The MiGs reappeared in the afternoon, this time to attack Meharnaf, where we had spent the night, with bombs and rockets; I saw the bombs bursting in the middle of the village and prayed that the inhabitants were safely under shelter. In the evening, after a violent thunderstorm and heavy rain, the clouds came right down over the mountain; we said good-bye to our hosts, enveloped in a blanket of mist, and slept in a village below. Despite rumours that a strong Egyptian-Republican force was going to attack us in the night, we were disturbed by nothing more than a few stray shells in the vicinity.

In the morning we were unable to hire donkeys for our three days' journey to Hajjah and had to get Sayid Hamoud to commandeer them for us; our destination now was the headquarters of Amir Hassan ibn Ismail, another of the Imam's cousins, who commanded all Royalist forces in that sector. We marched from 6.30 until 9.30, by which time the heat was so intense that we decided to rest in a village and continue in the evening. On the way the mountain landscape was green with terraces of coffee and grapevines straggling over the terrace walls; lizards about a foot long were basking on the rocks, their foreparts a deep azure and their tails a vivid orange; they nodded their heads at us in alarm as we passed. While we rested, a would-be mine-layer came to see me, by arrangement with Sayid Hamoud, carrying two large US mines of a type I knew only too well from the roads of Oman. I gave him a lesson in how to arm the mines, wished him luck and sent him on his way.

We moved on about 3.30, when the sun's heat was beginning to decline. I wasn't sorry to leave because, as always happened when we halted in a village, the entire population had turned out to stare at me, crowding into the room where I was trying to rest; I was the first European to be seen in these parts, and they made the most of me. Some of the tribesmen, I noticed, carried not only rifles but umbrellas, to protect them against both sun and rain on the road.

At dusk we reached the Wadi Maur, Yemen's largest and fastest flowing river, which we had to cross and recross at least ten times; the muddy water came up to the belly of my mule, and the current was so strong that we had to join hands to prevent being swept away. We halted at nightfall because we were too close to the enemy to risk lights and it was too dangerous to attempt further crossings in the dark. We slept in the open in a Bedu encampment near the river, where we were very well received; the sheikh even insisted on lending me his charpoy, but I found it hard to sleep because he and his followers, afraid I might feel lonely, crowded round me and talked through the night; moreover the wind was wafting over us the stench from a dead and decomposing camel.

We made another twelve crossings of the Wadi Maur next morning, during which time I observed four groups of red-bottomed baboons, with as many as twenty in one group. Then we turned up another *wadi* flowing with clear, clean water, and climbed onto a lush green plateau of maize fields; men were working in large conical straw hats like those of the coolies I used to see in Siam. All morning the sound of gunfire and bombing told us we were getting near to Hajjah. That afternoon two of our donkey boys deserted.

After a stiff climb from the plateau, which took us through orchards of fig and pomegranate trees, we came to the village of Mapien, where we were to stay the night. Mapien, perched on the top of a great cliff at an altitude of well over 10,000 feet, was the highest village in the Yemen. On one side of the mountain a pattern of green terraces climbed almost to the doors of the houses; another side plunged thousands of feet in a broad sweep of bare rock. The place housed a detachment of Royalist troops and was the target of the bombardment we had heard during the morning; there had been no casualties, Amir Mohamed Ismail, the Royalist commander, told me, although a small house had been demolished. He also told me that Sheikh Ahmed had brought us the wrong way, and we should have to make a long detour, costing us at least one extra day, in order to avoid the Egyptian and Republican positions.

In the morning, after I had watched a furious argument between my escort and some villagers over the hire of a mule, in which they almost came to blows, Amir Mohamed Ismail took me to the highest house in the village to point out the positions occupied by his own troops and by the Egyptians and Republicans. Inside the house he also showed me an old Turkish field gun, dating from before the First World War, which had somehow remained serviceable, together with its ammunition; from time to time the Royalists would fire off a few rounds — with greater danger to themselves, I should have thought, than to the enemy. From here we could see quite clearly the old walls and houses of the ancient fortress town of Hajjah, sprawled across the top of a mountain below us; in the rock-hewn dungeons of its grim castle previous Imams had imprisoned, and often murdered, those who incurred their

180

anger or suspicion. Sallal himself had lain there for seven years under the Imam Ahmed, until al Badr had persuaded his father to release him.

From what Amir Mohamed Ismail had shown me, it looked as though our route out of Mapien would take us down a valley dominated by two forts held by the Republicans and that we should have to pass alarmingly close to them — a matter of a few hundred yards — in broad daylight. My friends agreed this was so, but told me not to worry because the Republican garrisons had agreed not to fire on any Royalists, and were only waiting for an opportune moment to change sides.

My friends were right, for we passed the forts undisturbed, although there was a battle in progress down below and we could hear small arms and artillery fire. Through my glasses I watched Egyptian tanks and self-propelled guns firing from Hajjah, and saw their shells bursting in orange flashes and puffs of dark smoke in and around Mapien. We marched downhill until lunchtime, when we halted for the afternoon at the house of a Sheikh who had declared for the Republicans; he had done so under duress because they held his son in jail in Hajjah, and his house was within artillery range of the Egyptian barracks there. Secretly, however, he helped the Royalists in every way he could, mainly with information.

We left as darkness was falling, and walked for four hours along a tributary of the Wadi Maur; the moon was in its third quarter and gave us enough light to do without torches. I felt entranced by the beauty of the moonlit landscape — the black silhouettes of the mountains towering on either side, the clear, still water reflecting the rifles, bandoliers and *jembias* of our escort, the dark shadows of mules and riders on the path; huge trees and dead tree trunks loomed up out of the still night like the skeletons of prehistoric monsters. The only sounds were the croaking of frogs, the light patter of hooves from mule and donkey and an occasional sharp cry from our escort, answered immediately from some village or fort in the hills above.

I slept on the roof of a fort full of soldiers, declining their offer of a meal in favour of a tin of pineapples. I depended to a large extent on tinned pineapple; with rare exceptions, the meat was almost uneatable — tasteless and cooked to the consistency and toughness of shoe leather, and served usually with a sauce of very hot spices.

The headquarters of Amir Hassan Ismail was a cluster of small stone houses and rock caves seven thousand feet up among the cliffs of the Jebel Maswar. It took us three hours to climb up there. On the way I watched a MiG diving repeatedly on a village across the valley and saw its rockets explode among the houses. There had been pleasanter sights as well to attract my attention — a waterfall 300 feet high and a giant euphorbia tree.

A *feu-de-joie* from the Amir's bodyguard heralded my arrival and the Amir himself emerged from his cave to greet me. He was a handsome young man of about 25 who fairly sparkled with vitality and charm; but there was a bit of the swashbuckler in his high spirits, as he demonstrated that afternoon, when I saw him urge on a lethargic bodyguard by firing a burst from his tommy-gun a few inches behind the man's heels. When he took me shooting rock pigeon he was preceded by twenty-five soldiers of his bodyguard singing to the accompaniment of three drums and a trumpet. Like all his tribesmen, he was a first-class shot.

Perhaps as a result of my work with the Good Food Guide I soon came to give star ratings for comfort to the various caves I visited; Amir Hassan Ismail's I rated three-star, if not five. It measured some twelve yards by six, and I could easily stand up inside; the floor was deep in carpets and matting, and rich curtains lined the walls. By comparison, the Imam lived in a hovel. Moreover, Amir Hassan's coffee was the best I had tasted — genuine Yemeni coffee, spiced with cardamom seeds.

That he was also a serious soldier was obvious from the number of Russian and Czech weapons displayed in and around his cave; he and his men had captured them from the Egyptians the previous week, he explained in hesitant English, in ambushes around Sana. He seemed to have sound ideas on guerrilla warfare, I thought, at the end of our long discussions, and he was not distracted by the romantic Royalist dreams of capturing cities. But I was disturbed to learn that he was without either mines or demolition explosives, especially since I had seen plenty of both in the dumps around Mabda.

This remarkable complex of caves and cave houses on the steep face of the cliff was fashioned, Amir Hassan told me, some forty years ago as a refuge against RAF attacks from Aden; this was a war I knew nothing about. I had a room to myself in one of the houses, where I slept well despite the cold; in the afternoon the clouds had been well below us.

I awoke to the sound of rifle and automatic fire, and threw on my clothes, to discover that the shooting was only greetings for the Amir Abdullah Hussein — yet another of the Imam's cousins and commanders — who was arriving on a visit from his headquarters north of Sana. I looked out of my window to see a long column of tribesmen winding up the track towards us, led by drummers escorting a standard-bearer with the Royalist banner — a red flag with the Sword of Yemen and an Arabic inscription embroidered in white. As they came nearer, the volume of firing increased. Amir Hassan loosed off two drum magazines from one of his captured machine guns, then ran headlong down the track to greet his cousin; in ten minutes he was back, exhausted but in time to fire off another drum. Even Mohamed Zabara, not to be outdone, emptied several magazines from his Springfield. Red flags had already appeared on the roofs of a village lower down the track and mingled with the shooting I began to hear the shrill ululations of women; now, as the sound rose in intensity and pitch, I looked up and saw the roof of my own house black with the draped figures of women and girls with their hands in front of their lips, warbling this barbaric, exciting welcome.

Amir Abdullah's purpose in coming here was to reorganize his troops, who had taken heavy punishment in recent battles; he commanded the Royalists around Sana in all sectors from the north-west to the north-east of the capital. I was particularly glad that he had come because I was intending to visit him immediately after leaving the Jebel Maswar; now I was saved a journey of three or four days and could return direct to Qara.

A serious-looking young man of 28, with glasses and a sparse beard, he spoke the best English of all the princes I had met so far, a result of his education at the American University in Beirut. He frankly admitted that his command had virtually disintegrated as a result of his reverses, but he intended to rebuild and retrain it in the safety of these mountains. He claimed to have ten thousand men under him but I found these figures, like all estimates of Royalist strength, required adjustment, largely because they made no distinction between Royalist soldiers and loyal tribesmen. The Royalist soldier received pay from the Imam, through his local commander; he left his village to enlist and he fought wherever he was sent — although that was usually in his own tribal area. Moreover, he was not only armed with a modern rifle, but often had training in the use of heavier weapons and mines. The loyal tribesman remained in his village and was called up only when it was threatened. Soldier and tribesman dressed alike, since there was no uniform.

That afternoon Amir Hassan Ismail said good-bye to me; he was on his way to fight another battle. I left the Jebel Maswar next morning, 6 July, on the last leg of my tour. As we walked down towards the fort two Ilyushins were dropping heavy bombs on the mountains across the valley. After nearly four days of hard marching we reached Qara, but not without one unpleasant incident which taught me that, even without Egyptians or Republicans, these mountains were not always safe.

On the morning of the third day we were passing a maize field in a depression among rocky, boulder-strewn hills when we were hailed by about a dozen men working in the field; they asked, as was the custom, who we were, where we came from and where we were going. When we answered they called on us to halt, but Zabara replied that we were in a hurry and must press on. However, they ran after us, shouting and waving their rifles, and so Zabara told our two bodyguards to stop and talk to them. When, after ten minutes, the two men had not rejoined us, Zabara and I dismounted and walked back with Sheikh Ahmed and Ali, our donkey boy, who was carrying my binoculars.

We found our two bodyguards stripped of their rifles and *jembias*, standing disconsolately among their captors. In a minute we ourselves were surrounded by ten shouting, threatening tribesmen, but Zabara and I held them off with our rifles levelled. I heard them snarling '*gem houri!*' at us, and understood they were accusing us of being Republicans.

'Show them our letter from the Imam,' I told Zabara; but they refused to look at it and continued shouting '*gem houri!*' at

185

us. Meanwhile they had stripped Ali of his *jembia* — he carried no rifle — and, to my fury, taken my binoculars as well. We had been arguing for some twenty minutes when Zabara, perhaps unwisely, announced that we were going on to Qara, whence we would return with soldiers to take their rifles and punish them for their insolence. Thereupon eight of the ten spread out and took up positions behind trees and boulders; the other two demanded our rifles.

'We must not give up our rifles,' whispered Zabara. 'We shall have to fight them now.' He turned and began to unload ammunition from his mule while I looked around desperately for suitable cover. The situation looked bad for us, with ten of them against three; we had to discount Ali. However, we had semi-automatic rifles and I was resolved that, if I had to die here, I would at least take some of them with me; I had already selected my first target, a big, black-bearded villain who kept on shouting insults at me and who, what is more, had my binoculars.

For what seemed a lifetime we confronted each other in the heavy midday heat; perhaps the mention of the Imam's name and the sight of his letter, even though they hadn't read it, caused them to hesitate. Just when the tension was becoming unbearable and I was sure the shooting was going to start, there came a shout and I saw, on the brow of a hill a couple of hundred yards away, a man on a donkey with a group of some twenty armed followers. Zabara called back to him and after a brief conversation turned to me with a huge grin.

'He is one of the Imam's officers.' He let out a great sigh of relief. 'And he has two hundred men with him. We are saved.'

Within minutes our opponents were surrounded and deprived of their arms and we had all our belongings back. Zabara explained to the Royalist leader what had happened, adding that in his opinion our attackers had never believed we were Republicans; they were simply robbers, he thought, who preyed upon anybody who passed that way. The Royalists must have thought so too, because they put the leader of the band in shackles and threw him into prison, disarmed the others and billeted themselves on them for the next two days, eating them out of house and home and beating them from time to time.

That evening, in a small hut where we rested for the night, I listened to the BBC commentaries on Wimbledon and the Test Match, a soothing contrast to all the Arabic I had been hearing and couldn't understand. In my diary I wrote:

> As I write this the sun is setting, the thunder of guns keeps up in the distance, and all around me they are saying their evening prayers. Most of our party are good Moslems and say their five prayers a day. They are quite unconcerned by my presence and often in a small room they will be prostrating themselves around me while I carry on reading or writing. In fact, I very often say my own prayers at the same time as they are saying theirs. At this moment I think of Moy and the children, and pray all is well with them. I hate being so completely out of touch, but tomorrow I should reach Qara, Billy may be there, and with him I hope to get a letter from Moy.

At Qara, where I arrived at five in the evening of 9 July after a fourteen-hour march, Yahya al Hirsi told me McLean had already been and gone; but he had left me a long letter from Moy, which banished all my exhaustion. Not even the sight of my servant in shackles could depress me; he had been condemned to wear them for four hours for failing to get the Imam's pressure lamp going.

I spent more than two hours that night in a final conference with the Imam; I was to leave next day for Mabda and Jizan, but the Imam asked me to visit a village on the way where the Egyptians were alleged to have dropped poison gas. He agreed with my own suggestion that I should try to see General von Horn in Jedda; von Horn was a personal friend whom I had known well in Stockholm, and I was sure he would at least listen to anything I had to say.

On al Hirsi's advice I left next morning at 6.30 in order to be clear of Qara by 7.30, when the Ilyushins regularly paid it a visit; I had no wish to be caught by them in the open. I was at Mabda by lunchtime, having stopped on the way to inspect the village of Kauina, where the Egyptians had dropped poison gas bombs on 3 June. I examined and photographed the hideous sores and eruptions on the skin of children and animals who had been exposed to the gas, and I collected samples of the bomb casing to show von Horn and the authorities at home. I also sniffed one of the craters as I was crouching over it to pick up pieces of metal from the bomb; there was a pronounced smell of geranium, and suddenly I felt queer and almost fainted. There seemed little doubt that these were gas bombs.

At Mabda I found McLean at last, with some more of the Royal Princes. We made plans together for me to return on further visits, and later McLean and I discussed in private the report I was preparing for Amir Sultan.

'I shall emphasize,' I summarized to McLean, 'what I think are the Royalists' three main failings: first, their tactics, which are to waste men and effort in futile and costly attacks on towns for prestige reasons, instead of concentrating on the Egyptian lines of communication, which are extremely vulnerable; second, the lack of co-ordination in their operations, and the Imam's inability to control them, which only wireless sets can put right; and lastly, their supply system.

It's ridiculous to see so much stuff lying about in dumps in the rear when there are acute shortages at the fronts.'

'What are their most urgent needs, would you say?'

'Wireless sets — and that includes trained operators — and medical supplies. The Imam told me the Saudi authorities in Jizan have forbidden Yemeni merchants to trade there, which means the Royalists can't buy medicines. I must check on this.'

'What about the Egyptian bombing? Does it scare them?'

'The bombers don't worry the fighting men any longer, now they have learnt to take cover; they know they're pretty safe in their caves, and anyway the bombers fly so high they seldom put their bombs anywhere near their targets. The MiG cannon and rocket attacks on villages are another matter. First, they're pretty accurate and secondly they're directed against the civilians, who seldom have time to get under cover. They do have a serious effect on civilian morale and indirectly on the tribesmen, whose families are the sufferers; word of each attack gets passed around and of course is exaggerated in the telling. On the other hand, every air raid increases their hatred of the Egyptians and their determination to resist them to the bitter end.'

'What do you think is going to happen now?'

'That depends on whether both sides keep to the UN agreement. If the Egyptians do withdraw — highly unlikely, I think — then the Royalists could have Sana in a week. But if they don't withdraw and the Saudis still suspend supplies, I don't think the Royalists can hold out for more than a month. If, as seems the most likely, the Egyptians stay and the Saudis resume supplies, we're in for a long war.'

'I entirely agree. It seems we've both come independently to the same conclusions. You'll be leaving by truck tonight for

Jizan and home, so I'll wish you *bon voyage*. We'll be meeting soon.'

I reached Jizan too late to catch the regular passenger plane to Jedda, but flew instead to Taif, the mountain capital, in a Saudi Air Force Dakota, sent especially for me — or so they told me. But I couldn't help noticing I shared it with three prisoners, shackled hand and foot. They were Yemeni saboteurs, sent from Sana to blow up Saudi ammunition dumps in Jizan, and they had been caught with explosives on them. One was in a bad way, with bruises and dried blood all over his face and head; some of the cuts had required stitching. They were all tried in Taif, I heard afterwards, and executed.

In the Ministry of Defence I had a long interview with Amir Sultan, who asked me for an immediate report in writing on Egyptian activities in the Yemen for his brother Amir Feisal to show the American Ambassador the next day; the US was, after all, a party to the Saudi-Egyptian agreement which the Egyptians were so flagrantly breaking.

The following night I flew to Jedda with my friend Zeid Sudairi, Amir Sultan's ADC, whom the Amir had instructed to arrange a meeting for me with the United Nations representative there. The meeting took place the next day, 15 July, in the Foreign Ministry, in the presence of the Deputy Foreign Minister. I handed to the UN representative, a Norwegian major on von Horn's staff, some of the bomb fragments I had collected from Kauina, together with a personal letter I had written to von Horn. I received no acknowledgement of either. I wrote two more letters to von Horn, neither of which he answered. Since he was a good friend of mine, as I have said, I realized he must be acting under orders. Much later, after he had resigned in disgust, he came to stay with me in Scotland and told me he had been expressly forbidden to have any contact — or allow his officers to have any — with the Royalists.[29]

---

[29] See also von Horn's own comments, op. cit. pp. 344-5 and 355-6.

Chapter XII: 'The Sword of Islam'

Before I left Jedda I had already been invited by both the Saudi Government and the Yemeni Royalists to make another tour of the Yemen before the end of the year. Meanwhile, on my return to England I tried to arouse some public feeling against the Egyptian bombing of civilians and the use of poison gas; I published several articles in the Press and a letter to *The Times* and made two appearances on television describing what I had seen. My revelations were received in most quarters with scepticism, and even dismissed as Royalist propaganda. I marvelled at the reluctance of the British Press and people to believe that those who wished them ill could be capable of dishonourable conduct, reserving their moral indignation for their allies. Thus although they wouldn't believe that the Egyptians had bombed or gassed civilians in the Yemen, they would glow with righteous anger at every report of French or American brutality to civilians in Algeria or Vietnam.

There had been some progress, while I was away, in the despatch of mercenaries to help the Royalists. Ahmed al Shami, the Royalist Foreign Minister, had raised some in France with the help of a Colonel Roger Falques, who set up an office in Paris for this purpose; they were a tough bunch of professionals who had seen service in Indo-China, Algeria and the Congo. Jim Johnson in London was enrolling ex-officers and NCO's of the British Army, most but not all of them from the SAS, and sending them out to Aden; from there they were flown to Beihan State where the Ruler, Sherif Hussein and his son, Amir Saleh, both of them staunch Royalist supporters, had set up a 'safe house' for them to stay in until the time came for them to cross the border into the Yemen. Johnson's representative in Aden, who arranged their accommodation and passage on to Beihan, was Tony Boyle, an ex-Regular officer of the RAF who had previously been ADC to the Governor; on retirement he became Johnson's second-in-command.

When I returned to the Yemen in November, 1963, I went in through Aden and Beihan; by then I had met Johnson and Boyle, who had informed the mercenaries in the field of my impending visit. The first of the British to arrive there was Major Johnny Cooper, who had commanded one of the SAS squadrons that served under me in the attack on the Jebel Akhdar in Oman. Shortly after that operation he had left the SAS, having reached the age limit, but returned to Muscat as one of the Sultan's Contract Officers and did extremely well. He later became the first of Johnson's recruits. At the time of my arrival in Aden he had already established his headquarters with a wireless set and operator in the Khowlan area, not far from Sana, with one of the princes.

It is worth recording that at the height of the mercenary effort, when I was commanding them, they never numbered more than 48, of whom 30 were French or Belgian and 18 British. They were broken down into small missions — usually one officer, one NCO wireless operator, and one NCO medical orderly — and deployed according to the wishes and needs of the Royalist commanders. It is important to realize that none of the mercenaries actually fought in the war; their job was to advise the commanders, train their troops and provide communications and medical services. The medical situation in Royalist areas was particularly desperate; there were virtually no trained doctors. Until quite late in the war the International Red Cross operated only in Republican territory;

but even when it sent a mission to the Royalists its hospital was situated a long way from the fighting and the doctors spent most of their time treating the local civilians for endemic diseases. This was no fault of the Swiss doctors, who would gladly have served at the front, but of the Red Cross directorate, which gave them categorical instructions not to go near it.

At the time of my second visit I had no personal connection with the mercenaries, but later on, as I have said, I became their commander; my paymasters were the Saudi Government, and so I was in the fullest sense myself a mercenary. In view of the odium attached to that word in recent years, I will take this opportunity of stating my own attitude. 'A hired soldier in foreign service' is the Oxford Dictionary's definition of the term, and so it must include such fine infantrymen as the Gurkhas and such distinguished British soldiers as General Gordon and, in our own day, Glubb Pasha. I am very happy to be in such company. Although mercenary excesses in the Congo brought discredit on our calling, I maintain that it can still be an honourable one — with the important provisos that the mercenary's own conduct is honourable, and that what he is doing is in the interest of his own country, or in the defence of his own ideals. Speaking for myself, I was — and am — certain that what we were trying to do in the Yemen was in the interests of Britain. Nasser's ambitions there were aimed against the British position in Aden and the Gulf, and if he had succeeded there would have been a serious threat to Britain and the West from him and his Soviet patrons. The fact that there is now a hostile presence in Aden, owing to circumstances we could neither foresee nor control, does not invalidate my point.

During the four months between my first and second visits to the Yemen there had been a considerable improvement, both politically and militarily, in the Royalist position. A number of Republican tribes had defected outright to the Royalists, and others had made contact with them with a view to defecting at an opportune moment; some had even sent their children as hostages to Royalist Amirs as a pledge of their good faith. Royalist morale had soared and there were high hopes of an Egyptian withdrawal and a collapse of the Republicans. This improvement was a consequence of important military successes. In July the Egyptians had launched a general offensive on all fronts, presumably in the hope of destroying the Royalists as an effective fighting force and enabling themselves to leave the Yemen securely under the control of their Republican protégés. The offensive was a failure, gaining very little ground at the cost of very heavy casualties, but it did force the Royalists to expend so much of their heavy ammunition that they were unable to follow up their success and were obliged to remain on the defensive. However, they were now receiving clandestine supplies from the Saudis, while their two main weaknesses, training and communications, were beginning to improve since the arrival of the first mercenaries. One of the purposes of my second visit was to have a closer look, on the ground, at this mercenary activity.

I flew to Aden on 14 November, and on to Beihan two days later. There I spent the night in the village of Naqub, twenty miles north of the State capital, in the 'safe house' allocated to the mercenaries by the Ruler. I shared it with three Frenchmen, who were in wireless contact with Johnny Cooper and the other missions, and seven British, who arrived in the middle of the night after a drive of three days in a lorry from Aden; in the morning another Frenchman joined us — Colonel Bob

Denard, a veteran of the Congo who now commanded all the mercenaries in the Yemen except the British. His Frenchmen and Belgians, though very polite to me, were seldom chatty or communicative outside their own circles; some of them, I knew, had belonged to the OAS[30] and so had little love for General de Gaulle, but I never discussed politics with them. Their attitude to the work was strictly professional; they were there for the money, but they meant to give good value in return. Most of them, as I have said, had seen service in the Congo, and many of them alternated between the Congo and the Yemen, serving now in one theatre, now in another. The reason, I discovered, was that in the Congo they had all the drink and women they wanted, but seldom received their pay; whereas in the Yemen they had regular pay but no women or drink. And so when they had earned enough in the Yemen they went off to the Congo to enjoy it.

The British, on the other hand, were more often inspired by enthusiasm for the Royalist cause or a simple thirst for adventure, although there were some deplorable exceptions — one fairly senior officer, in particular, was strictly on the make; unfortunately mere enthusiasm was an unreliable guide to efficiency, and I discovered later on that, while the NCO specialists did excellent work, the British officers who proved their worth were those who understood some Arabic.

I left Naqub on the evening of 17 November in a convoy of four open Ford trucks, with a party of Yemeni tribesmen and one Englishman whose *nom-de-guerre* was Jack Miller; a quiet, reserved young man in his late twenties, he turned out to be the son of an old friend of my mother's and to have been at school with one of my nephews. Our destination was the

---

[30] *Organisation Armée Secrète* — the anti-Gaullist faction who opposed the concession of independence to Algeria.

Royalist headquarters at Amara, in north-eastern Yemen, where I hoped to find the Crown Prince al Hassan; we had a 400 mile journey ahead of us across the desert on the fringe of the Rub al Khali. We travelled for three nights and two days, with occasional halts for rest, and more frequent stops to cool the engines or dig the trucks out of sand drifts; several times we lost the way. The only living creatures we saw were four unlucky gazelles, which we shot after a chase and ate.

The Royalist headquarters, where we arrived soon after sunrise on the 20th, was in a labyrinth of caves among some gigantic boulders and curious rock formations like huge toadstools that rose sharply out of a desert of sand and camel thorn; the smooth, round tops of the rocks, on tapering pinnacles, and the clear delineation of the rock strata must have been the result of erosion by wind and sand. We were able to drive our trucks right up to the entrances of the caves under the overhangs of rocks; the inhabitants enjoyed perfect protection and ideal camouflage from the air. The camp was in the foothills of a great mountain range running westwards towards the High Yemen; to the east, as far as the horizon, stretched the featureless waste of the Empty Quarter.

In a tent hung for us between two enormous boulders Jack Miller and I washed and shaved and breakfasted while we awaited the arrival of the Royalist commander, another of the Imam's many cousins. We waited all day, our situation complicated by the fact that no one in the place spoke a word of English; but at dusk the Amir's brother appeared, a pleasant young man to whom I showed my letter of introduction from Ahmed al Shami and explained the purpose of my visit, in the face of frequent interruptions from the followers who filled his tent and from petitioners who crowded in to present their *warragas.*

About 9.30 we set off with him in the darkness to his own camp, a two-hour drive into the western hills. There Jack Miller and I parted. He remained in the camp, waiting to go south to his operational area in the Jauf, and I drove on for another fifteen miles up a river bed to the village of Odlah. I spent the night outside it, in a tent full of soldiers, and had my first good sleep since leaving Naqub.

On waking next morning I discovered that one of my four companions in the tent was in shackles — a punishment, I understood, for having tried to knife an opponent in a brawl; the shackles were on his feet — only in severe punishments were the hands also chained — and he hobbled along by lifting a string attached to the shackle bar and so taking the weight off them. Our tent was one of three in a *wadi* with steep rock cliffs on either side. About two hundred yards away, at the confluence of this *wadi* with a larger one, stood the high, square, mud houses and tall, round watchtowers of Odlah.

Al Hassan's headquarters was at the village of el Burg, more than eight hours' march to the top of the Jebel. I waited all morning in the tent for the guide, donkeys and escort who were to take me up there. We started at last around 2 in the afternoon, only to stop in Odlah five minutes later for another hour while the guide and escort took coffee.

We climbed for three hours up the *wadi*, passing on the way several of the Amir's outposts — groups of about twenty soldiers, who turned out of their tents to salute us as we went by; it was hard going, over rock as tough and unyielding as the Jebel Akhdar, and I was glad when we came out onto a plateau and stopped at another tented outpost, where the soldiers gave us tea and coffee. It was dark and bitterly cold when we resumed our journey across the plateau with only the dim light of a quarter moon to guide us; I cast an envious glance, as we passed the welcoming flames of a camp fire, at the silhouetted forms of the Bedu and their camels seated round it in a comfortable circle. We went through two silent, sleeping villages, the patter of our donkeys' hooves sounding unnaturally loud in the stillness among the darkened houses, and came at last to the outskirts of a third village. There we halted at the foot of a tall, square tower whose mud-brick walls gleamed palely in the faint moonlight. My escort motioned me to follow them inside.

They led me to the top of the tower — I counted seventy-five steps on the way up — and showed me into a small, crowded room where the Crown Prince was sitting among his bodyguard and counsellors. He read my letters of introduction and welcomed me effusively, but also with some embarrassment because, as he explained apologetically, no one had thought to warn him of my coming.

Saif al Islam[31] al Amir al Hassan ibn Yahya, to give him his full title, was a portly, well-built figure of about my own height, with a hawk nose dominating a plump round face, and an impressive growth of grey beard. Despite a benevolent, almost paternal manner he was a formidable soldier who had shown great skill and gallantry in the days of his father, Imam Yahya, when he had commanded a Yemeni force that ejected the Saudis from Najran in 1934. Although he was now approaching 60 and in poor health from duodenal ulcers his vitality and courage had not deserted him, and he was the most respected of all the Royalist leaders. He firmly resisted all attempts by his family to send him abroad for treatment, and remained indomitably cheerful throughout his constant suffering and discomfort.

---

[31] 'The Sword of Islam', the designation adopted by the Crown Princes of the Yemen.

After his years of service in the United States he was convinced he spoke perfect English; in fact he spoke it very fast and very inaccurately, with a confusion of phrase and idiom that left me baffled. As soon as I was seated he beamed affectionately upon me and asked, 'You would like some apple pie?' Tired and hungry as I was, the thought was irresistible and I nodded eagerly; it seemed too good to be true. It was. Only when he produced the ubiquitous tin of pineapple did I realize that what he had said was 'apple pine'.

I had a six-hour discussion with him alone on the following day, mostly about the situation in the Sada sector, which he commanded, and his requirements in arms and supplies. We went into minute details of each item and problem, which I found an exhausting process because I could scarcely understand his English; I found it easier when he spoke Arabic. He was full of optimism about the future and pointed out that now the Royalists had demonstrated their ability to hold their own against the Egyptians, the tribes that had been sitting on the fence were pouring in to join them. I had evidence of it that evening as I stood on the roof before sunset and watched bands of warriors converge upon the house from every direction, many of them singing. In the Yemen, as elsewhere, nothing succeeds like success.

While I watched I observed a strange ritual when one of the tribes came in to swear allegiance — strange to me, but apparently usual on these occasions. Ahead of the main body marched six men in line abreast, carrying their rifles at the slope and chanting, followed by a single man driving a sheep. At the foot of the house about fifty of them formed a half circle, still chanting, round the sheep. Then, as one of the singers advanced upon it with a drawn *jembia*, the singing ceased suddenly and there was a tense, expectant silence. With his free hand the man seized the sheep, threw it on its back in a single motion, and cut its throat. As the blood spurted in a great fountain over the ground, a strange howl arose from the circle of onlookers, part cheer and part song, while one of their number sounded a trumpet. The weird music continued for several minutes, while the poor beast kicked in its death throes; but as the last faint struggles subsided the noise died away and the tribesmen dispersed, leaving the corpse lying in its spreading pool of blood.

The Crown Prince told me he had given the sheep to the tribe that day, when they came to pledge their loyalty; later they would collect the carcase and eat it. Since the poorer tribesmen seldom had meat in their houses this was something for them to celebrate.

El Burg and the two villages on the plateau which I passed on my way down to Odlah next day had received their share of attention from Egyptian bombers; although only a few houses had direct hits, the earth was pitted with huge craters, and walls and vineyards showed the scorches of napalm. A truck took me from Odlah to Amara, where I arrived in the middle of the night and spent the whole of the following day. I didn't enjoy my stay there, for it was the filthiest camp I had yet seen. Sheeps' carcases, scraps of food, and human and animal excrement littered the ground within a yard or two of the tents and caves we lived in, and the clouds of flies that fed on this garbage, together with the stink of it, made life nearly unbearable; I wondered there was not more disease in the place. I took refuge in my tent for much of the time, listening to my radio in the company of a charming black and white lamb, who seemed even more absorbed by the music than I; whenever I turned it off, he would nudge me to turn it on again.

On the wireless I heard the shocking news of President Kennedy's assassination. But the tribesmen, who also heard it on their transistor sets, were delighted and celebrated the tragedy with cheers and *feux-de-joie*. They regarded him as the architect of the American policy of support for Nasser; but if they imagined his death would change that policy they were in for a disappointment.

My next destination was the mercenary training camp at Khanja, an area of gravel desert, rock, and scrub situated between the Jauf and the Rub al Khali, more than four hours' drive south-east from Amara. I arrived there by truck in the small hours of 25 November and lay down to rest on the floor of the mess tent, declining the offer from a Frenchman, whose sleep I had interrupted, to take his bed.

I was awakened at 5 am by a bugle calling reveille, and the tent began to fill with French instructors snatching a hurried breakfast before starting the day's training. I went outside to examine the camp. It was spread out among some large formations of rock and boulders on the edge of the desert. Accommodation for men and stores was provided by caves or rock overhangs protected by stone walls; or by tents, such as the one I had slept in, slung between the boulders. There were about 150 Yemenis drilling on the plain and undergoing instruction in the use of light and heavy machine guns, 81 mm mortars, and two types of weapon ideal for guerrilla warfare which I hadn't seen before — the 57 mm and 75 mm recoilless rifle. There was no doubt the instructors knew their job, but their efforts were hampered by an acute shortage of ammunition, so that their pupils weren't allowed to fire any of the weapons; also, most of the recoilless rifles were without sights.

Training ceased at 7.30 am — the usual visiting hour for Egyptian aircraft — and was not resumed until 4 in the afternoon. A week earlier a bomb had burst right outside a cave full of ammunition; the resulting explosion had killed eight men outright and wounded ten, among them the most brilliant of the Royalist commanders, Amir Mohamed ibn Hussein. He was rushed to hospital in Saudi Arabia, but was able to return later to his command.

In the camp I met Jack Miller again. He seemed in low spirits and behind his reserve I discerned a growing disillusionment with the Yemenis; revolted by their dirt and irritated by their persistent unreliability, he tended to keep himself apart from them. As time went on this became all too common a reaction among the British mercenaries. Colonel Bob Denard, on the other hand, had no illusions to shed. He and his second-in-command, Guy Mauré, were typical 'Centurions' from the pages of Lartéguy's great epic; battle, betrayal, and disaster in Indo-China and Algeria had forged inside them a steely cynicism and a contempt for causes and catchwords. They worked for money and they worked extremely well. I understood their attitude and in consequence found them easy to get on with, and invariably friendly and helpful.

At Boa, some twenty miles south-west of Khanja, in another complex of rock-bound caves was the headquarters of Amir Abdullah ibn Hassan, brother of the Amir Hassan ibn Hassan whom I had met in his castle on the Jebel Ahanoum during my first visit to the Yemen. Denard and Mauré drove me to Boa the morning after my arrival at Khanja. I had to wait from 9 am until three in the afternoon before I could see the Amir because he worked all night and slept through the morning. While I waited, two MiGs flew over and a pair of Yaks circled the area several times, but they made no attempt to attack, and

203

although Mauré opened fire on them with a .5 Browning he didn't appear to score any hits.

When he had woken up and read my letters of introduction Amir Abdullah gave me a very civil welcome. He was a serious, intelligent young man who had been educated in Cairo. He had served for a time under his father in New York on the Yemeni Delegation to the United Nations, and he had a little English — more intelligible if less fluent than his father's. At this first meeting between us, which lasted five hours, he gave me a very clear picture of the military situation in his area and of his own plans. He intended to move his headquarters shortly to the Khowlan, and attack the town of Jihana, about twenty-five miles south-east of Sana.[32] Like the Royalists at Amara he was delighted by the news of President Kennedy's death.

He later became bitterly and intemperately critical of the Saudis, whom he would openly accuse of fighting their war against Nasser with Yemeni blood; not surprisingly, they eventually dropped him. Towards the end of the war he was murdered, though whether by Saudi or Republican agents is obscure.

While we were at Boa Denard, Mauré and I examined a fine natural air strip, more than two kilometres in length, which lay beside a mountain in the desert about five miles in the direction of Khanja; the French were already preparing it for use. We spent the night there and returned next day to Boa, where we picked up a guide to take us on a reconnaissance of Egyptian positions at Agaba, ten miles farther west.

Flat on our bellies behind a rock on a hill above Agaba, we peered through our field glasses at the Egyptians spread out in a hollow below us; there was a battalion of about 800 men, we calculated, supported by half-a-dozen tanks. Overlooked on

---

[32] He captured it on 2 January, 1964, but held it for only a few days.

three sides by mountains held by the Royalists, they presented a perfect target for a textbook attack.

'What military cretin,' exclaimed Denard in a voice of wonder, 'could have chosen such a tactical disaster as a site for his camp? We could trap them down there, and not one would escape. But,' he sighed regretfully, 'without supporting fire from our heavy weapons our attack would not succeed, and at this moment our heavy weapons have no ammunition.'

'I will make this a matter of first priority,' I assured him, 'in my report to Amir Sultan.'

We returned to Khanja that evening. On the way Denard said to me with a grim smile:

'You will see what can happen to an Egyptian column in a successful ambush. There was one some time ago in a valley an hour's drive from our camp. We will take you to the scene of the battle tomorrow.'

The sight was indeed impressive. The Royalists had set their ambush in a valley between sand dunes and basalt rocks that looked like small volcanoes on the surface of the moon, and the grim relics of the battle littered the sand on either side of the track. There was a wrecked T34 Russian tank and the burnt-out shells of several armoured personnel carriers, and I counted — with my handkerchief to my nose — more than fifty decomposing bodies, half buried by sand and half eaten by jackals. I saw, also, six decapitated corpses — executed Republicans, they told me. From this grisly spectacle we drove on to some caves where the Royalists were holding twelve Egyptian survivors of the disaster. Although shackled, they seemed to be in good condition, well fed and clothed; one of them, who spoke English, told me his only complaint was that he couldn't go home to Egypt.

The following evening, 30 November, I said good-bye to the mercenaries and, with an escort and a servant, drove two hundred miles across desert and scrubland to Najran, a fair-sized town of mud houses and date gardens set in foothills a short distance inside the frontier of Saudi Arabia.

Next morning I was summoned to the presence of the Governor, Amir Khaled Sudairi; I found him in his camp in the desert near the airfield, about five miles out of town. Slighter in build than his younger brother Mohamed, whom I had met in Jizan, he was by far the more intelligent of the two; but paradoxically he was an enthusiastic hunter, happier in the field and in camp than in the city, whereas Mohamed seldom moved far from the luxury of his beautiful villa. Khaled, unlike his brother, spoke a few words of English, but he had two sons who spoke it well; one of them had been to an American military academy, the other to Cranwell. On this occasion, however, we used the services of a Jordanian interpreter.

Amir Khaled treated me with some reserve at first, but thawed considerably when he had read my letters of introduction from Ahmed al Shami, Crown Prince Hassan, and McLean. When I explained that I wanted to pay another visit to the Imam at Qara before returning home, he arranged to have me flown to Jizan immediately. Before I left he offered me a bath in the improvised *hammam* beside his tent; it was the first I'd had for a fortnight, and an extra attraction was the presence in the *hammam* of two tethered gazelles and four hawks perched on stools beside the bath.

At Jizan Amir Mohamed Sudairi found me a truck and a driver to take me to the Royalist roadhead at Mabda; but at the first town we reached after crossing the frontier we heard that heavy rains and floods had washed away the road. The only way I could reach the Imam now was by donkey — a journey of five days, for which I couldn't afford the time; I felt I owed it to my family to be home at least for our children's Christmas holidays. Indeed, among all the dangers and deprivations of my journeys in the Yemen I found the lack of contact with my family the hardest to endure. And so I drove back to Jizan and flew on to Jedda the same afternoon.

I spent six days in Jedda, waiting for permission to go to Riyadh and present my report in person to Amir Feisal. During this time I called on the British Ambassador, who took me to see his American colleague, Mr Hart. The latter questioned me closely about my impressions and gave me in return an interesting picture of the other side; he told me frankly he had strongly advised the State Department not to recognize the Republicans, but had been overruled by the President himself. As he was speaking, I pictured in my mind those wildly jubilant tribesmen at Amara and their triumphant *feux-de-joie*.

Chapter XIII: How to Lose a War

I waited in vain at Jedda for permission to see the Prime Minister in Riyadh, but in the end I had to hand my report to his Chief of Intelligence. Later I heard Amir Feisal had wanted to see me, but officials in the Saudi Ministry of Foreign Affairs had concealed my arrival from him. As was usual in Arab politics, there was a faction among the ruling family that disapproved, or were afraid, of Crown Prince Feisal's attitude towards the Royalists and towards Nasser; I was, of course, only a minor instrument in his policy, but as an unprejudiced source of first-hand information from the Yemen I must have had some significance: enough, apparently, for the opposition to keep the two of us from meeting on that occasion. And so on 8 December I flew back to London.

My report, however, reached the Crown Prince and as a result of it, and of representations from Ahmed al Shami, I was invited to return to the Yemen early in 1964. In England I found a much greater interest in the war, particularly among Government circles, than when I had last been home; the Prime Minister, Sir Alec Douglas-Home, listened carefully to my account, and asked me to contact him personally whenever I returned from future visits.

I flew to Saudi Arabia at the beginning of March, and on the 4th I had an interview in Riyadh with Crown Prince Feisal. I stressed again the necessity, in my view, for the Royalists to concentrate their efforts on attacking the Egyptian lines of communication rather than towns. The Amir agreed, and asked me to urge the Imam and his commanders to intensify their pressure on the enemy during the next two months; he was to meet President Nasser at the end of April and wanted to negotiate from a position of strength. With this brief I entered the Yemen from Jizan on 7 March, accompanied by Ahmed al Shami's cousin Yahya, who acted as my interpreter for the first few days.

I reached the Imam two days later, and found him installed in a new headquarters about two miles distant from his old one. He now had a wireless, with a competent Yemeni operator who spoke English, and was in contact with Naqub and with Saudi Arabia. He was also issuing his own postage stamps and had appointed a Postmaster-General to frank them. He had made himself very comfortable in two large caves, one of which he slept in; the other he used for receiving visitors. Instead of a pressure lamp he had electricity, provided by a Honda generator, and he had invented his own very effective air-conditioner — a long canvas vent which sucked in air from outside; the floors were well carpeted, and brightly coloured cushions were placed around the walls, which were hung with photographs — most of them taken by me. He had trimmed his long hair almost to a crew cut, and seemed thinner and fitter than before, although much greyer.

The new Headquarters was on a spur facing north, about 6,500 feet up, with splendid views in every direction; from one side I could see a range of mountains fifty miles away. But we had to take care when walking about the camp at night, for on two sides there were sheer drops of several thousand feet only a few yards from our sleeping quarters. Above us rose sandstone rocks crowned with small watch towers, and the mountainside below was green with terraces of coffee, *qat* and maize.

I received a heart-warming welcome from the commander of the Imam's bodyguard, Mohamed Khowlan, a tall erect figure with a fierce moustache and the manner and qualities of a first-class sergeant-major. Almost alone among the Palace Guard he had stayed with the Imam during the perilous hours of the *coup* in Sana, and continued to serve him throughout the war with unshakeable loyalty. He had a firm grip on the bodyguard, who fairly jumped at his commands, and although he spoke no English I came to rely upon him more than on anybody else at Qara.

'*Salam elykum*, Daoud Ismail!' he cried 'You will find some changes here since we last saw you. We even have doctors now; come, let us visit them.'

An important new feature of the base was an International Red Cross Unit, established in a house beside a well on the other side of a valley, about half an hour's walk from the camp. As we went over there I noticed tracks converging on it from all directions; they showed it was well attended, but they must also have shown the Egyptian air force that it was a significant target — especially since it bore no Red Cross markings. A mere two weeks later it was attacked with high explosive and incendiary bombs, some of which landed only fifteen yards from the house.

Inside I found a middle-aged Englishman playing with a puppy; he was Arnold Plummer, a volunteer male nurse who had served with the RAMC during the Second World War and with the Red Cross in the Congo. A most competent and devoted man, he was strongly critical of the Red Cross directorate in Geneva and particularly of Dr Rochat, their Swiss representative in Jedda, whom he described as an enthusiastic supporter of Nasser and equally opposed to the Royalists and to the British; Rochat, he told me, was trying to transfer their unit from Qara, where it was doing useful work, to the base hospital at Uqd, near Najran, a long way from the fighting. While we were talking Plummer's two colleagues joined us, both of them Swiss: Dr Wolfenburger from Zurich and another male nurse, Fredi Moser from Basel. They were, like Plummer, very friendly and helpful to me and very enthusiastic about their work in a battle area, but they shared his fears of a transfer to the base at Uqd, and they were right. Dr Rochat had his way and thereafter the only casualties they treated were the few tribesmen who could survive the battering journey by camel and truck from the fronts to Uqd.

I had several long interviews with the Imam, during which I tried to hammer home my own views and Amir Feisal's on the tactics his troops should employ. His reaction was to ask me to go down to Hajjah, which his troops were about to attack.

'Why', I asked, 'is it necessary to attack Hajjah?'

'Because', he replied blandly, 'it has great prestige value. Its capture will put heart into my people and encourage many Republican tribes to come over to my side; it will also have a good effect on opinion abroad.'

'What makes your Majesty think,' I persisted, 'that your men will be able to take it?'

'The Egyptian garrison has been encircled for several weeks now, and they are in a very bad state.'

This was not true, as I soon discovered. The main road from Hodeidah was still open and Egyptian transport were using it. However, I suppressed my doubts and agreed to go.

I started early on the morning of 13 March with an escort of four soldiers and a donkey boy — a lazy, insolent youth who carried a sword stick instead of a rifle and was forever holding up our progress while he slipped away to buy *qat* in the villages we passed. We travelled over much of the same country I had covered on my first visit in June and July of the previous year, and after three days very hard going, during which I suffered terribly from sunburn, we came to the village of Mapien. Since I was last there Egyptian bombing had reduced it to a heap of rubble, though fortunately with very few casualties, and it was now completely deserted. One of the bomb craters I examined was thirty yards in diameter and more than twenty feet deep, the largest I had ever seen. In some caves just below the village was the headquarters of Amir Mohamed ibn Ismail, brother of the gallant and flamboyant Hassan Ismail, whom I had met in July on the Jebel Maswar. Like his brother Amir Mohamed spoke excellent English, and he too lived in a three star cave — which he invited me to share; unfortunately he did not have Amir Hassan's military ability or courage.

Amir Mohamed was commanding the northern group of the Royalist forces in front of Hajjah, while his cousin Amir Abdullah Hussein, whom I had also met on the Jebel Maswar, was commanding the southern group.

Between them they had worked out a plan for a co-ordinated attack on the town, which they explained to me at intervals during the next three days. The details seemed sadly lacking in precision. As I have explained, Hajjah stood on the southern slopes of a great mountain, 8,000 feet high, which dropped almost sheer to a river bed; deep valleys surrounded it on all sides, and the heights across the valleys were all in Royalist hands. The mountain on which Hajjah stood had nine peaks, each crowned by a village of solid stone houses which the Egyptians and Republicans had converted into strong points; they dominated the town and so no attack on it could succeed until they were taken. On the south-west slope the road to Hodeidah wound steeply down the mountainside in a series of sharp hairpin bends; this was the only route which vehicles could negotiate, and to protect their vital supply line the

Egyptians had camps along it in platoon and company strength.

In outline — it was never more than an outline — the Royalist plan was for all their heavy weapons — the 75 mm and 57 mm recoilless rifles and the 81 mm mortars — to open a bombardment on the evening of Friday 20 March, while the tribes moved forward at dusk to assembly points for the night attack. The northern group, under Amir Mohamed Ismail, was to attack seven of the nine villages commanding the mountain; Amir Abdullah Hussein's southern group was to capture the remaining two and assault the town of Hajjah. The southern group, which was the larger, had the additional but vital tasks of cutting the road to Hodeidah in four places, attacking three of the Egyptian camps on the road and laying mines on it.

With Amir Mohamed I found Jack Miller; he seemed to devote most of his time there to the valuable but hazardous business of defusing unexploded bombs. The three of us, with a strong bodyguard, spent two days reconnoitering the Egyptian positions from vantage points on our mountain. On the second day we climbed for an hour up a steep and narrow track, while eagles and ravens hovered and circled around the crags below us; at the top we found a perfect observation post in an old fort on the edge of a cliff. Spread out beneath us were Hajjah and the fortress villages defending it, the road to Hodeidah and the Egyptian camps strung out along its length; those camps were perfect targets for guerrillas, I commented hopefully to Amir Mohamed. I made a number of sketches of the town and the enemy positions around it for my own and the Amir's use, and we discussed the siting of his guns for the attack. All the while the Egyptian artillery kept up a steady fire from the west of Hajjah into the hills to the south, where Amir Abdullah Hussein and his tribesmen were assembling.

On 18 March I left Mapien for the southern sector, to watch Abdullah Hussein put in his attack. The journey involved a breathless scramble down a precipitous track into the Wadi Shirras, where I arrived with my legs shaking uncontrollably; I was also shedding skins like a snake from the sunburn. I spent the night there in a small hovel, where Jack Miller joined me; he had delayed his departure from Mapien to defuse two more bombs. We started at six the next morning, following the Wadi Shirras through green plantations of coffee and banana trees. But while we were having breakfast in a village where my escort had insisted on stopping, an Ilyushin flew over and unloaded its bombs on us; two of them fell uncomfortably close, and so unnerved one of the escort that he refused to accompany us further, pleading a bad leg. They did no damage to the houses but left huge craters among the plantations, where they knocked down or blasted the foliage off most of the trees.

After a steep climb over a col and down the other side, we came soon after midday to Amir Abdullah's headquarters in some caves near the village of Haddad. He was still asleep at that hour, but when he awoke he received us and explained his plan of battle. It seemed a bit hazy to me, the more so because we were interrupted by a constant stream of petitioners; on one occasion the Amir broke off for two hours to deal with their *warragas* before resuming his discussion with us. He looked even more tired than when I had last seen him, after his reverses on the Jebel Aliazid. However, he finally agreed to give me a guide in the morning to take me to a village overlooking Hajjah where his guns were sited, and where I could get a good view of the attack.

About eleven the next morning, after a stiff uphill climb, Jack Miller and I reached the fortified hamlet of Ernica, from which we had a superb view of Hajjah on its mountain, a mere two kilometres across the valley. There were aircraft overhead throughout the morning, but no bombs landed on our village; a few shells came our way from Hajjah, but the enemy was firing at random, and we suffered no damage or casualties. In the late afternoon I took station beside a big Russian 82 mm mortar and waited for the preliminary bombardment to begin.

At five o'clock the Royalists opened up on Hajjah with their mortars and recoilless rifles. As far as I could judge, they were firing quite wildly and indiscriminately on the town, instead of selecting their targets from the enemy positions which were clearly visible; the mortar beside me consistently dropped its bombs short, except for one, which landed on a house in the town and probably added another family to the Imam's enemies. The Egyptians replied vigorously with artillery, mortars, cannon and heavy machine guns, causing us to keep our heads well down as bullets and splinters whirred around us and smacked into the rocks and houses of Ernica. I was using a ciné-camera to film the operation and went into a house to change the reel; I was closing up the camera when there was a thump and a crash outside, and plaster came flaking off one of the walls. The house had received a direct hit, luckily from a small calibre shell, which had made scarcely any impression on the thick stone masonry.

As dusk fell I watched the tribesmen moving up for the attack. They padded silently through the defiles among the rocks, their rifles on their backs or shoulders, many of them with the familiar bulge of *qat* in their cheeks; they didn't look very aggressive to me, and no war songs came from their ranks — rightly so in the circumstances. Low clouds covered the mountains, bringing showers of rain, and soon it was too dark for me to see across the valley. I returned to the house where I had changed my film, heated up a tin of soup, and then lay down in my sleeping bag on the floor. The shooting had died down, but the attack was presumably going in; perhaps I shall visit Hajjah in the morning, I thought, as I slipped into a deep and dreamless sleep.

That fond hope disappeared as soon as I went outside the next morning, to see across the valley a lone Egyptian lorry slowly climbing the twisting road up to Hajjah; not one shot was fired at it. If the Royalists had not even cut that road, which was the first objective before they even mounted the attack, it was unlikely they had been successful elsewhere; as if in confirmation, Egyptian artillery opened up a moment later from the town. Gloomily I set off on the three-hour walk down to Amir Abdullah's headquarters, passing on the way several large bodies of tribesmen squatting on the ground chewing *qat*; it seemed to me they ought to be attacking Hajjah.

Reckoning the Amir would still be sleeping at that hour, I went into a small house above his cave where he had lodged me and Jack Miller two days before. While I waited there I heard the blast of a trumpet and, looking from the window, saw Amir Abdullah moving off down the mountain with all his men. He had not even thought to send me word that he was leaving, whether through embarrassment or mere forgetfulness I was too angry to speculate. However, I ran after him and managed to head him off on the track. He had the grace to look a little sheepish as he halted in front of me.

'What happened', I asked, 'in the attack on Hajjah?' He hesitated, and I thought he seemed ashamed.

'My men did not attack,' he muttered.

'Why not?'

'Because Amir Mohamed's men were held up on the other side.'

Memories came flooding back of similar scenes in Albania.

'What are you going to do now?' I enquired.

'I am returning to Beit Elageh.' This was the village on the Jebel Maswar where I had first met him with Amir Hassan Ismail the previous summer.

'Why?' I asked in my most wooden manner.

'Because,' he replied haughtily, 'there are more important things to do there.'

I was determined not to let him off so easily.

'What did your men actually do in the attack?' I persisted.

'They cut the road to Hodeidah,' he answered defiantly. Respectfully I told him this was not so, for I had seen an Egyptian truck using it that very morning. He merely shrugged and suggested I follow him later to Beit Elageh. Then he went on his way with all his men and I returned to my house, where I decided to spend the night. To cheer myself up I turned on my radio and listened to a running commentary on the Grand National, won by Team Spirit.

'Precious little Team Spirit,' I said to myself, 'in the attack on Hajjah.'

We had been on the road for an hour the next morning, following the track Amir Abdullah had taken to Beit Elageh, when two twin-engined Ilyushin 28's flew overhead and began to bomb the village of Haddad we had just left; I took photographs while my party took cover. Most of the bombs fell outside the village, but one landed a few feet from a woman and two small boys as they were running away in panic. Through my binoculars I saw the bodies fly up into the air and spiral slowly back to earth in a shower of rocks and debris. I wondered how their families would feel if I had to tell them that the United Nations found this sort of thing morally quite acceptable as a means — so the Egyptians proclaimed — of bringing peace and prosperity to the Yemen. An hour later, as we plodded on, two MiGs zoomed over us to blast Haddad again, with rockets and machine guns; there was nobody there but women and children. The Egyptians knew very well there were only civilians in the villages — the fighting men lived in caves or out on the mountains; their bombing was a calculated policy of terror, designed to strike at the tribesmen through their families. To ensure maximum casualties they selected market days for their heaviest raids, when the streets were sure to be crowded. The policy certainly affected the Royalists' morale, although it aroused in them such hatred of the Egyptians that they were often unwilling to take prisoners. It didn't worry the great Powers in the least.

Amir Abdullah looked so desperately tired when I found him at Beit Elageh that I almost forgave him for nearly leaving me in the lurch the day before; he told me he had not slept for twenty-four hours, which was indeed surprising for one of the Yemeni princes, who seemed to spend so much of their time sleeping. He expected the attack on Hajjah to continue that night, but he seemed to have very little idea of what was actually happening there; he had received reports that Egyptian reinforcements were advancing to relieve the town, which was his excuse for his precipitate retreat to Beit Elageh. He made no excuse for not telling me he was going.

I stayed in the same room in the small house just outside his cave which I had occupied on my first visit to Amir Hassan Ismail the previous July; only this time, instead of having it to myself, I had to share it with six of the bodyguard. One of them had a khaki jacket he had taken off a dead Egyptian, with large silver buttons on it, which he proudly handed me to examine: round the badge in the centre of each button ran the legend: 'Southend-on-Sea Transport Corporation'.

Soon after our talk Amir Abdullah left Beit Elageh, again without letting me know. In the afternoon I heard heavy gunfire from the other side of the valley, which I supposed was connected with his sudden departure. That evening I was sitting in my small room, reading a copy of *Fanny Hill* I had bought in Beirut, when quite suddenly there was an almighty explosion just outside the house and most of the plaster from the ceiling came down on me and my companions. Within seconds I was alone in the room, but I reckoned that, whether it was a shell or a bomb, two seldom fall in the same place; and so I gave myself time to collect my briefcase and camera before walking over to the Amir's cave, where I found my former companions huddled together with some of his servants. As I stood in the entrance a second shell landed, farther away than the first. From this I deduced that we were not the target, and stayed outside photographing the bursts — most of them in or around the unfortunate village immediately below us. I should have preferred to spend the night in the cave, but I heard the Amir was returning, and so I had to go back to the house, where I spent a very disturbed night, with shells landing uncomfortably close at times, until towards dawn a heavy thunderstorm put an end to the bombardment.

I found Amir Abdullah next morning plunged in gloom. We talked to the accompaniment of a renewed bombardment and the sound of shells bursting in the village and on the mountain around our cave.

'My men have suffered a heavy defeat,' he told me sadly. 'We have lost all our heavy weapons, except a few that are still employed in the bombardment at Hajjah.'

He went on to explain that a large force of Egyptians and Republicans, with at least twenty tanks, were attacking from the south and east in an attempt to relieve the pressure on the garrison. His tribesmen, encircled by the enemy, had fled in the night, giving up four important mountains and abandoning their heavy armament, including four of the precious recoilless rifles, three heavy mortars, and three heavy machine guns — a very serious loss indeed when these weapons were so scarce.

'I have very little money left now,' he concluded, 'and without money the tribes will not fight. Will you please go directly to his Majesty at Qara and beg him to send me quickly more money, more heavy weapons and more ammunition.'

He was right, I knew, about the money. Generally speaking, the tribesmen fought out of loyalty to their Sheikhs, and the Sheikhs fought for money; although both were influenced to some extent by loyalty — or hostility, as the case might be — to the Imam, and all of them nursed a bitter hatred for the Egyptians.

I set off the following morning and reached Qara three days later, after an exhausting journey which involved a good deal too much of what I had come to call 'wadi-bashing', following river beds where the going was hard and monotonous, without any wind to cool us. We spent one night in the house of an old sheikh who displayed on the wall of his guest room not only the customary photograph of the Imam but also a large silk square decorated with portraits of Queen Elizabeth and the Duke of Edinburgh.

At Qara I was able to piece together the details of the Royalist debacle at Hajjah. It was a depressing story but in the circumstances hardly unexpected. In the first place there had been no security and therefore no surprise; since every tribesman for miles around had known for days in advance both the date and the time of the attack, it was inevitable the Egyptians should get to know them too. Secondly, the Royalists had sited their heavy weapons much too far from the enemy positions; and most of the weapons, particularly the mortars, had no sights. As a result, the preliminary bombardment was inaccurate and ineffective, especially as it was directed on the town instead of the positions defending it; those shots which didn't fall short landed on civilian houses and probably infuriated the inhabitants without damaging the Egyptians. Thirdly, and most significant in view of all I had told the Imam, the tribesmen didn't press home their attack and many of them didn't even start it.

Each tribe, well equipped with rifles, ammunition and money, had its own allotted target; but in the event many of them, notably those under Amir Abdullah, made no attempt to advance or even to mine the Hodeidah road. On the northern sector there was limited success when one tribe overran an Egyptian position, killing twenty of the defenders and capturing some artillery; but finding themselves unsupported on either flank, they had to withdraw, abandoning the captured guns. I discovered later the reason the two supporting tribes failed to materialize — a very typical one. They had killed a sheep, which took longer to roast than expected. Although their attack was planned to start at a certain time, in conjunction with their allies, they considered it more important to eat the sheep than attack on time. After the battle Amir Abdullah's men chanted exultant war songs praising their prowess, but I didn't see one bandolier among them which had an empty slot in it to indicate that a cartridge had been fired. The only consolation in a depressing story was a report, which arrived just before I left Beit Elageh, that the Hodeidah road had been demolished in four places and mined in others.

Would the Royalists, I wondered, at least draw the obvious conclusions from their failures, and change their tactics?

I spent most of the day following my arrival at Qara in a series of discussions with the Imam. Our interpreter was Abdullah al Khibsi, whom I had already met during my first visit to the country. He was a cheerful young man with a ready laugh and a jolly, round face; even in Yemeni dress, with his flower pot hat, he had a western appearance because, although he wore a small moustache, he had no beard. He spoke the best English of all the interpreters I used. I warned him I had some unpalatable things to tell the Imam.

'I know it is customary for your Majesty's subjects,' I began, 'to tell you only what you would wish to hear. I intend to tell you the truth, which will not be pleasant for you, and to be brutally frank about it. Shall I proceed?'

This made him laugh.

'Yes,' he urged me, 'please go on.'

'Your organization has four main weaknesses — planning, supplies, tactics and leadership. These are aggravated by three weaknesses in the character of your supporters — ignorance, inefficiency, and indolence. It is not for me, Sir, to criticize the Arab way of life or to try to alter it; but unless your men change their habits you have little hope of winning the war. Time has no meaning for them; "ba-den, bukra, inshallah,"[33] those three words typify their attitude. But in war, time is a vital factor and they must learn a sense of urgency. Their leaders, too, must learn to think and plan ahead.

'Supplies sit for weeks in villages where they aren't needed, while there are shortages at the front. Stores are wrongly split up, so that I saw guns and mortars without sights, mines

---

[33] 'Later, Tomorrow, As God Wills'.

without fuses, explosives without detonators. This is the result of inefficiency and ignorance.

'The failure of the attack on Hajjah confirms that your tactics are wrong. We have to remember that your soldiers aren't professionals, but peasant farmers with rifles. They haven't the training or the discipline to carry out attacks of that sort. But they are superb guerrillas and should be used as such — to mine roads, ambush convoys, or attack isolated camps on the roads; then they will kill Egyptians and get their equipment.'

The Imam was listening with close attention and no sign of resentment, and so I was emboldened to raise the subject of the princes in positions of command.

'These young Amirs are keen and intelligent,' I told him, 'But they labour under immense difficulties. They have to show themselves among their tribesmen, whose morale depends a lot on seeing them; and so they have to spend too much time travelling around. The rest of their time is too much occupied by petty details — endless *warragas* and letters. Wars can't be won by writing letters,' I added, which made the Imam smile.

'They really need both military advisers and an administrative staff to deal with correspondence. Some of them also badly need a rest, notably Amir Abdullah Hussein, who had not slept for three days when I left him. He has been fighting without a break for more than a year; could he not go on leave, say to Beirut?'

I was quite surprised at the good humour with which His Majesty received all these criticisms; he laughed a great deal at some of my sallies and interrupted several times to express agreement with me. Perhaps his sunny mood was due in part to the news which he had just heard on his wireless about the RAF attack on the Republican fort at Harib. This incident which, as I have already mentioned, roused the United Nations

Assembly to a pitch of hypocritical fury, delighted the Imam; his only complaint was that the RAF had, quite deliberately, given so much warning that the fort was empty when they bombed it. I took advantage of his happy frame of mind to persuade him to pose outside with his bodyguard for some photographs and ciné film, which later appeared in the British press and on television; I was quite proud of my achievement because this was the first time in three months that the Imam had emerged from his cave.

Chapter XIV: An American Moslem

It was a year before I returned to the Yemen. Most of the changes which took place in the interval were political rather than military. The most important from my point of view was the abdication of King Saud of Arabia in November, 1964, and the accession of Crown Prince Feisal to the throne; in future there would be no opposition from within the country to Feisal's Yemen policy, however much the policy itself might vary with circumstances.

Inside the Yemen the Royalists' morale had improved considerably. They had won no spectacular victories but their continued success in resisting Egyptian military pressure was encouraging more of the tribes to join them. The powerful Hashid confederation, which was almost wholly Republican in sympathy at the beginning — the Paramount Sheikh was one of Sallal's ministers — was on the point of switching its allegiance.[34] Morale was correspondingly low among the Republicans, who were already disenchanted with Sallal, and even more with his Egyptian masters; throughout the summer of 1965 they made a number of attempts, all of them abortive, to get rid of both.

Their disenchantment sprang partly from the tactless and arrogant behaviour of the Egyptians and the arbitrary rule of Sallal, who had made himself into a dictator, partly from disillusionment with Egyptian failure in the field. The last great

---

[34] All the tribes of the central and northern mountains belonged to one or other of the two great confederations, the Bakil and the Hashid; the Bakil, which was the stronger, had rallied to the Imam from the start and formed the backbone of his armies.

Egyptian offensive had taken place in the late summer of 1964. Mounted from the town of Haradh in the extreme northwest, its purpose was to kill or capture the Imam and to cut and occupy the Royalist supply route from Saudi Arabia. In both objectives it failed. Bogged down in mud from heavy rains and ambushed by the Royalists in two ravines, the Egyptian and Republican columns withdrew in confusion to Haradh with heavy losses, including half their armoured cars and ten of their tanks.

At the beginning of March, 1965, therefore, there had been little change in the positions of the opposing forces on the ground. The Egyptians and Republicans controlled the coastal plains, most of Southern Yemen, and the principal towns along the valley road running from Sana to the ancient capital of Sada in the north. They also maintained garrisons along the road that branched off from it to run south-eastwards to Marib and Harib; the most important of these garrisons was at Hazm, in the Jauf — an area of semi-desert between the mountains and the Rub al Khali. Most of the time they managed to keep these roads open for their supply convoys, but sometimes the Royalists would close them with demolitions, mines or ambushes and oblige the Egyptians to supply their garrisons by air.

The Royalists were firmly established in the mountains of the northern, central and eastern Yemen, and in the Jauf — apart from the isolated Egyptian garrisons. These mountains were more populous and more fertile than the Republican areas. The Royalists organized their own administration, appointed *walis* to all the provinces, maintained law and order through the tribal sheikhs and their own regular soldiers, and collected taxes in the Imam's name.

The number of Egyptian troops in the Yemen now exceeded 60,000, well supported by armour and artillery and by their Air Force; all their arms, equipment and aircraft were Russian. The Royalist fighting strength was difficult to estimate because their leaders would always exaggerate the strength of their commands for propaganda purposes. But at the time I assessed it at 50,000 Regulars, and a further 200,000 tribesmen who could be summoned to fight in their own tribal areas.

The Royalists had no aircraft, of course, and their only antiaircraft weapons were .5 calibre Browning machine guns, effective only against low-flying planes. As a result, their villages suffered cruelly from Egyptian bombing, and most of them were — or soon would be — reduced to rubble; tens of thousands of civilians — but very few fighting men — had perished in these raids.

In England I had seen a great deal of Jim Johnson and his second-in-command, Tony Boyle, and had become well acquainted with the details and problems of the British mercenary organization. When, therefore, I received another invitation from King Feisal and Ahmed al Shami to return to the Yemen, Johnson suggested I should spend some time with his men inside the country and let him have my views and any ideas for improvement; he would fly out there himself and meet me at Amara around the end of March. The *Daily Telegraph* again provided me with accreditation and a cable card. On 3 March, 1965, I flew out to Jedda on my fourth trip to the Yemen — my last in the passive role of an observer.

I waited in Jedda a week for news of McLean, who had written to me from the Yemen in January suggesting a meeting. While I was there I was drawn, reluctantly but inevitably, into the politics of war.

227

Certain prominent Republicans, including former members of Sallal's government, were in Jedda at this time for discussions with the Royalists and the Saudis about the possibility of forming a 'Third Party' to produce a United Front against Sallal and get rid of the Egyptians. The chief obstacle to agreement was the insistence of the Republicans that no member of the ruling Hamid ud Din dynasty should be included in the proposed new government. Without committing themselves the Saudis appeared interested, even sympathetic, to this new development. I was afraid it might weaken the Royalist war effort by causing their leaders to look over their shoulders, and by splitting what had been a united front.

My old interpreter, Mohamed Zabara, was involved in these negotiations on behalf of his present employer, Kemal Atham, the chief of the Saudi intelligence services. Kemal Atham, a brother-in-law of King Feisal, was considered by many to be the King's *eminence grise*. I came to know him well during the next two years. He was of mixed Albanian-Turkish descent, with blue eyes and a small, carefully trimmed, fair beard; his thin drooping moustache, melancholy eyes and withdrawn expression often gave him the appearance of a pensive mandarin. He spoke very slowly and deliberately, but his English was excellent. His position was not official, but he was very powerful and very rich, and he enjoyed the complete confidence of the King. He had a brilliant and cultivated mind, shrewd intuition and deep cunning, and he manipulated the many strings of his intelligence network with consummate skill. It was in his house that we installed the first wireless set operating to the Royalists — and later also to the British mercenaries — in the Yemen. In Oman we had captured a similar type of set in the Jebel Akhdar, and I often wondered whether the rebels on the mountains there had been in communication with this same house.

I had several long discussions with him during this visit to Jedda, and others with the Deputy Prime Minister of the Yemeni Royalists, Amir Abdurrahman. The youngest of the great Imam Yahya's fourteen sons and half-brother to the Crown Prince al Hassan, Amir Abdurrahman was still in his early thirties; but he had considerable experience of foreign affairs, having travelled extensively in America and the capitals of Europe, and he had a good knowledge of English. Although he held no military command, he made frequent visits to the field commanders and readily shared their hardships and understood their difficulties. His house in Jedda was the control station for the Yemeni radio network.

From him I learned that the Imam had left his cave headquarters and was now staying at Jizan. The Egyptians were claiming that their last offensive from Haradh had forced him to flee, but the Imam maintained he was sick and had come to Jizan only for medical attention; meanwhile the Royalists had told the Press that he was still in the Yemen with his troops. It was important, therefore, to keep his presence on Saudi territory a secret, because it could embarrass King Feisal if it became known abroad, especially to the Egyptians.

I wanted to see the Imam as soon as possible, and when I heard that McLean was travelling in the Khowlan area, east of Sana, I decided to leave at once for Jizan, in the hope that by the time I returned he would be in Jedda. I left on 10 March in a large four-engined aircraft which made the journey to Jizan in a record two hours — though it wouldn't have made it at all if the American flight engineer hadn't discovered, minutes before take-off, that two of the petrol tanks were empty.

The Imam was staying in the town in the house of his father-in-law, Yahya al Hirsi. His appearance left me in no doubt that his illness was real, not diplomatic; he looked both sick and desperately tired, and he told me that he had a kidney complaint as well as malaria. He rejected my suggestion that he should be treated at the Red Cross hospital at Uqd in the Yemen, where he would receive good medical attention and, at the same time, be back in his own country. But he readily agreed to my request to be allowed to visit the Royalist positions in front of Haradh, and asked me to see him again on my return.

I set off at seven the next morning in a Ford truck with a siren which was evidently a source of great pride to the driver, for he kept it blaring almost the entire journey until we reached Meshaf, the first town in the Yemen, about noon. Soon afterwards we heard the sound of aircraft and of bombing from about five miles away, and so we pulled off the track and camouflaged the vehicle. We had barely disembarked when there was a loud explosion on the track behind us as a mortar bomb landed barely a hundred yards off; the dust from our truck had given us away.

A climb of twenty minutes brought us to a great overhang of rock, under which was the headquarters of Sayyid Hassan Ismail Al Madani, Commander of the Royalist forces on the Haradh front. Formerly a merchant who had fled from the Yemen in the reign of Imam Ahmed, Sayyid Hassan was nevertheless proving a most capable leader, with a reputation for constantly visiting all sections of his front line. A quiet, unassuming man who spoke his mind with perfect frankness, he impressed me most of all by his calmness and confidence. Unlike so many Royalist commanders who complained ceaselessly about shortages of arms and money, he told me he was quite able to hold any Egyptian offensive with his present supplies — although, he added, if he had more he could drive the enemy back to Haradh.

After a discussion lasting two hours he summoned a soldier to take me up to a hilltop from which I could observe the Royalist and Republican positions. They faced each other along two ridges of dark brown rock separated by a green *wadi* thick with camel thorn; the Egyptians were grouped behind the Republican lines, across a plain. Apart from some mortar and machine gun fire, there seemed to be little activity.

The following day I gave my impressions to Amir Mohamed Sudairi in Jizan: 'The Egyptians have little chance of driving the Royalists from their present positions,' I concluded, 'But they might try to cut their supply route by a thrust through Saudi territory towards el Kuba, where the flat country would be ideal for their armour.'

The Amir agreed. 'I will send to Riyadh,' he said, 'for more troops.'

I was unable to keep my promise to see the Imam, because he had been obliged to leave Jizan hurriedly for the Yemen. His flight was caused by the indiscretion of one of his most devoted supporters, the American Moslem Abdurrahman Condé, who had chosen this moment to bring a party of Scandinavian journalists to Jizan, on their way to 'visit the Imam in the mountains'; it would not look good if they found him inside Saudi Arabia instead.

One of the most colourful characters of this war, Abdurrahman Condé was a highly intelligent man — notwithstanding this unfortunate lapse of judgment — who had acquired a profound knowledge of Arab, and especially Yemeni, affairs and a good command of Arabic. Born in California and christened Bruce Condé, he served in the

231

Second World War as a major with the U.S. 82nd Airborne Division and studied Arabic afterwards in Beirut. A consuming interest in postage stamps, which was shared at that time by the Crown Prince al Badr, brought him an invitation to visit Yemen in 1953. He was well received by the Imam Ahmed and settled there to develop a business in the export of Yemeni stamps and to become postal adviser to the government. He was passionately interested, also, in the archaeology of the country and always hoped to be appointed Yemen's first Director of Antiquities. In 1958 he renounced his American citizenship, without any ill-feeling towards America, and became a Yemeni subject; about the same time he embraced Islam and exchanged his Christian name of Bruce for the Moslem Abdurrahman.

A year later, however, he was expelled from Yemen. He wandered round the Middle East for a while as a stateless person, but when the civil war broke out he offered his services to the Princes and helped them to raise money from the printing and sale of Royalist stamps. He also acted for the Imam, quite brilliantly, as a public relations officer, and showed great initiative and skill in cultivating the foreign Press. This work inevitably involved a good deal of embroidery, if not exaggeration, which, also perhaps inevitably, tended to colour his accounts of his own achievements and background. He claimed to have discovered a lineal connection between himself and the great Prince of Condé, and, adding a couple of fresh names to his own, began to call himself 'Abdurrahman Bruce Alphonso de Bourbon-Condé'; later, with the amused acquiescence of the Imam, he assumed the title of Prince and the style of Serene Highness. He made similar advances in military rank until, when we met in Jizan, he was signing himself, 'Major-General Prince Abdurrahman Bourbon-Condé'.[35]

He was thin and wiry and always wore Yemeni dress — a black turban, khaki *iz-zar* and khaki shirt. The Imam and the Princes liked him although they laughed at him; indeed, he was a most likeable and good-hearted fellow, and he did many small kindnesses for me. For example, he had connections with the Yemeni Jews, who were permitted, even under the old Imamate, to distil brandy in their villages; when he came to see me he would often bring me a bottle. Unfortunately, he suffered terribly from trachoma, which was endangering his sight, and when I last heard of him he had gone to Barcelona for an operation. I hope it was successful.

On 15 March I flew back to Jedda, where I had an interview with Kemal Atham who wanted my advice about a new French bazooka which he had a chance of buying. It looked like a good weapon and I suggested he should order a hundred of them. He promptly ordered two hundred.

McLean was still in the Yemen, but on 18 March Jim Johnson flew in from London on his way to see King Feisal in Riyadh. I arranged a rendezvous with him at Amara and, deciding to wait no longer for McLean, left immediately for Najran.

On the aircraft I found an old friend and brother officer, Kenneth Timbrell, who had served as a major on my staff in Muscat. He was now a brigadier in the service of King Feisal and the senior British officer in the *Geish al Abyad*, the 'White Army', an elite body of Bedouin troops utterly devoted to the King, which acted partly as a palace guard and partly as an emergency striking force. Timbrell had enlisted as a trooper in

---

[35] Dana Adam Schmidt, op. cit. p. 132.

the Blues in 1936, when I first joined the Regiment, but had been commissioned into the Royals as soon as war broke out, and seconded to the Transjordan Frontier Force. Thereafter he had spent most of his time in the Arab world, except for a period after he left Muscat, when he commanded the Royals in Malaya.

The picture of a smart cavalry officer, with a trim moustache and erect, unmistakeably military bearing, he was always perfectly dressed and his manners were impeccable. He was a firm bachelor, his first love was horses, and he had the run of King Feisal's stud at Riyadh; but his value to the King lay in his outstanding military qualities, both as fighting soldier and administrator.

We parted company at Najran, where he told me he would be busy making plans for troop deployments on the frontier. I wondered whether this was a result of my talk with Amir Mohamed Sudairi.

I left Najran the same night, driving for two hours and a half across the desert to Amara. This was the Royalist headquarters to which I had driven in the opposite direction when I came in from Aden eighteen months ago, and where I had noticed the strange toadstool formations of the boulders. I found a great improvement now on the filth and squalor that had so disgusted me on my previous visit, and the cave where I slept had a comfortable bed, electric light, and — best of all — a clean *hammam*.

I also found Amir Abdullah Hussein, looking, if anything, even more tired, ill and dejected than when I had last seen him after the fiasco of his attack on Hajjah. I suggested he should go to Uqd for treatment at the Red Cross hospital, which he agreed to do.

While waiting for Johnson to arrive I paid another visit to the Prime Minister, Amir al Hassan. He had moved his headquarters to Ketaf, an eight-hour climb from the road-head at Odlah — although in fact it took me twenty hours because my guide lost the way and we had to camp out on the mountain. I found the Amir in bubbling good spirits and spent an entire day talking with him. He was very anxious for the Royalists to seize the heights overlooking the Harib-Marib road, and so re-open the supply route from Beihan. Would I please go to Khanja and discuss it with Amir Mohamed Hussein, who was commanding the 1st Army, which included all Royalist forces in eastern Yemen and the Jauf. Afterwards I might visit the Marib front, and then go to Beihan to see the Ruler, Sherif Hussein.

For part of my journey back to Amara I had an Egyptian prisoner as interpreter — a very good type of man, I thought, who spoke excellent English. He told me he had been twenty-two months in captivity, but was being well treated; the Red Cross visited him and brought him and his fellow-prisoners food, clothes, and cigarettes, and he received one letter a month from his family and was allowed to send one to them.

On 28 March Johnson turned up at last, accompanied by a British doctor whom I was particularly glad to see because he was able to give me medicine for a painful sore throat and cough that had kept me awake for the past fortnight. With them were two British mercenaries, Major Bernard Mills and his wireless operator, Sergeant James, both of whom I came to know well over the next three years. Mills, a stocky, dark-haired, quiet young man with remarkable powers of physical and mental resilience and an excellent knowledge of Arabic, had served in the Sultan's Armed Forces in Muscat; he and

Johnny Cooper proved incomparably the best of the British mercenary officers.

I told Johnson of my talk with Amir al Hassan and we agreed to drive to Khanja the following evening. Johnson had his own reasons for wanting to see Prince Mohamed Hussein.

'King Feisal is very dissatisfied with the Royalist war effort,' he told me. 'He says he's given them quite enough arms and cash to attack the Egyptians and so far nothing has happened. Unless they do something soon he's not prepared to waste any more. He does, after all, need a counter to bargain with Nasser.'

We left for Khanja at 3.30 the following afternoon, disregarding the risk from Egyptian aircraft because there was plenty of cloud cover. But we had frequent delays when the truck bogged down in the sand dunes, and so didn't arrive there until ten. From midnight until three in the morning Johnson, Mills and I harangued and brow-beat the unfortunate Mohamed Hussein, urging him to make an attack soon and justify the support King Feisal had given him over the last two years. Otherwise, Johnson warned him, all Saudi help would cease.

Mohamed Hussein, obviously embarrassed by our plain speaking, stressed the difficulties he was facing, especially in keeping the goodwill of the tribes, who were always demanding more money and were not above playing him off against the Egyptians in order to raise the price. But he assured us he was preparing an attack on the main Egyptian supply route from the north to Marib; he had drawn up plans for an ambush at a point where the road ran through a narrow gorge near Humeidat, and the British Liaison Officer attached to him had already made a detailed reconnaissance of the position. He himself had given orders to mobilize the tribes and move up

236

the necessary equipment to forward assembly areas. Under further pressure from us the Amir agreed to hasten his preparations and launch his attack within a week. Meanwhile, Johnson would return to Riyadh to tell King Feisal about it and I should stay with the Amir until the fighting started or until 4 April, when I should have to return in order to see the King before he left for Mecca on the *Haj*; but if there had been no attack by then, we warned Prince Mohamed, he could expect no further help from the Saudis.

It is only fair to say that although King Feisal had grounds for impatience with the Royalists for their inactivity on other fronts, I soon realized that Mohamed Hussein's difficulties here were genuine, and not mere excuses; he was certainly not lacking in courage or initiative, as he had already proved and was frequently to prove again. In fact, although he had no previous military experience, Mohamed Hussein was by far the most capable soldier and the most gifted and inspiring commander of all the Yemini princes. He had been educated in Cairo — indeed his dislike and contempt for the Egyptians derived from their failure to practise the liberal principles they had taught him — and later served the Imam Ahmed as his Ambassador in Germany. He spoke excellent English with a slight drawl, and his good-tempered, almost lazy manner and sleepy expression, enlivened by a ready and wholly charming smile, created a misleading appearance of indolence; only his strong features and shrewd though humorous eyes revealed the energy and ability behind it. He had been appointed Deputy Imam and worked very hard at his duties. He was very popular, but also very ambitious, and so he provoked jealousy among the other princes; it was said that he aspired to the Imamate — and that the tribes, if they had had the choice, would have preferred him to al Badr.

I was to see a great deal more of him in the future, and we became firm friends; but despite my admiration and affection for him I could never get used to his maddening sleeping habits. He worked all night and slept — even for a Yemeni prince — very late into the day. His servants were terrified of waking him and would send me in to do it; I would shake him until he awoke — when he would give me a sweet smile, turn over and fall fast asleep again.

Johnson and the doctor left for Riyadh the following day, and the rest of us accompanied Mohamed Hussein to new headquarters at Boa. Two days later McLean at last arrived there, after travelling most of the way from the Khowlan on a camel. He was in very poor shape, with a poisoned arm and a fever, and so we sent him off immediately to the hospital at Uqd. When I returned to the cave I shared with the Amir I found him playing with a three-foot snake. I thought he was being a bit rash because it was a sand viper, whose bite is considered fatal; however, he put it in a bucket and I reminded him lightly of an earlier remark he had made when I complained that our cave was infested with rats and mice. 'Good,' he had said, 'That means there won't be any snakes,'

We spent many hours together, going over his plans for the attack, which I thought had a good chance of success. But it was evident that he wouldn't be able to mount it before I had to leave on 4 April. Not only were there difficulties with the tribes, some of whom would only fight in their own area, so that he had to make last minute changes in his order of battle, but the supply problems were also formidable. Everything would have to be carried by men or animals from the road-head up the steep slopes of the Jebel Aswad[36] and the Jebel Ahmar[37] — heights which overlooked the road at the point of

---

[36] The Black Mountain.

ambush. However, I was sure the attack would take place, if only because by now the build-up had acquired such momentum that it was virtually impossible to stop it. It was to be coordinated with other Royalist attacks to the north and west, to distract the Egyptians, and if the Amir's men could hold their position on the Red and the Black Mountains in the face of air attack, they would effectively cut the Egyptian supply route to Marib and the south.

The Egyptians must have been suspicious, because we had several air raids during those days; but they did no damage, and our only casualties occurred when the European mercenaries, rushing out of the caves to shoot at the aircraft, would collide in the entrances with the tribesmen running inside to get away from them. On 6 April I said good-bye to Mohamed Hussein, confident that I could report favourably to King Feisal.

In the event I was proved right. The attack, launched on 15 April and well co-ordinated by radio with diversionary operations by other Royalist commanders, was an overwhelming success. Mohamed Hussein's men effectively cut the road and, after several days of bitter fighting, held on to their positions. There was one critical moment on the Red Mountain when only the personal courage of the Amir saved them from disaster. Early one morning, when the Royalist sentries were asleep, an Egyptian paratroop battalion, guided by a Royalist deserter, scaled the mountain. The defenders awoke to find the plateau swarming with the enemy and most of them fled. But Mohamed Hussein, gathering a dozen men of his personal bodyguard, threw himself at the Egyptians and engaged them with such spirit that they faltered, while the tribesmen, shamed by his example, rallied and drove them from the mountain.

---

[37] The Red Mountain.

Henceforward the Egyptians would have to depend on air supply to maintain their garrisons in southern and eastern Yemen. Mohamed Hussein had more than justified King Feisal's lavish help.

Chapter XV: The Red Mountain

While I was in Jedda on my way home in April, Ahmed al Shami and Amir Sultan invited me to take command of all the mercenaries in Yemen; Jim Johnson and his French counterpart, Colonel Roger Falques, agreed with this proposal. After talking it over with Moy I accepted the offer; but I insisted my contract should include a clause permitting me to come home on leave three times a year for a total period of four months, to coincide with the children's holidays.

After a month in Scotland I returned to the Yemen towards the end of May, and went immediately to see the Imam. He was at a new headquarters at Shedda, about five hours drive from Jizan and very close to the Yemen frontier, in a cave about half-an-hour's climb from the roadhead. With him I found Amir Hassan Hassan, whom I had met on the Jebel Ahanoum during my first visit to the country. Both of them bombarded me with complaints against the Saudis for keeping them short of money, rifles and ammunition; in return, I tried to persuade them to do some fighting. Eventually I extracted a promise from Amir Hassan Hassan that he would do so, but only on condition that he received 600 rifles first. Amir Mohamed Sudairi, when I told him, agreed to send them at once.

All the time I was in the Yemen I was subjected to this same argument from both sides. The Royalists complained ceaselessly that the Saudis wouldn't give them enough support; the Saudis maintained they had already given them vast quantities of arms and money, with nothing to show for it — although Mohamed Hussein's action at Humeidat should have reassured them. My own view was that the Saudis, for their own reasons, were giving the Royalists just enough help to prolong the war but not enough to win it outright; they also suspected, with justification, that some of the supplies they sent were misappropriated. I had no doubt that the main factor in winning the war was money, because in the last resort most of the tribal Sheikhs would fight for the side that paid them best; so much so that those of the mercenaries who had served in the SAS would say that their old motto 'Who Dares Wins' should be changed in this war to 'Who Pays Wins'.

On my return to Jedda I had discussions with Roger Falques and Amir Sultan about the purchase of heavy weapons for the Royalists. With the help of old Sheikh Hafiz Wahba, who acted as interpreter, I persuaded the Amir to order French 120 mm mortars; with their great range they could hit Sana from the existing Royalist positions. But we agreed they should be kept under European rather than Yemeni control.

I had decided to set up my headquarters at Amara, where Bernard Mills had already selected a suitable cave for me. I arrived there on 8 June. On the way I met Mills at Najran and heard from him the story of the Humeidat operation; he was the liaison officer with Mohamed Hussein, but was about to start a month's well-earned leave in England. With him was James, who drove back with me to Amara. A former SAS sergeant and a trained mechanic and radio operator, he was a young man of admirably calm and self-confident temperament, who had fought in Borneo and the Radfan mountains of Aden; during my period of command he was my principal companion, acting as radio operator, driver and bodyguard.

Our first stop after Najran was at Fida, the Royalist radio station just inside the Yemeni border. It was under the control of Stolz, a West German national in his late thirties with typically Aryan features but a most friendly and hospitable nature. He had worked as a radio specialist for the Imam Ahmed, but had stayed loyal after Sallal's coup; soon afterwards he had set up this broadcasting station, built and maintained with Saudi money, in a huge, well-cemented cave, from which he transmitted news, communiqués and propaganda with the most modern equipment. He frequently visited West Germany on leave or to buy spares; because he asked so many leading questions about our work many of us suspected him of working for West German Intelligence.

In addition to James my headquarters staff at Amara consisted of Chris, our very competent Anglo-Indian radio operator, a French radio mechanic, Jean, and two Persian officers. We depended heavily on Chris and Jean to keep us in touch with the other missions, to whom I transmitted my orders by radio and from whom we received news reports at 1300 hours each day. There were four Persians under my command in the Yemen at this time — Regular Army officers whom the Shah had sent, partly because of his natural sympathy for the Royalists and his fear of Nasser and his policies, partly because he wanted some of his officers to gain experience in guerrilla warfare. All had received previous training at the Special Forces School in the USA, where they had acquired some exaggerated standards of luxury that were quite unsuitable for work in the Yemen; for example, before coming into the field they had spent £500 in Aden on tinned food. However, they were pleasant companions and we certainly ate well in their company.

The mercenary training school had moved from Khanja to Amara, and so it was not surprising that on the morning after our arrival we had three separate air attacks. The first two were from MiGs, which dropped bombs and followed them with cannon and rocket attacks, and the third came from Ilyushins dropping bombs. We fired back at the MiGs, apparently without effect, but the Ilyushins were too high; their bombs, moreover, were so close that they drove us to ground in our cave, where the explosions dislodged most of the Persians' tinned food from the shelves. Otherwise we suffered no damage, although the cannon and rocket fire, like the bombing, was pretty accurate. The Ilyushins returned on two of the three following days, and although they caused no casualties their bombs fell near enough to shake us.

On 14 June I set out to visit Amir Mohamed Hussein at his battle headquarters on the Jebel Ahmar — the Red Mountain. I started at four in the afternoon, driving our Land Rover, with James beside me in the front and two tribal bodyguards sitting on a heap of baggage, petrol cans, and water containers in the back. A seven-hour drive across sand dunes and gravel desert brought us to the roadhead at Matarra, where we camped for the night under some high cliffs — to the consternation of a pair of hoopoes who were nesting in them.

A gruelling climb in the dark the following evening brought us to the top of the Black Mountain, where we spent the night beside a well at a height of over five thousand feet. Another sharp climb next day brought us onto the plateau of the Jebel Ahmar, and after a walk of two and a half hours across it we came to a cliff overhang honeycombed with caves, where Mohamed Hussein had his headquarters. While waiting to see him we breakfasted in one of the caves that housed the French mercenaries attached to him.

Their commander, known as Louis, had just returned from a very thorough reconnaissance of the Egyptian and Republican positions. He was a former major in the French Army, of about my own age, tall and slim, with his head clean-shaven, a practice adopted by all the French mercenaries as a protection against lice. An exceptionally efficient soldier who had a firm grip on his men and was greatly respected by them, he would jump heavily only on conduct that endangered security. He was certainly no thug, either in appearance or manner; on the contrary, he was a well-educated and cultured man who spoke good English and had excellent manners and enormous charm.

He greeted me with one of his cracking salutes. 'I have good news, Colonel David,' he began. 'An Egyptian aircraft has been shot down at Khanja five days ago.' Perhaps our shooting had not been so ineffective, after all. 'But, I must also report,' he went on, his smile fading, 'that the enemy has driven our Amir's men from some of their positions overlooking the road from Humeidat to Hazm. Perhaps you would care to accompany me tomorrow to observe the situation?'

After arranging the details with Mohamed Hussein, who seemed genuinely pleased to see me, I set off next morning with Louis and one of his men. The Egyptians, who seemed very nervous had kept up a steady and quite ineffective artillery barrage, accompanied by flares and tracer, all night, and they were still firing when we left on our reconnaissance. On the way we came under some heavy shelling which scared away all our six tribal bodyguards; but eventually we came to a Royalist position where a 75 mm gun was shooting at some Egyptian tanks at extreme range — a great waste of ammunition, we thought, because they were using H.E. and so even a direct hit would have done little damage; but it must have been good for morale. An Egyptian 105 mm battery was returning the fire and landed a dozen rounds within a hundred yards of us.

On the way back I noticed the plateau was literally covered with fossilized shells, including oyster shells; I collected some, and sent specimens of them to the Natural History Museum. The Museum later informed me that these shells were new to science, and had never been described or named in literature. They asked me to present them to the National Collection, and I did.

My next official visit was to the Prime Minister, Amir al Hassan; thanks to his ingenuity we were able to travel by a much shorter and easier route. Leaving Amara early on 21 June with James, Yahya the Persian and three tribesmen, we drove first to Najran and then south for half an hour to the foot of a great mountain. Here we loaded our kit on camels and climbed for four hours to a plateau, nearly 6000 feet high, where two trucks were awaiting us; on al Hassan's initiative they had been carried up in sections on camels and reassembled at the top.

The plateau commanded superb views in every direction; we seemed to be looking over the whole of north-eastern Yemen. Immediately below us to the north spread the Najran valley, and strung out along it I could see caravans of camels plodding towards us, laden with Saudi arms and flour. A slow and bumpy drive of four hours over camel tracks, followed by a donkey ride of an hour and a half, brought us, at an altitude of five and a half thousand feet, to the cliffs and caves of al Sadma, the new headquarters of al Hassan. This was only twelve miles north-east of Sada. It looked as though the Egyptians were pulling out of their forward positions and concentrating in and around the town, from which the nearest Royalist troops were now only five miles away.

Al Hassan greeted me like an old and valued friend, which didn't prevent an acrimonious argument developing between us over the future deployment of the new 120 mm mortars. He insisted that one mortar should be sent to each front, and I wholly failed to convince him that to be really effective they must operate together as a team. But I had to admit next day that he did know something about mortars. He took us to look at the Egyptian positions across the Wadi Nashur, a mile or so from his headquarters, from an Observation Post behind which an 81 mm mortar was emplaced. He ordered it to open fire, and not only worked out all the calculations with rangefinder and wind tables but insisted on sighting the mortar himself. His fire, at 3000 yards range, was extremely accurate, and we could see the Egyptians running as the bombs burst among them. He followed with an hour and a half's lecture on mortar firing. Although scarcely the job for a Prime Minister, this demonstration reminded me that he was an old warrior of great experience and personal courage, and it might serve as an example to some of the other Amirs, who seldom emerged from the safety of their caves.

Sherif Hussein, the Ruler of Beihan State in the Aden Protectorate, was a good friend of the Royalists, sending in convoys of arms to them in the early days of the war and providing accommodation and transport later on for the mercenaries infiltrating through Aden. It was time I went to see him. James and I started from Amara at the end of June with a small party in an old Ford truck.

Our way took us along the fringe of the Rub al Khali, over drifts and dunes where we often stuck in the sand, and where in the heat of the day the radiator boiled over every fifteen minutes and the petrol evaporated; we had to halt between 10.30 and 4 in the afternoon, but we found no shade from the sun or the scorching desert wind. Once we stopped where a solitary mountain rose out of the sand sea, its steep sides veined with streaks of coloured rock in red and blue and green; there were traces of ancient quarrying around its base and our *bedu* guide told us this was where they quarried the stone for the Queen of Sheba's palace at Marib, 70 miles away.

After a journey of thirty-six hours we crossed the frontier of Beihan State soon after midnight and entered the Aden Federation. At the check point, which had been attacked by MiGs on the previous day, the Beihani guard commander made us rest until sunrise.

'It is dangerous to go farther in the dark,' he warned us. 'There are mines on the road.'

One of the objects of my journey was to reconnoitre the Egyptians' positions in and around Marib and work out a plan to expel them from the town. I would need Sherif Hussein's help, for the Royalists in front of Marib came from three tribes — the Abida, the Murad, and the Jiham — who owed allegiance to him, although they lived on the Yemeni side of the frontier. In Naqub we enquired for him at the house he had allotted to our mercenaries, and eventually found him, after another twenty minutes drive, with his son, Amir Saleh, at Hajja.[38] This was the site of the ancient city of Timna, famous in the time of King Solomon; now the only traces of its former glory were a few ruins, half-buried in the sand among the dirty mud huts of the village.

With his luxuriant grey beard, dignified bearing and shrewd, twinkling eyes, Sherif Hussein might have been some venerable Old Testament prophet except for a warmth and benevolence uncommon among those austere figures. He readily agreed that I should visit the Marib positions, and made the arrangements so promptly that at 4.30 in the afternoon I was bumping over giant sand dunes — some of them over 150 feet high — in a Land Rover with three sheikhs from the Abida, Murad and Jiham tribes. Overhead RAF Hunters patrolled incessantly

---

[38] Not to be confused with Hajjah in northern Yemen.

until dark, when we passed the frontier into Yemen and halted for the night beside a stream in a deep, precipitous *wadi* in the hills.

Next morning we drove on down the *wadi* until it broadened into the Marib plain beneath the stupendous ruin known as the Queen of Sheba's Great Dam. Built about 850 BC, not in fact by the Queen of Sheba but by a predecessor, the first King,[39] it irrigated the land for nearly fourteen hundred years, making it the most fertile country in Arabia, until it fell into disrepair and finally burst towards the end of the sixth century AD. But its massive wall and buttresses of granite still towered over the plain like some huge Vauban fortress, the great stone slabs, six feet long and two feet wide, interlocking perfectly up to a height of over fifty feet; even the ancient cement still held them firm.

From the hills above the dam I looked through binoculars across the scrub-covered sand dunes and gravel desert of the plain to the town of Marib, prominent on a hill. I could see some tall stone columns rising out of the desert, which reminded me of Baalbek, and I would have liked to examine them more closely; unfortunately there were two Egyptian tanks cruising in front of them. Eventually we had to make a hurried move when shells began falling close around us.

The three sheikhs who were my guides insisted on taking me by camel to see all the Royalist positions whereas I was much more interested in Egyptian defences. Another irritation was that at every position we visited the garrison would open fire with all their heavy weapons, invariably bringing down upon us further salvoes of Egyptian shells, which fell much too near for comfort because they had the Royalists registered. At one point in our journey the shelling was so close that I had to

---

[39] Dana Adams Schmidt, op. cit. p. 142.

dismount. My escort ran for cover, but I continued at a walk, feeling I must preserve the dignity of my age and rank. However, I accelerated sharply when a shell landed fifty yards behind me, exactly where I had been a minute earlier.

After a brief visit to Harib, which was in Royalist hands, we returned to Beihan for the night. Next morning I took my leave of Sherif Hussein and drove back to Amara where I found all our tribal guards had gone on strike over pay — a Yemeni responsibility, not ours. I therefore sacked all eighteen of them and replaced them with two guard dogs, who proved much more effective.

A few days later I paid another visit to Al Hassan's headquarters near Sada, in company with James, Chris and two of the Persians. We were going there to receive a parachute supply drop — one of many we received during my years in the Yemen. The mercenary organization had spent a great deal of time, money and trouble in setting up the apparatus for these drops. It had been necessary to charter reliable aircraft with discreet pilots, to reconnoitre suitable dropping zones, and — most delicate of all — to obtain the agreement of a Middle Eastern country to the use of its territory for mounting the operations. But by the summer of 1965 everything was ready, and we had already received one successful drop, near Amara, a month previously.

This one presented more difficulties: in the first place we were so close to Sada that the aircraft would have to swing low over the town to make its run in; secondly, instead of open desert for the dropping zone we had to use a rocky *wadi* with steep mountains on either side. However, al Hassan had rounded up a force of eighty tribesmen to act as guards and to collect and carry the containers.

The aircraft was due at 1 am on 13 July. Throughout the previous day thick cloud and heavy rain drifted across the plateau, followed by a sandstorm; but the weather cleared at nightfall and we were all in position soon after midnight. Dead on time we heard the engines overhead and lit the fires to mark the dropping zone. The pilot made a perfect drop, landing all the containers in the *wadi*. Al Hassan was as excited as a schoolboy. '*Wallahi*! *Wallahi*!' he shouted, as each parachute glided down, and he insisted on supervising personally the opening of every package — a very wise precaution, because otherwise the contents would certainly have been looted.

His followers, however, were so busy cutting up the parachutes for themselves and quarreling over them that they had no time to spare for the arduous work of collecting the containers and loading them onto the waiting truck. We had to do it all ourselves, and it took us until sunrise.

However, we felt it was worth it when we counted the stores we had received: twelve Brens, ten bazookas, a hundred rifles and fifty mines, with plenty of ammunition, not to mention a welcome 'comforts' package for ourselves, with whisky, brandy, beer and — best of all — mail from home. We began to forget our anger with the useless Yemenis. For their part, they were exultant.

'*Wallahi*!' they boasted happily. 'With all these new weapons we shall drive the British out of Aden.'

Chapter XVI: The War of Gold

I suppose I had been lucky over the last two years not to have contracted any serious illness, given the conditions of life in the Yemen. But my luck gave out that summer of 1965, when I went down with bilharzia during my leave in Scotland. Instead of returning to Jedda in September, I had to spend three weeks in hospital with a series of agonizing injections which I found much harder to bear than the disease; had I contracted it only a year later I could have been cured painlessly with pills.

As a result it was mid-October before I returned to the Yemen, and the situation had altered radically in the meantime. The Royalists had resumed the offensive and inflicted more losses on the Egyptians, who began to withdraw their most exposed garrisons. Then, at the end of August, Nasser had flown to Jedda to meet King Feisal, a move which both the Yemeni Royalists and the Saudis interpreted as a confession of weakness. From this meeting emerged the 'Jedda Agreement', the main provisions of which were that the Egyptians would withdraw all their troops from the Yemen within ten months from 23 November, 1965; the Saudis would cease all military aid to the Royalists; there would be an immediate ceasefire; and, finally, a Conference would assemble, under joint Saudi and Egyptian supervision, on 23 November at Haradh, to be attended by delegates from both Royalists and Republicans. Its function would be to agree upon a system of government for the Yemen, pending a plebiscite at a later date.

Both sides observed the ceasefire at once, which gave rise to considerable uncertainty about the future of the mercenaries. Amir Sultan was reluctant to renew their contracts until he knew the results of the Haradh Conference; for the moment their only task was to keep open the radio network. It was my thankless duty as soon as I returned from England to persuade them to remain patient.

Before the situation was resolved I received a cable in Jedda from the *Daily Telegraph*, asking me to represent them at the Haradh Conference. I was still technically in command of the mercenaries, and so I had to consult my Saudi and Yemeni masters but they raised no objection. And so on 22 November I flew to Jizan, where a large party of delegates was assembled, together with a few Arab journalists and the BBC correspondent, Ken Brazier. The following morning we flew on to Haradh.

Although the Saudi and Egyptian armies had each provided a contingent of soldiers, the security arrangements were in Egyptian hands — a matter which caused me some qualms lest they should find out what I had been doing in the Yemen. Brazier and I, as the only two British correspondents, were in any case regarded with deep suspicion by the Egyptians, who checked our credentials no less than three times within an hour of our arrival.

The Conference took place in a vast camp, in which delegates and the Press were housed, or rather confined. Surrounded by barbed wire, with manned machine gun posts at each corner and sentries patrolling everywhere, it might have been designed for political prisoners rather than diplomats. However, the Camp Commandant, a friendly and hospitable colonel, arranged for Brazier and me to share a tent with the only other Western correspondent, Arthur Higbee of *Newsweek*; an Egyptian Army batman waited on us — a detail which afforded me some quiet amusement in the circumstances. Apart from ourselves the Press corps consisted of three

Russians, two East Germans, a large number of Arabs and two Communist Chinese.

Ahmed al Shami headed the Royalist delegation, which included several members of the 'Third Party'. But newsmen were not allowed to talk to any of the Yemenis, a prohibition I respected until, after a few days, the Egyptians allowed them to talk with Republican delegates but not Royalists; thereafter I circumvented it, usually by passing notes to my friends in the camp cinema, where there was a film every evening — nearly always B category with a strong element of anti-British propaganda. If Brazier or I attempted to speak directly with a Royalist there was invariably a watchful Egyptian 'Public Relations Officer' at hand to warn us off and even, on one occasion, threaten us with expulsion.

At first the Royalists and Republicans shared the same quarters, presumably to encourage informal exchanges between them, but they quarrelled so violently that they were eventually moved to separate accommodation. The Saudi Amir Abdullah Sudairi presided over the formal sessions. A nephew of my friends Khalid and Mohamed, he would hold long Press Conferences during the course of which he managed, with enormous charm, to say nothing at all; indeed there was nothing to report, for the Republicans, under Egyptian pressure, refused to compromise on any point. It became clear afterwards that the whole Conference had been no more than a manoeuvre by Nasser to gain a breathing space to regroup and reinforce his army in the Yemen.

Life in the camp, therefore, became very tedious, with the added irritation that all our cables were officially censored. The two Chinese left after three days, bluntly declaring they had been wasting their time; we missed them because they were friendly companions — as indeed were the Russians, with whom we used to swap whisky for vodka until they too departed.

One evening, when I had been there a week, Amir Abdullah Sudairi sent for me privately to warn me that the Egyptians now knew about my activities with the mercenaries; for my own safety I should leave at once, and he would arrange it first thing in the morning. And so on 1 December I slipped away from the camp at dawn, accompanied by a Saudi captain who brushed aside the sentries and put me on an aircraft for Jizan.

Before flying home for Christmas I had a meeting in Riyadh with Amir Sultan, at the end of which he agreed to renew the mercenaries' contracts for a further four months. I was preparing to return to my command in the middle of January when I collapsed out shooting in Scotland and had to have a cartilage removed from my knee. This was the second time in succession I had overstayed my leave through sickness, and I was afraid people would think I was malingering.

While I was convalescing I learned I had been appointed a Member of Her Majesty's Bodyguard — a Gentleman-at-Arms. Since the appointment involved my attendance at such functions as State Visits and Royal Garden Parties, I was in a dilemma: how could I reconcile these new duties with those of commanding the mercenaries? Fortunately most of the Bodyguard ceremonies took place in the summer, and so I decided to carry on in the Yemen until April, when my contract there would expire.

When I reached Jedda early in March, 1966, the Egyptians had already broken the ceasefire and resumed bombing in all areas of Royalist Yemen. For a brief period after the Haradh Conference President Nasser seemed to lose heart, and began withdrawing troops from the country; from its peak of 70,000 their number dropped to about 20,000 at the beginning of February. At that moment the British Government issued their notorious Defence White Paper, announcing our withdrawal from the Persian Gulf, and the situation changed overnight. Nasser saw a fresh opportunity to seize Aden, and began to reinforce in the Yemen until he had nearly 60,000 troops there. More important, the White Paper marked the final eclipse of British prestige among the Arabs. Only two weeks previously Goronwy Roberts, Minister of State at the Foreign Office, had toured the Gulf and given the Rulers positive assurances that the British would stay. Hitherto the Arabs had trusted the British, despite many disappointments, to the extent that the phrase 'word of an Englishman' had become a part of their vocabulary; after the White Paper it ceased to have any meaning.

I spent two weeks in Jedda, most of the time in conference with Amir Sultan, Ahmed al Shami and Jim Johnson. Kemal Atham presented me with a new Toyota Land Cruiser, which I camouflaged and from which I removed the roof, windscreen and windows — partly to enable me to spot hostile aircraft, and partly to lessen the risk of injury should I run over a mine. I decided to drive it to Najran, calling on the way at Taif, where the Imam was having treatment for nephritis; I intended to visit a mercenary base near Najran, and then drive on to the Yemen to see Mohamed Hussein, who was reported to be touring the Khowlan and the Jauf, rallying the tribes in areas recently evacuated by the Egyptians.

The seven-hundred-mile journey to Najran took me four days, including a detour through the mountains on the way to Taif in order to avoid Mecca, which as an infidel I might not enter. In Taif I saw the Imam who gave me a warm greeting, although he seemed far from well. The next two hundred miles of driving were the most gruelling I have ever done, over savage country where we bogged down repeatedly in sand or bumped agonizingly over hard volcanic rock. My knee hadn't yet recovered and was swollen like a balloon; each time we had a puncture I had to change the wheel alone while my guide, a venerable but arthritic tribal sheikh, quietly prostrated himself towards Mecca and said his prayers.

'You will need a good guide for your journey in the Yemen,' Amir Khaled Sudairi told me when I saw him in Najran. 'I am going to give you the best. His name is Jum Han, and he was with your famous countryman Abdullah Philby on many of his travels through Arabia.'

Jum Han was a *bedu* from Nejd, the heartland of the Wahabis and birthplace of the great Ibn Saud. He had a thick, well-trimmed moustache, a close-clipped beard and a wide mouth that contained several gold teeth. He was about my own height and carried himself erect with an air of pride and independence that matched the strong features and the fierce eyes crinkled by the winds and glare of the desert. His deep knowledge of the country, his courage and calm self-assurance, and his strong sense of humour made him an ideal companion for a hazardous and lonely journey, and although he held a poor opinion of the Yemenis his courtesy never allowed it to show in their presence. He also had a *bedu*'s contempt for soldiers, particularly those of the Saudi army, but in cold weather he always wore an old British khaki greatcoat with Royal Marine buttons.

The morning after my arrival at Najran I was awakened by the army firing saluting guns to mark the opening of the three-day festival of Id. The streets were crowded with men, women, and children, all wearing new clothes in celebration, and the houses were festooned with palm branches, some of them linked with rolls of pink and blue Andrex. Since all offices would be closed for the festival, I drove out with Jum Han to the mercenary base, some thirty-five miles to the east, and spent the next three days there. The mercenaries — British and French specialists — had a comfortable camp just inside the Saudi frontier, where they ran a workshop for the repair of vehicles and weapons, and where we were going to instal the new 120 mm mortars for trials and training.

We drove across the frontier into the Yemen on 4 April and reached Boa in well under six hours. Unlike some of my previous guides Jum Han was a real help, setting to with a will to dig the Toyota out of the sand whenever we became stuck; he even carried a puncture repair outfit in his kit, for which I had cause to be thankful. At Boa we heard that Amir Mohamed Hussein had gone to Hazm, now abandoned by the Egyptians, and so I decided to follow him. We turned east towards the Jauf, taking the old Egyptian motor road and passing several of their old camp sites and the wrecks of their transport. Just outside Hazm, where we had a puncture, a *bedu* guard told us Amir Mohamed had already left and so we accepted his invitation to sleep in his camp. We sat round a fire among the tents, drinking coffee and tea and talking with the Bedouin until I could keep awake no longer; I lay down beside the car, in the middle of a herd of goats, and immediately fell fast asleep.

The Jauf is semi-desert country with few villages; the tall houses are built of mud, quite unlike the solid stone fortress dwellings of the mountains, and the inhabitants are mostly peaceable herdsmen without the warlike spirit of the hill-men. Hazm, which we passed through early next morning, lies in a plain dotted with green shrubs and bushes between two high mountain ranges; I had only seen it before through binoculars, from the top of the Red Mountain, and I hoped we wouldn't run over any of the mines the Royalists had laid on the road before their successful attack a year ago.

We caught up with Amir Mohamed at last, half an hour's drive beyond Hazm; the village where he had halted was thronged with tribesmen come to swear allegiance, and around the tall mud house where he was staying I counted twenty parked vehicles — trucks and Land Rovers, some of them mounting recoilless rifles, others .5 Brownings. The Amir was putting on a fine show of strength to win over this area, so recently occupied by the Egyptians, and he told me that all the villagers of the Jauf had affirmed their loyalty to the Imam.

'The war has changed since you were last with us, Colonel David,' he continued. 'It is a war of gold now, rather than weapons. The Egyptians have learned that they cannot beat us in battle and their bombing only strengthens our hatred of them. So they have changed their tactics from bombing to bribery. You know that in the Yemen gold talks loudest of all and now they are giving money to the tribes to persuade them to desert us and fight for them. With all the resources of America and the Soviets behind him, Nasser believes he can offer more than we, who have only King Feisal to support us.'

His biggest problem, he told me, was with the Dahm tribe, who controlled a large area on his lines of communication. The Dahm were proverbial for their treachery, meanness and cruelty and had been responsible for most of the atrocities committed against Egyptian prisoners. Mentioned by Thesiger in *Arabian Sands* as a scourge of the Bedouin of the Rub al Khali, they were both aggressive and suspicious; but their loyalties were wholly mercenary and during this war they had changed their allegiance repeatedly, without warning or scruple, to follow whichever side proved the better paymaster. In the past they had received money simultaneously from the Egyptians and the Royalists, but now the Egyptians had departed they expected the Amir to make up the difference.

'It will be expensive,' he sighed. 'But they know I have no choice.'

After the Egyptian withdrawals the Royalists had moved forward towards Sana until their most advanced outposts were only five miles from the capital. Amir Mohamed now planned to isolate it by cutting the roads leading south to Taiz and west to Hodeidah, and reinforcing the Hashid tribes now operating against the road running north from Sana to Sada; at the same time he proposed to threaten Taiz, the southern capital, with a thrust south-west from Harib. In my view, which I set out in a report to Amir Sultan, he would first have to consolidate the areas recently evacuated by the Egyptians, in order to secure his rear. In the new phase of the war this task would require not arms so much as gold.

After consultation with Amir Mohamed I decided to travel southwest to visit the Royalist commanders in the Sana sector. My route would take me through the foothills of the High Jauf, across the Arhab plateau, through the mountains of Nehm, and finally into the Khowlan. When I told Jum Han, he shook his head and told me, sadly but firmly, that he could not go with me.

'I have enemies in that country,' he explained, 'and they would surely kill me.' He returned the same day to Najran.

I was very sorry to lose him, and far from reassured by the two young boys Amir Mohamed provided as guides in his place. However, the Amir gave me letters to the Royalist commanders and sheikhs whose help I would need, and then left the village with his motorcade. The noise was deafening, with repeated *feux-de-joie* from the villagers and a continuous blare of motor horns and the wailing of a siren, until they vanished in a thick cloud of dust.

We drove westwards in the blazing afternoon until the Toyota's engine began to falter, and finally stopped; it turned out that the great heat was causing the petrol to evaporate in the carburettor. The country around us was bleak and desolate, with no vegetation or landmarks. Looking about for somewhere to shelter from the sun I noticed some primitive stone cairns with beehive roofs, and crawled inside one of them, squeezing with difficulty through the low, narrow entrance. There was just enough room inside to lie down, and I was settling myself comfortably when my hand came in contact with some hard, knobbly objects beside me. I struck a light and saw I was lying among piles of human bones and skeletons, and realized I had entered some ancient burial chamber. For the rest of the afternoon I lay under the car.

The following evening we came to a village in the Wadi Hirran, where a clear river ran through fields of maize in which men were busy threshing. This was as far as I could take the car because the Republicans held the next village, four miles down the road. We were well into the foothills now, and my pocket altimetre registered 4,500 feet. After passing several suspicious sentries, including a fierce old man who balanced a rock in one hand and with the other brandished a tomahawk uncomfortably close to my head, I met the Royalist *naib*,[40] Sheikh Daoud. An alert and wiry little man, he gave me a warm welcome, which became even warmer when I handed him a note from Amir Mohamed and a bag of sovereigns.

He promised me his own riding donkey and two camels for the next stage of my journey, which involved a stiff climb into

---

[40] Local military commander (of any rank).

the mountains. After an enormous meal he took me to a small stone house for the night and led me up to the roof, where I said I would prefer to sleep.

'Take care you do not roll off in the dark,' he warned me as he left. 'It is a long way to fall.' I saw what he meant when I awoke at daybreak. I had in fact rolled in my sleep to the very edge of the roof and found myself looking down a sheer drop of 250 feet to the *wadi* bed.

At seven the camels were loaded, I climbed onto the donkey and we started off to cries of farewell from the villagers and a *feux-de-joie* from the sentries. Sheikh Daoud promised to take good care of the Toyota, although I had little doubt he would be using it as a taxi. For three hours we climbed steeply up a great escarpment, which took us out of the Wadi Hirran and on to the Arhab plateau at nearly 7,000 feet. For another hour we walked across a gloomy and deserted landscape of red-brown rock with only a few cactus bushes for vegetation, until we came to a village which bore the scars of severe bombing. Here I was lodged in a house while my donkey and the camels returned to Sheikh Daoud and my guides hunted for replacements. For the whole afternoon and evening my only companions in a small room were eight women, varying in age from about sixty to fifteen, who taught me to spin goat hair into yarn until they left me alone to sleep.

This was to be the toughest and physically the most exacting of all my journeys. For two more days we travelled across the desolate, rocky plateau, with the mountains of Nehm a blue line on the horizon ahead; only the rare green field of grass or lucerne softened the stark monochrome of the rock. We passed a few wretched villages whose crumbling houses resembled dilapidated stone forts, where I begged a cup of foul water, and sometimes we came to a stagnant pool where I shared a drink with the donkey. The rough walking was a severe strain on my knee, which I had injured again in a fall in the darkness of Amir Mohamed's house, and a strain on my lungs too, at an altitude of over 7,500 feet. On two occasions I saw MiGs in the distance and heard the sound of bombs, but there was no other sign of the enemy.

On the third day, 11 April, we left the Arhab — which I hoped I would never see again — and descended into the Wadi Harib, a deep ravine of rock and shale with a gently flowing river, which divides the plateau from the Nehm mountains. This was my fiftieth birthday, and to mark the occasion I took a photograph of myself while our party rested among the bushes beside the clear water. I also took from my pack an orange which I had bought in Najran and carefully saved as a treat for my birthday; but when I peeled it I found it had completely dried up.

Our pack transport was now reduced to a solitary and evil-tempered camel, which had to carry all our kit as well as a radio for the mercenary mission in the Khowlan. It was in 'must' and during the next stage of our journey, a steep climb into the mountains, it gave us plenty of trouble. Slipping its nose rope, it suddenly went berserk and charged, first the camel man, then my guide and finally me; I cracked it on the nose with my stick and then, like the others, took to my heels — wisely, I think, because in its fury it twisted round and seized a kettle from its load, grinding it in its teeth until it was quite flat. I was thankful I hadn't been riding it at the time; it had already thrown me by rising as I was mounting it, with the result that I had landed heavily on my bandaged knee.

The Nehm mountains were green and well-watered and the villages prosperous by comparison with the Arhab. In the evening we reached Jerbat Attala, the cave headquarters of the

Amir who commanded the Royalist forces in Nehm and Arhab; with him I found his cousin, Amir Abdullah ibn Hassan, whom I had already met and who was now in command of the Khowlan. In the course of a four-hour conference the same evening they told me they fully supported Mohamed Hussein's plans for isolating Sana, but left me in no doubt that money would play the decisive part in future operations.

I slept in the princes' cave, in the luxury of a bed, and left them the following morning to continue my journey to the Khowlan. They gave me an escort of fifteen soldiers together with two camels and three donkeys, one of which I rode. After climbing a steep range of mountains we crossed the wide valley of the Wadi Sharefar and entered the Khowlan. We passed several villages surrounded by vineyards, but had to keep well away from them because they belonged to the Republicans. Another climb, so steep that I had to dismount from my donkey, brought us to a village standing on a mountainside above terraced fields at an altitude of 8,200 feet, where we halted to feed the animals. It took three hours to feed each camel because its food — lucerne wrapped in maize leaves — had to be fed to it a mouthful at a time. As it was already late in the afternoon when we arrived, and we had been on the march for eight hours, we decided to stay there for the night.

Just before noon next day we reached Shawkan, headquarters of Brigadier-General Kasim Monasir, a bare eight miles north-east of Sana. The general's military bearing and his style of dress — a British army pullover under crossed bandoliers — singled him out from his companions as a professional soldier. Taller than most Yemenis, with a taciturn, even dour personality and the swarthy complexion and woolly hair of his black ancestors, this former Captain of the Imam's Bodyguard and one-time colonel in the Republican army was among the ablest of the Royalist commanders. His troops, who admired his personal courage and respected his firm discipline, had followed him enthusiastically in a series of energetic and imaginative attacks on the Egyptians, and had occupied a mountain range, the Jebel Jamina, which dominated Sana. There he had suffered a reverse, through no fault of his own. The Egyptians had bribed the tribes on that mountain to join the Republicans, and Kasim's men had been forced to withdraw, after inflicting heavy losses on the enemy.

'My problem now,' he told me through an interpreter, 'is that I have no supplies. I have only one 75 mm recoilless gun and no ammunition for it; I have very few machine guns and hardly any bombs for my mortars, which could do real damage to the enemy down on the plain below.'

I knew he was speaking the truth. I also knew that the princes, who looked down on him because he was not of royal blood, were jealous of his success and slow to send him the material he needed. However, I promised to arrange a parachute drop to get supplies directly to his base. Unfortunately I was too late. Disgusted with his treatment by the princes, General Kasim defected again to the Republicans, but was executed soon afterwards by his own tribe, who considered he had disgraced them by his frequent switches of loyalty.

Although he had been driven off the Jebel Jamina, his men still occupied some of the heights overlooking Sana. One of the objects of my visit was to observe the capital and the Egyptian airfield north of it, with a view to bombarding them later on with the 120 mm mortars. Kasim Monasir gladly sent me forward with an escort to one of his advanced posts, on a rocky outcrop which commanded a clear view over the

Egyptian positions in the foothills, and beyond to Sana and the airfield. They would be easy targets, I reckoned, if we could manage to keep the mortars supplied with ammunition, which would have to come up on camels from the roadhead. Immediately below me on a flat-topped hill were twelve T34 tanks — sitting ducks for the recoilless 75, I reflected sadly, if only we had the shells to fire at them.

The following day, after a six-hour march across two high mountain ranges, we reached Qarwah, the mercenary base for the Khowlan, and I handed over to the three British officers there the radio and equipment I had brought all the way from Najran; I also had my first good wash for over a week.

I left Qarwah on my homeward journey at 8.30 on the morning of 15 April, accompanied by three tribesmen and two donkeys. I was returning by a shorter route, which led over the mountain massif of the Jebel Lowse into the Wadi Sharefar and thence to the caves of Jerbat Attala I had visited four days earlier. A stiff, exhausting climb of five hours up a high pass brought us onto a fertile plateau green with neatly terraced fields and groves of almond trees — *lowse* is the Arabic for almond. Villages of square stone houses perched precariously on the edge of the high, rocky bluffs above the plateau, or straggled up the mountain slopes among vineyards and orchards that offered a pleasing contrast to the bleak, austere grandeur of the pass.

We had been on the move for five hours when we halted to rest in a village on the plateau. After a while my escort came to me with the news that there were Republican patrols along the route we should be taking, and therefore we must travel by night. It was still early afternoon so we lingered another three hours while I watched some men weaving a rug from camel hair, and later played hockey with a group of small boys.

Darkness overtook us as we were making the precipitous descent from the plateau into the valley of the Wadi Sharefar, where we had to cross a motor road used by the Egyptians. As we approached the road two trucks drove up and stopped a few yards away. Two of my escort went forward to parley, while I stayed with the others and the donkeys, blessing the darkness and the fact that I was wearing Yemeni dress. I waited in considerable suspense for half an hour, listening to the murmur of voices from the road; but at last I heard the engines start up and the trucks drive away into the night. A moment later my guards returned to explain we had narrowly escaped being rounded up by thirty Egyptian soldiers in two armoured personnel carriers.

After this episode I wound a cashmere shawl round my head as a turban before we moved on; I also accepted my escort's suggestion that if we were stopped again they should pass me off as their half-witted and dumb kinsman. It was lucky we took these precautions because twice we were halted by Republican pickets as we crossed the plain, and once a torch was flashed on me as I hung back with the donkey man and the animals while my guards did the talking. After a gruelling climb up from the plain, during which we were again challenged by armed Republicans, we reached Jerbat Attala at midnight; I was dead tired after a twelve-hour march, mostly on foot, and as soon as I had greeted Amir Abdullah Hassan, whom I found in the middle of a *qat* session, I went to sleep.

My arrival had coincided with the wedding of one of the young Yemeni princes, and the whole of the next day was taken up by the celebrations: an enormous lunch attended by over a hundred guests, all of us sitting on cushions in the

Amir's cave, followed by singing, tribal dancing and repeated *feux-de-joie*. I left Jerbat Attala on the morning of the second day and, after a strenuous scramble down the steep *wadis* of the Nehm mountains, followed by an easier descent through the foothills where we spent a night, we reached the roadhead in the High Jauf early in the afternoon of 18 April.

I had hoped to find my Toyota there, following instructions I had sent on ahead to Sheikh Daoud, but there was no sign of it. Much later I found out that he had, as I had feared he would, run it as a taxi until it broke down and had then abandoned it; a French mercenary mechanic had found it and driven it to Najran, where I saw it a year later in a garage, in several pieces. The local *naib* promised me a place in a convoy of trucks leaving for Najran the same night; increased Egyptian air activity, he explained, made it unsafe for us to travel through the Jauf by day. He might have added that it wasn't all that much safer by night, as I was about to discover.

We set off at 7 in three Ford trucks, each carrying one Royalist soldier and twenty-five unarmed civilians. Happy in the thought that my troubles were over, I sat back beside the driver and relaxed my aching limbs; I had forgotten we were now in the territory of the Dahm, the *bedu* brigands whose rapacity caused such problems for Mohamed Hussein. We had been going for half an hour when we came upon a barricade of stones blocking the road and behind it about twenty villainous-looking tribesmen who covered us menacingly with their rifles. The drivers stepped on their brakes, our guards jumped down, and a long argument followed, at the end of which I gathered that the Dahm were demanding a payment of one silver Maria Theresa dollar for each member of the party before they would let us proceed.

Our guards refused to pay and for a start sent the seventy-five unhappy civilians off on a three mile walk back to the road-head. The Dahm insisted, however, that I should stay behind with the guards and drivers, presumably as a hostage. I limped up to their Sheikh and, pointing to my bandaged knee, tried to explain in my halting Arabic that I was wounded and needed immediate treatment in hospital; my gesture provoked a good deal of merriment, but no other reaction. The drivers and I sat down to brew tea and after a while the Dahm sheikh joined us. The argument went on for three hours, while I went to sleep; eventually I was woken up to be told we were moving on and the Dahm had been persuaded, or threatened, into letting us through without payment.

Before I left for London at the beginning of May I told Amir Sultan I would not renew my contract with the mercenary organization, although I would be happy to go back to the Yemen later on as an independent adviser. In the first place I realized that in future the mercenary commander would have to spend most of his time on administration in Jedda and would have few opportunities for the field operations I preferred. Secondly, I didn't see how I could reconcile my duties as a Gentleman-at-Arms with a service contract in the Yemen; it would have been very difficult at best and might have caused political complications. Nevertheless, I was unwilling to leave the Yemen for good, and was greatly cheered when my Saudi and Yemeni friends assured me they would be inviting me back.

Chapter XVII: Murder, Mutiny and Manners

Almost a year passed before I saw Arabia again. In the interval I lived quietly at Branxholme while my knee recovered from the ill-treatment of my last journey. I even gave up working for the *Good Food Guide*. Early in 1967 Moy and I paid a visit to Spain and bought ourselves a plot of land on the east coast between Valencia and Alicante, on which we proposed to build ourselves a house.

Meanwhile, there had been another unsuccessful attempt to end the Yemen war by diplomacy. In August, 1966, the Saudi and Egyptian Foreign Ministers had met in Kuwait, on the initiative of the Ruler, to discuss terms for a disengagement. They reached an agreement, but it was rejected by both Royalists and Republicans, who were resentful that they had not been consulted beforehand. However, the lull in hostilities brought about by this and the Jedda Agreement had improved the position of the Egyptians at the expense of the Royalists.

Having withdrawn their troops from the more vulnerable tribal areas, the Egyptians were now concentrated in force in the triangle between Sana, Hodeidah and Taiz; in the north they had abandoned the important and ancient town of Sada but retained a strong garrison in Hajjah. But they had left behind selected political officers of very high calibre, who were offering lavish bribes to the Sheikhs to win them over. These able and courageous men were having such success that in some areas the Royalists could no longer safely use their old lines of communication. Where bribery failed there would be the threat of bombing, supported by heavy air raids when necessary, to terrorize the tribes into co-operation.

The Egyptians were also paying Yemeni agents to employ against the Royalists the same methods that the Royalists formerly had used so effectively against the Egyptians. Royalist convoys were being sniped, and even ambushed, and the roads they used were frequently mined.

The Royalists were primarily guerrillas and as such could only operate successfully with the support of the local population. With no fighting to occupy them, the tribes were losing interest in the political issues and were beginning to worry about the survival of their families. They needed money and if the Amirs could not give it to them they would get it from the Egyptians. The Amirs in their turn depended for money on the Saudis, who were rapidly becoming disenchanted with the Royalists and switching their support to the 'Third Party'. There were even signs of a movement among the Bakil and Hashid confederations to unite under Third Party leadership. If they were to survive all these pressures the Royalists must start fighting again, and soon.

Towards the end of March, 1967, I heard from McLean that he was leaving shortly for Saudi Arabia and the Yemen, accompanied by Duncan Sandys, the Shadow Minister for Commonwealth Relations. I was invited to join them and show Sandys something of the mercenary organization. We reached Jedda in the middle of April and I flew on ahead from there to Najran to make the necessary arrangements with Khaled Sudairi and Mohamed Hussein. Both Amirs gave me a warm welcome and we decided that as soon as they arrived I should drive with McLean and Sandys to the British headquarters at Amara and show them the Training School. They could stay at

Amara for a night, which was as long as Sandys could spare from his timetable.

They turned up on 18 April in time for lunch and a useful conference afterwards with the two Amirs. Then we drove to the mercenary base nearby, where the 120 mm mortars and their French teams were waiting to go into action. These mortars represented the heaviest fire-power at the Royalists' disposal, but they could not be deployed on the Sana front, where they were badly needed, because Mohamed Hussein could not guarantee their safe passage on the way, in particular through the territory of the Dahm.

When we had inspected the mortars we drove in the darkness across the desert to Amara, in a convoy of five trucks filled with Mohamed Hussein's followers. We arrived about midnight to find an excellent meal prepared and a comfortable cave for the three of us to share. In the morning I drove McLean and Sandys to the cave I had occupied two years before, which was still the headquarters of the British mercenaries, and introduced them to the staff. Later in the day we drove to the Training School, where we talked with the British and French instructors and watched the recruits — about a thousand of them — drilling and receiving training in the handling of heavy weapons.

That evening, after McLean and Sandys had gone back to Najran, I collapsed in my cave with acute dysentery and stayed there on my bed for the next two days, unable to swallow any solid food. On the evening of the second day a loud explosion shook the camp, followed fifteen minutes later by another, both of them close at hand. I listened to the shouting that followed and watched the guards running in all directions, but I was too weak and tired to investigate the cause; I only hoped that enemy guns or mortars hadn't found our range. It was not until the following afternoon that I learned that two time bombs had exploded at the entrance to Mohamed Hussein's quarters, which was also the entrance to the cave I had shared with McLean and Sandys. They had in fact gone off about thirty yards from the spot where I had been lying, but luckily had injured nobody. When I inspected the craters I thought they might have been heavy mines. Whether they had been intended for Amir Mohamed, Sandys and McLean, or even myself I would never know; but it was clear the Egyptians had been busy with their gold.

I was back in London in May, in time to be on duty in the front hall of Buckingham Palace when King Feisal arrived on his State Visit. His retinue included a number of my friends, among them Amir Sultan, with whom I talked privately in his hotel after the official visit was over. He asked me to make another reconnaissance in the Yemen the following month, and write him a report on the situation.

On my way through Najran from Amara in April I had spent a long time listening to Amir Mohamed Hussein's proposals for future operations. It was evident he had taken to heart our repeated advice that the Royalists should ignore prestige targets and concentrate on the Egyptian lines of communication; and he had developed in careful detail the plan he had discussed with me in April, 1966, for isolating Sana, neutralizing Taiz and sabotaging the port and airfield of Hodeidah. It was an excellent plan, well within the Royalists' capabilities, and if it had been implemented properly it might well have ended the war. Unfortunately it foundered on the rocks of Saudi-Yemeni suspicion and resentment; both partners were to blame for the failure.

The aftermath of the Six Day War, which broke out while I was in England, provided the Royalists with their greatest opportunities and they threw them all away. The catastrophic defeat of Egypt obliged President Nasser to withdraw the bulk of his troops from the Yemen — although it is likely that he took advantage of the occasion to extricate himself without loss of face from what had already become an embarrassing commitment. For just as the long-drawn-out struggle in the Yemen had fostered suspicion between Saudis and Royalists, so also had ill-feeling grown between Egyptians and Republicans. In October, 1965, immediately before the Haradh Conference, Sallal had found it prudent to retire to the safety of Cairo, where he remained for nearly a year. When he returned to Sana in September, 1966, to institute a reign of terror, with widespread arrests and executions of Republican liberals, the Egyptians were obliged to give him powerful military support. In particular, they launched heavy air attacks, with an extensive use of poison gas, against the villages of tribes supporting the Royalists; Sana radio went so far as to announce, as late as July, 1967, that gas bombs would be dropped on all areas harbouring Royalists — an admission which caused very little disturbance to the liberal conscience abroad and which the United Nations Assembly refused even to discuss.

Nasser extended his air war to Saudi territory; his aircraft bombed Najran and Jizan in October, 1966, and January, 1967, again without protest from the United Nations. But by June, 1967, he was thoroughly disillusioned with his expensive and unprofitable adventure in the Yemen. After their defeat by Israel the Egyptians began to withdraw, although they left Sallal with enough armour and modern weapons to equip his troops. By the end of the year, however, Sallal himself was overthrown and the Republicans were so demoralized that a determined onslaught by the Royalists would probably have captured Sana. Instead the Royalist commanders, deprived of Saudi support and fearful of incurring heavy casualties in the flat country around the capital, resorted to siege tactics. The delay gave the Republicans time to recover and reorganize their defences, with substantial help now from the Soviet Union. Those critical weeks of indecision cost the Hamid ud Din their throne.

I entered Yemen on 16 June by car from Jizan and, after two days at the roadhead waiting for a baggage mule, embarked on the long and arduous climb up to Qara. The scenery was as majestic and as beautiful as I remembered it — tall trees like chestnuts growing up the mountainsides and sparkling streams with green, grassy banks running through the valleys; but the climb seemed even stiffer than before and took much more out of me. To make matters worse, my guard and two donkeymen each carried a transistor radio, all of which blared incessantly at full volume, each tuned to a different station. It had become a status symbol among Yemenis to own a transistor and I felt a wry satisfaction when we were beaten in one-upmanship by a man we met coming down from Qara carrying a portable tape-recorder which drowned even the din from my own party.

The Imam was still sick in Taif and Amir Hassan ibn Hassan was in command at Qara. Al Badr had become little more than a figurehead since the formation in May, with Saudi encouragement, of an organization known as the 'Struggle Front for the Liberation of the Yemen', which embraced Royalists, Third Party and various Republican groups opposed to Sallal and the Egyptians. A committee of this organization, under the leadership of the Royalist Prime Minister al Hassan, was now responsible for the planning, direction and co-ordination of all activities against the Egyptians and the Sana regime. Amir Hassan Hassan had been appointed commander of the armies in the west and Amir Mohamed Hussein commander in the east.

While I waited for an interview with Amir Hassan I drank tea with the British wireless operators attached to the headquarters — a bearded Scot from Stirling, an ex-Welsh Guards NCO and a grey-haired Irishman with a huge moustache; they were a genial and hospitable trio. During the nine days of my stay I spent the greater part of my time waiting to see Amir Hassan, because he was busy holding a *majlis*[41] with sheikhs of the Hashid tribes who had come to offer him support. Our brief and infrequent meetings therefore had something of a conspiratorial nature, the more so because he used them to air his grievances to me with embarrassing candour. But he gave me one piece of good news — the Egyptians had just evacuated Haradh. Royalist forces had immediately occupied it and were following the retreating enemy, mopping up the Republican troops they had left as rearguard — most of whom were either in headlong flight or coming over to the Royalists.

I climbed down from Qara by a shorter but yet more precipitous route, which took us six hours. The journey, all of it in darkness, was sheer hell. I was soon soaked with sweat, my knee was a throbbing agony, and after an hour my torch failed, leaving me to stumble blindly along the winding, narrow tracks and rock-strewn *wadis*. When at last we reached the roadhead I firmly resolved never again to go up to Qara. The climb, and even more the descent, was far worse than the Jebel Akhdar in

---

[41] Literally 'audience' or 'assembly'. In fact, a democratic court at which any person, from the highest to the lowest in the land, can attend and present petitions, air complaints, or ask the ruler to arbitrate in disputes. King Feisal holds them to this day.

Oman, and although I told myself that my knee was to blame, I knew the real trouble was my age: I was no longer fit enough for this kind of physical strain.

On my way back I spent a few days in Jedda, where I found the principal Royalist leaders assembled for a conference with the Saudis to work out operational plans for the future. The proceedings were scarcely harmonious and ended with a Saudi threat to cut off aid unless the Royalists, particularly Mohamed Hussein, pressed their attacks more vigorously against the departing Egyptians. Before I left for home Mohamed Hussein extracted a promise from me to return as soon as I could.

In London I was approached by BBC Television with the offer of a temporary job as liaison officer to a team from the *Twenty-four Hours* programme which they were proposing to send to the Yemen in September. I accepted and promised to make arrangements with the Saudi and Royalist authorities for their reception. I was back in Jedda early in August to find that in the meantime the Royalists, unknown to the Saudis, had sent an emissary to Tehran with a request for help. The negotiations had ended satisfactorily with a promise from the Shah to send supplies.

On 10 August I flew to Najran, where I picked up my old guide Jum Han, and drove on to Amara to see Amir Mohamed Hussein. On the way back, two days later, we stopped at Uqd, where we found a pathetic party of twenty Burmese and Pakistani pilgrims stranded on their way to Mecca; half of them were young children and all were penniless, starving and parched with thirst. They begged us for water and we gave them what little we had. I mused on the power of a faith that could compel men to leave their homes in Burma and hitchhike with their families all the way to Mecca, with no certainty of return. I also remembered the unscrupulous traders in Muscat who would ferry pilgrims across the Gulf from Pakistan and leave them to find their way through the Rub al Khali.

I had to waste two weeks in Jedda trying to find out whether I was still supposed to be working for my old employers, the Saudis, or for the Yemeni Royalists. It turned out that I was to work in future for the Royalists, with the special assignment of Military Adviser to Mohamed Hussein. The first task he gave me, when I saw him again at Amara, was to do a reconnaissance of Royalist territory, including areas the Egyptians had just abandoned, and look for landing grounds for transport aircraft. It seemed the Shah might be sending his supplies directly to the Yemen.

While waiting to begin my journey I had a grim reminder of the danger that was a constant companion to travellers in this country. I was visiting the British radio operators in their cave one evening when a signal came in from al Hassan to say a truck had just arrived at his headquarters with the bodies of three British soldiers. They had left Amara that afternoon on the four-hour drive to al Hassan's base, taking with them Ali, the young Yemeni boy who made the tea in the British cave.

'Little Ali was the only survivor,' my hosts told me. 'We don't have any details at present, but it seems they were held up about an hour's drive from here and shot out of hand. We'll know more when Ali gets back.'

Amir Mohamed, horrified by the news, immediately sent out a posse of soldiers to track down the murderers, but it wasn't until the following afternoon that Ali arrived to tell us the full story.

Their Land Rover had been stopped near a village by a road block manned by three men, whom they thought at first were Royalist tribesmen. Since they had been expecting no trouble the Englishmen had brought only one rifle between them, although Ali had another. While two of the tribesmen kept the vehicle covered, the third approached and questioned them in English for about twenty minutes. Finally he asked for money to let them through, which they gave him, and then he demanded their rifles. Ali whispered, 'do not give him your gun,' and held on firmly to his own. But the Englishmen innocently handed over their rifles, whereupon the tribesman opened fire, killing one of them instantly and wounding the others.

Although hit in the leg, Ali managed to crawl behind a rock, but the two remaining British soldiers tried to shelter by their car, where a grenade finished them off. Ali exchanged shots with the tribesmen for some time, until a fourteen-year-old girl, daughter of the village sheikh, appeared on the scene and pleaded with them to let him go.

'Are you not ashamed?' she had cried. 'You have killed the three *faranghi* [Europeans]. Why would you stain your hands with the blood of this boy, who is one of our people?'

She had then walked calmly over to Ali, taken his rifle and led him by the hand to her village.

We heard him out in silence, too shocked to say a word. All the dead men were married with young children. One had been a good friend of mine who had served in the SAS under me in Oman. Like most of the British mercenaries he had come here to risk his life, not so much for the money, as for the adventure, and in the hope that he might be helping his own country as well; it was a tragic waste that he should lose it through trickery and murder.

There was deep anger among Amir Mohamed's followers, not only at the manner of this cold-blooded killing but also because they regarded the victims as their guests and therefore their responsibility. They told us they knew the names of the murderers, who were Republicans from that same village; they would be hunted down, they assured us, and brought to justice. They were never found.

The following night, 28 August, I left Amara on my first airfield reconnaissance and headed south towards Hazm, Sirwah and Harib. Although the Egyptians had withdrawn from this part of the country, they were offering large rewards for attacks on Europeans, and after the recent murders Amir Mohamed was taking no chances; he sent me off with two trucks carrying an escort of twenty soldiers and tribesmen, including four sheikhs, and two heavy machine guns.

On the second afternoon, two hours' drive beyond Hazm, we came to the ruins of Baraqish standing on a huge, flat-topped mound in the middle of the desert. This was the ancient city of Yathil, which they say was built by Queen Belgis of Sheba nearly three thousand years ago and was the capital of Ma'in, a powerful kingdom on the Incense Route. The magnificent outer wall of the city, thirty feet high and still almost intact, was built from great blocks of stone. It ran the whole circumference of the mound, reinforced at frequent intervals by square bastions that threw sharp shadows in the strong sunlight across its ochre face. Inside, among the remains of buildings, I found wall surfaces carved with inscriptions in curious geometrical hieroglyphics; a tall, circular tower stood out from the ruins close beside the peeling domed shell of a mosque.

Soon after noon next day, after I had examined three excellent airfields formerly used by the Egyptians, I passed the remains of the two-thousand-year-old fortress city of Sirwah; the walls and fortifications had survived in good condition until the Egyptians systematically blew them up before they withdrew, leaving only one corner standing.

That evening Ali, our *bedu* driver, insisted we should dine with him in his camp. We all sat on camel rugs in the firelit darkness among the black tents, from which the grinning faces of small children peeped furtively to catch a glimpse of their first European, while camels and goats wandered freely between the stacked piles of our rifles and machine guns. There were twenty families in the camp, Ali told me, numbering about a hundred and fifty all told. We drank endless cups of tea while two hubble-bubbles smoked in the centre of the rectangle formed by our bodies. I was given a camel saddle, covered with a bright yellow eiderdown, to prop my back, and while I wrote up my notes in the dim light the others rose to pray in the direction of Mecca — first asking me to check the direction with my pocket compass, as they often did in this country where, instead of 'North' or 'South', they would say 'towards Mecca' or 'towards Aden'.

Four sheep had their throats cut in front of us, and three hours later we ate them roasted, cut up and served with piles of rice. The meal, according to my guide, would have cost Ali and his co-driver 700 Saudi riyals — £60 in English money. When we had eaten we drove on for four hours in the dark, and at 1 am we bedded down in the open, killing several scorpions as we laid out our sleeping bags.

The following day, after reconnoitring Harib airstrip and examining the old fort which the RAF had bombed in 1964, we entered Beihan State and spent the night at Naqub in a palace belonging to Sherif Hussein's brother. We did not see Sherif Hussein but his brother and his son, Amir Saleh, who ruled the State on behalf of his father, lodged us in comfort and fed us well, spending many hours in conversation with me.

Only when I reached Najran two days later and found the Sherif and all his family there as refugees did I learn that all the time we were being entertained by them, they were preparing for a hasty flight. Even while I was bathing and eating in the palace the National Liberation Front had seized power in Beihan, aided by the Federal Army, whose officers had only the previous day pledged their loyalty to the Sherif. Our hosts had carefully hidden from us the slightest indication of what was going on, for under the Arab code of hospitality personal disaster takes second place to good manners.

Chapter XVIII: The End of a Dynasty

I arrived in Najran on the same day as the BBC Television team. Amir Mohamed Hussein was also there and they were most anxious to interview him, apart from the fact that we needed his authority to travel in the Yemen. However, although I immediately sent him an urgent message asking for a meeting it was three days before anybody remembered to give it to him; meanwhile, whenever I called at his house I was told he was sleeping. I explained to the team that all this was part of the Arab way of life and they took it extremely well.

There were four of them. In charge was Tony Summers, the producer, a 25-year-old graduate of New College. With his fashionable long hair and drain-pipe jeans he cut a bizarre figure among the ragged tribesmen of the mountains and desert; but he was clever, efficient and easy to get on with, and he controlled his team with firmness and tact. David Lomax, the six-and-a-half-foot-tall reporter and interviewer, was four years older; he had served in the RAF and with Radio Newsreel. Intelligent and likeable, he suffered agonies trying to fit his enormous frame into the front of a truck beside the three others, as he often had to do, and in bending double to talk with the diminutive Yemenis.

'You should carry around a portable hole for your interviews,' the cameraman, Derek Banks, used to say to him. A stout and phlegmatic young man who had been four years with the BBC, Banks had the most exhausting job of them all and would work at it until he almost dropped with fatigue. The most experienced member of the party was Fred Downton who was responsible for sound. Ten years' service with the

Corporation had taken him all over the world — Vietnam, Kashmir, Canada, Mexico and Brazil were only a few of the countries he had visited. He shared with Banks a good, dry sense of humour, and he was the only bachelor in the team. I enjoyed very much the weeks I spent in their company and came to admire their stamina and resilience and the good humour with which they endured the discomforts, dangers and above all the frustrations of work in the Yemen.

On 9 September we left Najran for Amara, where the team recorded an interview with Amir Mohamed in the afternoon. Next morning I took them to the Red Cross hospital at Uqd and introduced them to the Swiss doctors. In the afternoon the Training School put on a demonstration for them, which almost ended in tragedy when two hundred recruits who were staging a mock attack seemed to go berserk. They surged towards the cameras chanting wildly and firing their rifles from the hip, and the team had to make a quick dash for safety to avoid being overrun or shot. To help them get over it we took them to film some machine gun practice; their recovery was complete after the first burst when a recruit innocently squatting behind a bush in the target area leaped up and ran for his life.

Mohamed Hussein decided to send us to Sada, now in Royalist hands, and gave us three trucks and a strong escort for the journey. It took us two days, grinding up narrow passes and over a rocky plateau, to reach al Hassan's headquarters at Quaddum, an hour or so from the town. I found the old man so stricken with asthma that he could barely talk, but he gave me an affectionate welcome.

Sada, seat of the Zeidi Imams from the eighth to the seventeenth century, was a city of square, mud-brick houses and fine palaces, approached through a narrow gateway commanded by two great tall round towers. A mud and stone fort on a mound of rock overlooked the town and the white-domed mosque with its red and white minaret. Around the entrance of the fort was strewn the wreckage of Egyptian trucks and APCs abandoned in the hasty retreat. After a full day spent in exploring the buildings and narrow streets and alleyways we drove south for two hours on the Sana road to the village of al Safra where we arrived before dawn.

The Egyptians had been bombing villages in the vicinity and so we climbed into the neighbouring hills at sunrise to await the Ilyushins. Banks took some effective shots of the bomb explosions about half a mile away and when we visited the stricken villages in the afternoon he and Lomax recorded an interview with me standing among the piles of rubble; we also found some unexploded bombs with Russian markings.

After a fourteen-hour journey from Sada over roads little better than camel tracks we arrived back at Najran, where I left the team for two days while I flew to Jedda with their film and tapes. As soon as I returned, on the 18th, we started out for the Wadi Hirran in the Jauf, in two trucks with an escort of six men and two sheikhs from the Dahm tribe to ensure safe passage through their territory.

We drove through the night and stopped on the road near Haggerla for a few hours' sleep. But at dawn we were woken up by flocks of goats and sheep and a few camels walking over us. One of the Dahm sheikhs was groaning in agony with stomach pains and his men were heating stones on the fire and placing them on his abdomen — a common treatment for a variety of ailments among the Yemenis, many of whom bear livid scars from its burns. We took the road again at noon and drove for the rest of the day and on into the night in acute discomfort, enveloped in a cloud of fine dust and shaken stupid by the continuous jolting and lurching. About one in the morning our truck ground to a halt with the differential cover broken off and so we slept in the open beside it.

We were now in the Wadi Hirran. After a welcome bathe in the clear, flowing water while our driver miraculously repaired the damaged truck, we left before midday and drove for three hours to the Royalist headquarters; this was the roadhead at the village of the rascally Sheikh Daoud, where I had left my Toyota just before my fiftieth birthday in April, 1966.

We stayed there two days before returning to Najran, and the team spent the time travelling around and taking photographs of wrecked tanks, artillery and transport left behind by the Egyptians. They also visited one of the villages nearby which had suffered gas bombing a few months earlier; they interviewed survivors, took a great deal of film, and told me they had found ample evidence to convince them that gas had indeed been used. When they returned to England the BBC showed their film, including their findings on the Egyptian use of gas. And so this atrocity at last received the publicity of television, four years after I had first reported it. The International Red Cross had long been in possession of the facts but had refused to make any public disclosure of them on the astonishing pretext that this was a 'political' issue and so beyond their competence; only after their own doctors had refused to enter the Yemen without gasmasks did they admit the truth, in a leak to the New York Press. Even then the British Government refused to take up the matter, either directly with Egypt or in the United Nations, and a Saudi attempt to raise it in the General Assembly failed for lack of support; meanwhile the liberal intellectual establishment in Britain and the United States, with its traditional devotion to double standards, chose to ignore the Yemen bombing and concentrated its indignation on Vietnam.

After saying good-bye to the BBC team in Jedda I waited there for two weeks before I received my next assignment from Amir Mohamed Hussein. This was to take a Persian officer to see the airfields I had examined on my previous reconnaissance; he would report back to his superiors if he considered them suitable for transport planes. We were also to look for possible dropping zones in the Royalist territory around Sana, which would give me an opportunity to visit the Hamdan and the Heimatain, where I had never been.

By the beginning of October the Egyptians had almost completed their withdrawal from the Yemen, although they were still continuing their air attacks. At the last of the Saudi-Egyptian summit conferences, the Khartoum Conference of 29 August, Nasser had given a firm undertaking to withdraw his troops before the middle of December in return for a quarterly subsidy from Saudi Arabia and Kuwait to compensate him for the loss of the Suez Canal revenues, linked with a promise from King Feisal to cease his aid to the Royalists. King Feisal made sure that Nasser would keep his promise by withholding payment of the subsidy until all Egyptian troops were out of the Yemen; while for their part the Saudis were not unwilling to abandon the Royalists, who they felt had let them down by their supine inactivity in the field. The Royalists had therefore turned for help to the Shah, who had his own good reasons for fearing Nasser.

I met Major Mahmud, the Persian officer, in the waiting room at Jedda airport. A thick-set man in his late thirties with strong, fleshy features, he greeted me with easy familiarity.

'Colonel Smiley? I think we met before, in London, with Jim Johnson.' He spoke with a pronounced American accent.

He was one of four Persian officers, I now remembered, whom Johnson and I had interviewed two years before in a Kensington hotel. We had advised them at the time to return to Iran. He didn't hold it against me, however, and even seemed grateful to have a companion on his forthcoming journey. He told me he was married, with a three-year-old daughter and another child on the way, and so he might have felt lonely by himself. A Regular officer who had received military training in the United States, he had a sophisticated western outlook while retaining the good manners and easy charm peculiar to his countrymen. He was undoubtedly a fine soldier, with a sense of humour and an equable temper which was nevertheless inclined to fray under the stress of Yemeni irresponsibility and incompetence. Although he was usually tactful with the Yemenis I could sense that he looked down on them, and in private conversation between ourselves he would speak of 'them' and 'us'; I doubt if they came out well in his reports.

On 6 October we flew to Najran, where we had a conference with Amir Mohamed and Billy McLean. McLean was remaining there, but we agreed that I should take Mahmud to Amara and the Jauf airfields by truck, after which we would do a reconnaissance on foot of the Hamdan and Heimatain. We had to be back in Najran by 25 October. At 5 the next morning, as soon as our conference was over, Mahmud and I drove to Amara with an escort of three soldiers from Amir Mohamed's personal guard who were to accompany us throughout our journey. On the way we stopped to inspect the airfield near Amara, which Mahmud found suitable for landing supplies.

In the afternoon we went to the Training School to inspect the first consignment of Iranian arms, which had arrived the previous day by truck from Jeddah. It included the heaviest weapons yet to reach the Royalists — six 107 mm recoilless rifles with a range of eight kilometres, four 120 mm mortars with a twelve kilometre range, and six Vickers heavy machine guns.

The following morning, after a good night's sleep which we both badly needed, we left Amara in a convoy of one military and two civilian trucks; to ensure our safety through the territory of the Dahm the military truck mounted a .5 Browning and carried an escort of ten soldiers under the Naib of Sirwa, who was to look after us for the first part of our trip. In the afternoon we halted to inspect an airstrip to the northeast of Boa, which Mahmud agreed with me would serve very well. We drove on across the flat desert through the evening and well into the night before bedding down in a *wadi* under some thorn trees.

When day broke we found we were beside the *bedu* camp where I had been entertained on my last visit at the end of August. The *bedu* again insisted on our joining them, first for breakfast — innumerable cups of excellent unsweetened coffee, which we drank seated on the ground in front of one of the big black tents — and then for lunch; with the result that it was afternoon before we could take to the road on the two hours' drive to Sirwah.

It was a rough ride, over black volcanic rock in a landscape harsh as the surface of the moon; sometimes we had to reduce speed to ten miles an hour. On my previous trip I had found three airstrips near Sirwah which seemed possible for transport aircraft, and I was delighted when they all passed Mahmud's critical inspection. We had now reached the southernmost point of our reconnaissance, and began to retrace our steps towards the Wadi Hirran and the north. After three hours the volcanic rock gave way to open desert, and after another two hours' driving in the dark we decided to halt for the night, and spread our sleeping bags comfortably in the soft sand.

The cold woke me at 5.30 and we left at six. After two hours we came to the splendid ruins of Baraqish, or Yathil, which had so deeply impressed me before, and stopped a while to take photographs. A further eight hours, four of them along the appalling road through the Wadi Hirran, brought us at sunset to the Royalist headquarters where I had stayed with the BBC Television team just a month before.

A fierce argument now arose between the new village *naib* and myself; he insisted we must sleep in the Amir's cave, in case of an air raid, whereas I was determined to sleep by the river. At the end of an hour, when tempers were rising dangerously, Mahmud persuaded me to give in for the sake of peace. However, I wouldn't go into the cave, but sat outside in a sulk. After about ten minutes he scrambled out in something of a hurry.

'David,' he gasped, wriggling and scratching himself in a frenzy, 'I'd rather face any air raid than stay in there. It's fairly crawling with fleas — and, look, so is my shirt!' We compromised with the *naib* by sleeping on top of the cliffs above the cave, where we were much more comfortable although, at an altitude of over four thousand feet, we were frequently woken up by the cold.

Listening to the BBC news on my transistor radio in the morning, I learned that Che Guevara had been killed in an ambush in Bolivia. I told Mahmud.

'As a guerrilla yourself, I figure you'd have a kind of fellow-feeling for him,' he commented with a smile.

290

'My feeling is, he couldn't have been a very good guerrilla to get himself killed so easily. Which reminds me,' I went on, 'We'd better clean the dust and sand out of our pistols because we may need to use them soon. Some of the Hamdan tribes are not at all friendly to the Royalists.'

In the afternoon we drove on to the village of Coulat Hamama, the new roadhead, where we had to leave the trucks. We said good-bye to the Naib of Sirwa and his men, thanking them for having looked after us so well, and at eight in the evening began our climb onto the Arhab plateau.

We had a fresh escort of twenty soldiers, with three camels for our baggage and three riding donkeys — one each for Mahmud, myself and our new interpreter Abdul Kerim, an irresponsible, very young man who told us he was one of twenty-six children sired by his father from two wives. After only three hours of easy going up a gradually sloping *wadi* we halted for the night. It was bitterly cold in the open at that height, but half a mug of Mahmud's whisky soon sent me off to sleep.

We set off at five for another three hours' gentle walk up the *wadi*. Bare mountain slopes frowned above us on either side, but green trees and shrubs grew in the ravine, interspersed with the orange and red of aloes. Only the cooing of doves, the grumbling of the camels and the occasional bray of a donkey broke the stillness of the morning. We halted briefly in a village at the head of the valley, at a height of eight thousand feet, before embarking on our wearisome journey across the bleak, rock-bound wilderness of the Arhab plateau. Even at noon the cold was intense, biting through my thin shirt and *iz-zar*, although the sun was strong enough to give me a headache. Soon after midday we came to the sombre, grey stone village of El Rajou, where we stopped to eat in the house of one of our camel men — the first meal Mahmud and I had had for twenty-four hours.

We stayed there all day, while Abdul Kerim went off to gather information about the next stage of our journey. At midnight he returned and told us we could leave, but first I must try to disguise myself as a Yemeni because we should be crossing Republican territory. The best I could do was to wind a cloth round my flower-pot hat to make a turban and thrust a *jembia* through my belt.

For six hours we walked over the freezing plateau. I rode for the first ten minutes until my donkey stumbled in the dark and threw me to the ground, after which I preferred to go on foot. At seven we made a brief halt in a village for coffee and a breakfast of cheese and tinned tunny fish. Another two hours' painful walk across the hard, unyielding surface of black and brown rock brought us to the edge of the Arhab plateau and the Hamdan village of al Yahees, perched on a cliff high above the Sana plain. Below us was a sheer drop of a thousand feet or more to the bare brown foothills; beyond them terraces of vines and fruit trees sloped gently towards the flat country and the distant greyish blur that marked the capital.

We had come to the most dangerous part of our journey. To reach the Heimatain we had to cross the Sana-Sada motor road, passing through hostile territory on the way. We left al Yahees at 4.30 in the afternoon and walked steadily downhill until dark, when we came to the village of Monakea, close to the road. It was Republican in sympathy, but we had arranged to pick up two guides there who would take us across and lead us to a Royalist village in the Heimatain for a fee of five sovereigns. Our escort and guides showed increasing nervousness as we approached the road and I confess I felt very exposed as we hurried across the open country on either side. But we passed unchallenged and began a steep climb up into the mountains. On the way we split into two groups, with Mahmud in the leading party and my own following some distance behind. When we stopped at midnight to sleep on the mountainside I discovered that my mattress and sleeping bag were with Mahmud's party; and so I passed an uncomfortable and wakeful night curled up among the rocks.

We were off again at dawn but after two hours our guides halted us. We must pay them another five sovereigns, they insisted, or they would not go on. When we protested we had already paid them the agreed price, they blandly pointed out that they could easily find some Republican soldiers who would pay much more to have us as prisoners. I was sorely tempted to shoot them but we were still in enemy country and so I had to watch in helpless fury while Abdul Kerim handed over the money. After another three hours we came at last to the village of Beit Saad in the territory of the friendly and hospitable Beni Matr.

I had hoped to get an hour's rest here but the irresponsible Abdul Kerim, unknown to me, had told the villagers I was a doctor — he said he thought it would seem less suspicious. I was stripping down for a shower when a young girl appeared at my door complaining of stomach-ache and insisting I should feel her tummy. I had no idea whether it was Entero-Vioform she needed or cascara — or whether perhaps she was pregnant; however, I gave her some aspirins and she went away happy. Soon afterwards a woman brought me her baby to examine, and a little boy came in suffering, as far as I could judge, from rickets. I gave them all aspirin and sent them away.

When we had eaten we went on for another hour and a half, which brought us to our destination, Beit al Yursi, in the safety of the Heimatain. Here I found Mahmud and the rest of our party, including a small boy aged about ten, who had walked with us barefoot all the way from el Rajou. We stayed the night at Beit al Yursi, and set out at 8.30 the next morning to meet the Royalist commander in the Heimatain, General Mohamed Abdullah Sharda.

The journey took more than eight hours, along dangerous narrow tracks, little wider than ledges, cut in the face of the cliffs. We climbed to over ten thousand feet, with the icy wind numbing our faces and hands and cutting clean through our thin clothing, while our lungs laboured painfully in the thin air. Thousands of feet below us terraces of maize and sorghum wound sinuous patterns of green and brown along the lower slopes of the valleys; brightly coloured flowers gleamed in the crannies of the rocks, and wild thyme, sage and aloes grew along the banks of the *wadis*; sparkling streams cascaded down the mountainside to fill the irrigation channels among the tiered fields of crops.

General Sharda came out to meet us on the way with a formidable escort and led us to his headquarters. This was a cave on top of the Jebel Januk situated, at a height of over seven thousand feet, just behind the crest of a huge precipice falling almost sheer to the Sana plain. It was only five miles from Sana itself. The view, when the clouds permitted, extended right across the plain to the mountains beyond. With his emaciated figure, thick, round glasses and austere expression the General resembled a village schoolmaster rather than a guerrilla leader. Yet he had proved himself a capable commander and he took great pride in his men; for their part they were smart and well-disciplined and their morale was excellent.

We spent a day and a night with the general, who was an excellent host. He clearly believed in the value of showmanship and 'Public Relations', for he made sure that we met successive delegations of Heimatain sheikhs and enthusiastic groups of loyal tribesmen who would greet us with, I suspect carefully stage-managed, *feux-de-joie*. After one of these exhibitions Mahmud and I had to patch up two bleeding warriors whom their overzealous comrades had inadvertently shot in the head; luckily they were only scalp wounds. There was nowhere suitable for a landing strip in that wild, mountainous terrain, but we saw some possible dropping zones, although the strong wind, which was a permanent feature of the Heimatain, might easily blow the containers into deep ravines where they would be difficult to recover.

We were in a hurry to get back to Najran and accomplished the homeward journey in very good time and almost without incident. We passed safely across the Sana-Sada road and covered the distance between the Jebel Januk and el Rajou, in Arhab, in less than twenty-four hours. It involved over twelve hours of walking, with only a tin of bully beef between the two of us; indeed, by the end of our journey I had taken in my pistol-belt four holes. Twice on the road a pair of Ilyushins flew low over our heads but we waved at them in the hope that they would take us for Republicans and they left us alone.

We spent the night at el Rajou. When we awoke in the morning we found a note from Abdul Kerim to say he was tired and would not be accompanying us any farther; and so we were left without an interpreter. In view of Mahmud's importance to the Royalists it was foolish of Mohamed Hussein not to have provided us with someone more reliable; Abdul Kerim didn't even speak good English. I believe this was one among many incidents which influenced Mahmud in the unfavourable report which I believe he later submitted.

We walked for another ten hours that day, climbing down from the Arhab plateau into the Wadi Hirran, where we spent the night. At two in the following afternoon, 20 October, we climbed into a civilian truck and drove for eighteen hours to the radio station outside Najran. Soon after we had left the *wadi* for the track across the Jauf desert four Dahm tried to hold us up. They stood in our path, shouting at us to stop and threatening us with their rifles; but our *bedu* driver put his foot down hard on the accelerator and charged them, scattering them before they had time to shoot and only a few bullets clanged ineffectively against the bodywork as we sped on our way.

Three days later Mahmud and I said good-bye in Jedda. He was returning to Tehran to report on his visit, I to London for duty at the State Opening of Parliament.

In this, my last important journey in the Yemen, I had been lucky to have Mahmud as a companion. His unfailing good temper and keen sense of the ridiculous had made our difficulties and frustrations a lot easier to bear. We were both lucky, too, in the three soldiers of Mohamed Hussein's bodyguard who had accompanied us all the way from Najran; they were courageous, efficient and always helpful and it was a great pity Mahmud wasn't able to meet more of their kind.

On 5 November, two days after he had left Sana on a visit to Baghdad and Moscow, Sallal was overthrown in a bloodless *coup d'état* by Republican army officers. They set up a Presidential Council of three members, which soon came to include one implacable enemy of the Hamid ud Din, General Hassan al Amri.

At the end of December, 1967, the Royalists held Sana encircled. Their most advanced positions were only five miles away. They had taken the town of Amran, fifteen miles to the north on the road to Sada; they were bombarding the principal airfield outside the capital and they had cut the road to Hodeidah; they were even sending commandos and sabotage groups into the streets of Sana. Still Mohamed Hussein hesitated to attack. His situation, already weakened by the withdrawal of Saudi help and by the doubts and jealousy of his own colleagues, was further compromised by Britain's evacuation of Aden at the end of November, 1967, and her replacement by the hostile government of the National Liberation Front. The position of the Republicans, on the other hand, progressively improved. Their army began to fight back instead of disintegrating as the Royalists had expected, and their air force grew stronger with the arrival of MiGs from the Soviet Union and Yemeni pilots, trained in Russia, to fly them.

The Soviet Union, hoping to step into the vacuum left by the departure of the British and the Egyptians, spared no effort to bolster the Republican regime and sent not only arms but advisers and instructors to help General Amri. On 8 February, 1968, a strong column of Republican troops, supported by armour and artillery, forced its way up from Hodeidah to Sana and cleared the Royalists from the road.[42] The 'Siege of Sana' was over. Mohamed Hussein had lost his last chance.

I visited the Yemen for the last time at the end of that month and stayed only four days in the country; I could not even travel far enough to reach Mohamed Hussein because of the hostility of the tribesmen on the way. I returned to Jedda and flew home, deeply saddened that at the end I had been unable

---

[42] "The organization, conduct and efficiency of this relieving force had a lot to do with the assistance and planning of Soviet and other foreign supporters." Edgar O'Ballance, *The War in the Yemen*, p. 197 (Faber, 1971)

to help this ablest and most courageous of the royal princes; he was the most ambitious too, which may have contributed to his failure. The cause which McLean and I had tried for five years to help was dying; even our reason for helping was scarcely valid any longer, for the Russians were already in Aden, at the invitation of the NLF. At least the experience was familiar to us both: the enthusiasm, the excitement, the hardship, the danger — and the final disappointment. The wheel had turned full circle, back to Albania.

While the military stalemate continued over the next year, the Royalists' hold on the countryside steadily weakened; they lost Hajjah in December, 1968, and Sada in the following September. The tribes began to drift away, some to their homes, others to join the Republicans; some of the Princes, deserted by their followers, left the country. In March, 1969, Mohamed Hussein resigned his position on the Imam's Council, abandoned the Royalist cause, and retired to live in Saudi Arabia; in July Amir Abdullah Hassan was assassinated.

At last King Feisal, who had no wish to see the Russians take Nasser's place in the Yemen, arranged a conference in Jedda between leaders of the opposing factions, in order to put an end to the war. The outcome was a coalition government of Republicans, Third Party and Royalists. One of its earliest and wisest moves was to install Royalist governors in areas with Royalist sympathies; it also appointed the former Royalist Foreign Minister, Ahmed al Shami, as its first Ambassador to London. Moreover, as the fighting died away and the new government felt more secure, it hastened to rid itself of Soviet influence. The present regime in Sana, which enjoys the support of King Feisal, is at least sympathetic towards the West and deeply suspicious of the Communists and their allies.

And so perhaps McLean and I can feel our efforts were not entirely misdirected.

The Hamid ud Din family, however, is excluded from the government. The Imam al Badr, last of a dynasty that ruled for well over a thousand years in Yemen, now lives quietly in Bromley; a few miles away in Hampstead lives his father-in-law Yahya al Hirsi.

Acknowledgements

First and foremost I would like to express my gratitude to my good friend and wartime companion, Peter Kemp, who helped me to put this book into a condition acceptable to the publishers. For the Oman chapters contemporary notes and letters were used, combined with my memory; for the Yemen chapters I kept a detailed diary of all thirteen trips I made to that country.

I would also like to thank Julian Amery in the case of Oman, and Billy McLean in the case of Yemen, for giving me the opportunity of going to these two countries, as a result of which this book was written.

I am also most grateful to my wife, Moy, and my sons, Xan and Philip, for their patience while this book was being written, and especially for their help in reading and criticising the draft and correcting errors.

Last but not least my sincere thanks to Mrs Irma Harewood for her enthusiasm and meticulous care in typing the script.

DAVID SMILEY

1974

If you have enjoyed this book enough to leave a review on Amazon and Goodreads, then we would be truly grateful.

The Estate of David Smiley

Sapere Books is an exciting new publisher of brilliant fiction and popular history.

To find out more about our latest releases and our monthly bargain books visit our website: **saperebooks.com**

Made in United States
Troutdale, OR
09/30/2024